The
Road
to
Righteousness

An Ancient Path
to the Next Great Awakening

"But for you who fear my name, the sun of righteousness
will rise with healing in its wings."
Malachi 4:2

TIMOTHY LOYAL TINGELSTAD

xulon
PRESS

CONTENTS

Preface

America is in trouble, but the problem is not what we think it is. Terrorism is on the rise and no military action can eliminate it, but it is not the terrorists that we should fear. Our economy is not sustainable and will eventually crumble, and no amount of government regulation will prevent it, but the greed on Wall Street is not the real problem. Epidemics, physical and mental disease and cancer are on the rise, and the best that medical science can do is slow them down. Americans have shed the innocent blood of millions of babies, and the land cries out to God for justice. Our highest courts have followed the court of public opinion and rejected God's definition of marriage and family. Religious liberty is about to disappear, and the Church has become powerless to impact the culture. America is in trouble, and in need of the Next Great Awakening.

For decades the call has gone out for more prayers for God's deliverance of our nation, but God has not yet moved to heal our land. Why has God not responded? Could it be that our pending destruction, whether it is from terrorists, economic collapse, epidemics, or natural disasters, will actually be executed by the hand of God, Himself? Could it be that **it is not** the actions of the terrorists, the other political party, those in favor of same sex marriage or pro-abortion advocates that will bring the sword of judgment upon our land? Is it possible that this sword is directed at God's own people? History tells us that harbingers are given as a warning by God to His people before they are judged, for it is always God's people who must repent, by turning back to the true God. But before God's people can repent, they must first be awakened to the truth that they have drifted away from the true God and away from His great salvation plan.

Only when this Next Great Awakening has taken place will we understand why the countless prayers for God's intervention to save us from this great decline and destruction have been to no avail. The purpose of this sword is both to awaken us to the nature of our own sin, and also to persuade us to repent of that sin. The prayers of the people, no matter how numerous or sincere they may be, will not remove this sword until this two-fold purpose has been completed. This was true of God's people, Israel, throughout Biblical history, and it will be true of God's people today. God's word, spoken through Ezekiel, now applies to today's American Christians:

> As surely as I live, declares the Sovereign Lord, I take no pleasure
> in the death of the wicked, but rather that they turn from their ways
> and live. Turn! Turn from your evil ways! Why will you die O house
> of Israel? Ezekiel 33:11

But what are the *evil ways* from which today's Christians must turn? This is the question that will be answered in the Next Great Awakening. We have redefined God and we have changed His plan of salvation from one based upon our repentance from sin to one based only upon God's forgiveness of our sins. The goal of Christianity has been changed from producing a righteous and God-fearing people, to a goal of producing sinners saved by grace. We have come to accept sin as an inevitable part of our walk with the Lord, and we have rejected the call to a walk of complete obedience to God's commands.

History tells us that there was a time when the people of Israel had created and worshipped Baal, a false god of their own design. Today's Christians have done the same thing. We have created and are worshipping a false god, whom we have created in our own image and likeness. The word of the Lord, spoken through His prophet, now applies to us:

> The Lord is with you, if you are with Him. If you seek Him, He will
> be found by you. But if you forsake Him, He will forsake you. For a
> long time Israel was without the true God, without a priest to teach
> them, and without the law. But in their distress they turned to the
> Lord, the God of Israel, and sought him, and he was found by them.
> II Chronicles 15:2-3

Today's Christianity has redefined God, and it has rejected His Law, which is the foundation of His great salvation plan. The false god of today's Christianity now tolerates the sins of His people rather than demanding and empowering them to repent from their sins. Today we teach that salvation comes through saying a one-time prayer rather than from a complete change in the way we live. The fear of sinning against God has been lost, and without this fear of the Lord in our hearts we have become powerless to overcome our sins and powerless to walk in the righteousness that God both desires and requires of His people. Christianity has become a label rather than a lifestyle of obedience to God.

We too have been for a long time without the true God, and God cannot return to us until we return to Him. The only way we can return to God is by accepting Him as He has defined Himself, and by accepting His great salvation plan, which is established upon the foundation of His unchanging Law. God hates lawlessness, and Christianity has become a religion of lawlessness. The Church must repent from teaching a plan of salvation which is only from the punishment of our sins, but not from the sins themselves. The sword that is coming upon us is actually the fruit of our own schemes, the fruit of our new salvation plan. The word of the Lord, spoken through the Prophet Jeremiah, now applies to us:

This is what the Lord says: Stand at the crossroads and look. Ask for the ancient paths, ask where the good way is and walk in it, and you will find rest for your souls. But you said, 'We will not walk in it." I appointed watchmen over you and said, 'Listen to the sound of the trumpet.' But you said, 'We will not listen.' Therefore, hear O nations, observe O witnesses, what will happen to them. **Hear O earth, for I am about to bring destruction upon this people, the fruit of their schemes, because they have not listened to my words and have rejected my law.** (Jeremiah 6:16-19) (emphasis added)

God is now exposing our drift away from Him and from His great salvation plan by allowing the fruit of this new salvation plan to ripen. The fruit of today's new salvation plan is lawlessness. The public acceptance of abortion and the meteoric rise in the acceptance of same-sex marriage, even within the Christian Church, are examples of this fruit. The court of public opinion has established abortion and same-sex marriage as the law of the land. Yet the Church has failed to see that this is the fruit of its own teachings. History tells us that the Church is responsible for the culture we live in.

The Church has had no moral authority to speak against changing the definition of marriage because for generations it has taught believers that God will not punish our sins so long as we are *Christian sinners*. Homosexuals are correct in accusing the Church of hypocrisy on the issue of same sex marriage because the Church has made the sin of homosexuality an exception to its teaching of God's grace and of His unconditional forgiveness of Christian sinners who continue to live in disobedience to His Law. If God's great salvation plan is to simply forgive us while we continue to walk in our sins, then the Church has no moral authority to stand against same-sex marriage. But if God's great salvation plan is actually to save us from our sins, then the Church has the moral authority to stand for God's definition of marriage as between one man and one woman.

The sword of God's judgment **is not** coming upon us because many people in our nation have chosen to live a homosexual lifestyle, or because of those who have lobbied for the shedding of innocent blood of millions of aborted babies. The sword of judgment is about to strike this nation because the Church has chosen to reject the true God and to reject His Law, the foundation of His great salvation plan. When God's own people formally reject Him and reject His Law, then all hope for revival will be gone. The Church is like the root of a tree that has been bearing bad fruit in the culture for generations. God has been patient so long as the root of the tree has been good. But when the root of the tree becomes evil, then the tree must be cut down.

God is now giving us the fruit of our own schemes, the fruit of our decades of teaching a salvation plan which does not require true and complete repentance from all sin. This may be our last warning. God is not waiting for the non-believers to repent, He is waiting for His own people to repent, by returning to Him and to His great salvation plan. This is what God is saying to His people in II Chronicles 7:14:

> If my people, who are called by my name, will humble themselves
> and pray and seek my face and turn from their wicked ways, then will
> I hear from heaven and will forgive their sin and will heal their land.

Many today will deny that there is anything wrong with the way Christianity now defines God or with our contemporary plan of salvation. Until the Church stops blaming the culture for our problems there will be no hope for our nation. Yet it is not too late, if we choose to listen carefully to God and are willing to humble ourselves and to let go of our traditional beliefs, if those traditional beliefs are not consistent with the truth of God's Word. For those who are willing to take this step of humility, the invitation is made to experience The Next Great Awakening.

Introduction

Without a Vision the People Perish

> *"Where there is no vision, the people perish:*
> *But he that keepeth the law, happy is he."*
> **Proverbs 29:18 (KJV)**

God has a story to tell, and that story is called *History,* His story. It is a story that has been unfolding for 6,000 years. It is a story about God's people, those He created with the responsibility of taking dominion over His creation, in accordance with His commands. Throughout history, God's people have periodically drifted away from God, often for long periods of time. But God has always had a plan to bring His people back to Him and to the purpose for which He created them. This truth was once revealed by God to His people through the Prophet, Azariah, who declared to King Asa, the King of Judah,

> *The Lord is with you, when you are with Him. If you seek Him, He will be found by you, but if you forsake Him, He will forsake you. **For a long time, Israel was without the true God, without a priest to teach, and without the law**. But in their distress they turned to the Lord, the God of Israel, and sought him, and he was found by them.* (II Chronicles 15:2–4) (emphasis added)

Every Great Awakening throughout history has had a time and place of beginning. The purpose of this book is to be a catalyst that will spark the next Great Awakening within God's people. This spark will begin in the form of a question, which if answered in accordance with the truth of God's Word, will lead us back to God and to the purpose for which He created us. The question this book seeks to both ask and answer in accordance with the Word of God is raised from II Chronicles 15:2–4.

Is it possible that American Christians today, like God's people of the past, have been for a long time without the true God, without a teaching priest, and without the law?

The next Great Awakening will take place only if we are willing to first ask ourselves this question and then answer it through the study of God's Word. Many have been praying for the next Great Awakening to come for many years, without really understanding what it is they have been asking for. What exactly is a *Great Awakening?* History tells us that true awakenings are about more than just a short-term stirring up of our emotions. A truly Great Awakening is a point in time when there is an abrupt change in the hearts and in the lives of the people, over a long period of time. In a true awakening there is *something* that we are awakened to, and this book is about identifying what that *something* is.

It may have been wise to have placed a warning label around this book for those who have considered reading its content. That warning could read **Caution: The words you are about to read may cause great discomfort!** This is true because if this book is read carefully, a great collision is about to occur in the lives of its readers. Two very powerful principles in our lives are about to collide with each other. These two principles are **Tradition** and **Truth**. When our traditions are grounded in the substance of truth, these two principles empower us to live the lives we were created to live. But when our traditions have drifted away from the truth of God's Word, then we will eventually reach a crossroads in our lives and in our culture. We have come to such a crossroads in today's Christian culture. The next Great Awakening will require us to make a choice in the direction we are traveling, and the decision we make will determine both our destiny and the destiny of generations to come.

There is a passage of Scripture, spoken through God's Prophet, Jeremiah, which now applies to us, and it will form the outline of the message of this book:

This is what the Lord says:

> "**Stand at the crossroads and look;**
> **ask for the ancient paths**,
> *ask where the good way is, and walk in it,*
> *and you will find rest for your souls.*
> *But you said, 'We will not walk in it.'*
> *I appointed watchmen over you and said,*
> *'Listen, to the sound of the trumpet!'*
> *But you said, 'We will not listen.'*
> *Therefore hear, O nations;*
> *observe O witnesses,*
> *what will happen to them.*
> *Hear O earth:*
> *I am bringing disaster on this people,*
> *the fruit of their schemes,*
> **because they have not listened to my words**

and have rejected my law." (Jeremiah 6:16–19)
(emphasis added)

A great drift has taken place within the Christian faith today. Just as God's prophets called His people to stand at a crossroads and awaken throughout history, we too are standing at such a crossroads. Will we look for the ancient path, and then walk in it? Will we listen to the sound of the trumpet that is giving us warning that the sword of judgment is about to come upon us if we do not change our path? Will we take warning? This theme of *listening carefully* to the Word of God will be repeated frequently throughout this book. Casual reading will not be enough to guide us in the choices that we must make. This is why the most important points and passages of Scripture throughout this book will all be repeated at least three times. It is to ensure that these critical points are not missed.

The times are urgent, and many Christians today have lost hope that we will ever experience another Great Awakening. But God has prepared an ancient path for us to walk on. It is the only path that will lead us back to God and to the blessings He desires for those who choose to be His people. Walking on this ancient path will not be easy. But walking on this path will be worth every amount of effort that we can give. For this ancient path will lead us back to a life in God's Kingdom, both now and forevermore.

May it be in us as God has said!

The Call

"Many are the plans in a man's heart, but it is the
Lord's purpose that prevails."
Proverbs 19:21

This passage of Scripture has been foundational in my life, and while I have made many plans during the past ten years of preparation and writing this book, my hope is that God will use it for His purpose of awakening His people. The message of this book actually began to take form on a beautiful Minnesota Saturday morning in November of 2003. The snow was falling as I headed out for my morning walk along the east shore of Lake Bemidji, where the Mississippi River reaches its northernmost point before turning south toward the Gulf of Mexico. My intent was to begin the day with prayer and to meditate on scripture memory verses, but something very unusual happened instead. I did not hear an audible voice, but these are the words that formed in my mind: "Pray to your Father in heaven, that He would let you carry the light of His truth to the highest court of the land."

I had never experienced anything like this before. It is difficult to explain how these words were different than just another thought in my mind, but they were. All I can say is that they were not my words. I recall at the time thinking that this might be the way the Lord spoke to people in Bible times. When we read the Old Testament, prophets say that *the Word of the Lord came to me* . . . Was God placing a call on my life? If so, what was God calling me to do?

A short time later, as I was doing my daily devotions, I came upon Psalm 43:3, where King David prayed, "*Send forth your light and your truth, let them guide me; let them bring me to your holy mountain, to the place where you dwell.* " The words of this Psalm were very confirming because they were so similar to the words that had formed in my mind earlier. I have accepted these words as a call upon my life to carry the *light* of *truth,* which is the *power* of God's *Word,* to the highest court of the land. This call has led me on a decade-long journey of seeking to know God, to know Jesus, and to understand God's great plan of salvation. While this journey has only just begun, it has totally changed the way that I think and the way that I live.

This call has also led me on four statewide campaigns for a seat on the Minnesota Supreme Court, the highest court in the land I could seek to carry the light of His truth. In 2003, I had been practicing law in northern Minnesota for seventeen years. With experience in both private practice and as an assistant county attorney, as well as having served the State of Minnesota as both an administrative law judge and as a magistrate, I chose to carry this message to the people of Minnesota by campaigning for a seat on the Minnesota Supreme Court. At that time I felt that this would be the highest hill that I could carry the message of God's light and truth, and that if I were to receive the honor of being elected by the people of Minnesota, I could be an instrument of justice on our state's highest court.

I soon learned how difficult it would be to carry the light of truth into the political arena. While Minnesota's State Constitution gives the people of Minnesota the right and the responsibility to elect their Supreme Court Justices, the judicial election process in this state had historically made it very difficult for a challenger to unseat an incumbent justice. Needing a little over a million votes to win a seat on the Minnesota Supreme Court, I received the votes of approximately 890,000 Minnesotans in the 2012 election. And while this may have been a moral victory, it was very disappointing to fall short of the necessary votes after the many hours of traveling across the State of Minnesota over four elections cycles. But as I look back, I can see how this experience has prepared me to answer the call upon my life. I have now come to the conclusion that the highest court of the land may not be the Minnesota Supreme Court. In America, the highest court of the land is actually the court of public opinion, which is held in the hearts of the people. Both our United States Constitution and our state constitutions begin with the familiar words, "We the People . . .," and this makes the hearts of the people the highest hill that can be climbed in our land. This is the place that the light of truth, the power of God's Word, must be carried if our nation is to experience the next Great Awakening we so desperately need.

The problems and challenges we face today are both numerous and great. We are facing economic instability; a decline in our physical health due to disease, illness, and stress; a great social and moral decline; a raging battle with natural disasters that seem to be intensifying each year; and an increasingly violent and fragmented world with both foreign and domestic threats. The foundational institution of our culture, the family, is crumbling, and the Church appears powerless to save it. While it is not the purpose of this book to focus directly on any of these great challenges on the horizon, it is the purpose of this book to identify the real underlying cause of all of these problems. The real problem is that God's people, the Church, has drifted away from God's Word. For some this may be a bold statement that will be received with great skepticism. For others, it will be received as a statement of the obvious, but that will be ignored unless it is supported by new evidence that will provoke them to take action. But for those who have ears to hear, awakening to this underlying problem will itself lead to the only solution.

I have read many very good books over the years, which have helped me greatly in my search for truth. I have participated in many great Bible studies, which have also helped me come to the place of understanding of God and of His purpose and plans. I have been blessed to have spent the past decade learning from the many great authors and teachers of both the present and past generations. Until now I have not felt that I have had anything to add to the wealth of information available to our generation. Until now, I had nothing to write that has not already been written. And while there is always a benefit to saying important things in a new way, I have not felt that this was my call. More importantly, I am convinced that there is only one book that has the power to really make a difference in our lives and our culture, and that book is the Bible. I have always believed that if people would simply study the Bible, everything would change.

As I have grown in my understanding of the truth of God's Word, I have begun to see the many problems that we face in a new way. I have come to the conclusion that if a book is to become a spark toward the next Great Awakening, it will need to be more than a book of more information. Today's culture is not lacking in information; it is lacking in the ability to correctly process the information we already have.

We have lost the ability to *listen carefully* to the information we have. Thousands of people today are diligently studying the Bible, yet there has been little or no change in the culture. Something is wrong. Something is missing. Even the Bible seems to be lacking the power to change lives and to change our culture that it once had. And while I was slow to accept it, the truth is that we are now living in a post-Christian culture. But this can change! And this will change, if we are willing to humble ourselves and learn to listen carefully to God's directions for life!

The Word of God should have the power to change everything from the life of an individual to the climate of a culture. This truth is boldly proclaimed by God in Isaiah 55:10–11:

> As the rain and the snow come down from heaven, and do not return to it without watering the earth and making it bud and flourish, so that it yields seed for the sower and bread for the eater, so is my word that goes out from my mouth: It will not return to me empty, but will accomplish what I desire, and achieve the purpose for which I sent it.

How could God's Word have lost its power? What has changed? The answer is that God's Word has not lost its power! And neither God, nor His Word, has changed. But for the Word of God to accomplish its purpose on earth, it must fall upon ears that are able to hear those words. The problem is not in the Word of God; the problem is in the ears that hear that Word. We have lost the ability to *listen carefully* to the words God has spoken. The time has come to stop reading what we already believe, and to start believing what we are actually reading.

The Drift

T here are two Bible passages that will emphasize the listening problem we face today. These two passages will form a foundation and an outline for the message of this book. The first passage, which we have already heard, is the Word of the Lord spoken through the Prophet Jeremiah:

> This is what the Lord says, "**Stand at the crossroads**, and look. Ask for the ancient paths. Ask where the good way is, and walk in it, and you will find rest for your souls." But you said, "We will not walk in it." I appointed watchmen over you and said, "**Listen to the sound of the trumpet**." But you said, "We will not listen." Therefore, hear O nations, observe O witnesses, what will happen to them. Hear O earth, for I am about to bring destruction upon this people, the fruit of their schemes, **because they have not to listened to my words and have rejected my law.** (Jeremiah 6:16–19) (emphasis added)

Consider who God is speaking to in this passage. It is not to the pagans or to the unbelievers. God is speaking to His own people. He warns them to *listen* and to wake up to what is about to happen to them if they do not change the way they are living. God had appointed watchmen over His own people to sound the trumpet of warning, but they refused to listen. And He is doing the same for His people today. But will God's people today have ears to *listen carefully* to what God has told us since the beginning of time?

It should also be noted from this passage that it was God who was bringing destruction upon His own people who would not walk on the ancient path and who would not listen to the warning sound of the trumpet. The sword was not in the hands of foreign enemies. It was God Himself who was about to bring destruction upon His own people. The destruction would come as a result of the people's own actions and plans, but the consequences would be executed by God's hand. But why would God bring destruction upon His own people? This is a difficult concept for today's Christians to accept. Yet God clearly gives the two reasons for this destruction. He says that it is because, "*They have not listened to my words, and have rejected my law."* Could it be possible that American Christians today are guilty of these same two great errors?

There is a second passage, this time from the New Testament, which also points us to the real foundational problem that faces today's Christian culture. This passage comes from Hebrews 2:1–4, and it forms the outline of the message of this book:

> **So we must listen very carefully then, to the truth that we have heard, or we may drift away from it**. The message God delivered through angels has always proved true, and the people were punished for every violation of the law, and every act of disobedience. **What makes us think that we can escape if we are indifferent to this great salvation,** that was announced by the Lord, Jesus himself, it was passed on to us by those who heard him speak. And God verified the message through signs, wonders, various miracles, and by giving gifts of the Holy Spirit, whenever He chose to do so. (NLT) (emphasis added)

This passage warns us again to listen very carefully to the truth, to God's Word, or we may drift away from it. Could it be possible that we, as American Christians, have drifted away from the truth, without knowing it? What is this message God delivered through angels that has always proved true? Could it be that we too have become indifferent to this great salvation message? These are some of the questions we must ask and answer if we are to experience the next Great Awakening.

Before we begin our walk on the ancient path, it is important to hear the words of God's watchman, the Prophet Ezekiel, who was appointed by God to warn the people of the impending danger. These are the words of warning, the sound of the trumpet, which God's people must respond to:

> The Word of the Lord came to me, "Son of man, speak to your countrymen, and say to them: 'When I bring the sword against the land, and the people of the land choose one of their men and make him their watchman, and he sees the sword coming against the land and blows the trumpet to warn the people, then if anyone hears the sound of the trumpet and does not take warning and the sword comes and takes his life, his blood will be on his own head. Since he heard the sound of the trumpet but did not take warning, his blood will be on his own head. If he had taken warning he would have saved himself. But if the watchman sees the sword coming against the land, and does not sound the trumpet to warn the people, and the sword comes and takes the life of one of them, that man will be taken away because of his sin, but I will hold the watchman accountable for his blood.
>
> Son of man, I have made you a watchman for the house of Israel; so hear the word I speak, and give them warning from me. When I

say to the wicked, 'O wicked man, you shall surely die,' and you do not speak out to dissuade him from his ways, that wicked man will die for his sin, and I will hold you, accountable for his blood. But if you warn the wicked man to turn from his ways, and he does not do so, he will die for his sin, but you will have saved yourself.

Son of man, say to the house of Israel, 'This is what you are saying: "Our offenses and sins weigh us down, and we are wasting away because of them. How then can we live?" Say to them, 'As surely as I live, declares the Sovereign Lord, I take no pleasure in the death of the wicked, but rather that they turn from their ways and live. Turn! Turn from your evil ways! Why will you die, O house of Israel?"

Therefore, son of man, say to your countrymen, 'The righteousness of a righteous man will not save him when he disobeys, and the wickedness of a wicked man will not cause him to fall, when he turns from it. The righteous man, if he sins, will not be allowed to live because of his former righteousness. If I tell the righteous man that he will surely live, but then trusts in his righteousness and does evil, none of the righteous things he has done will be remembered and he will die for the evil he has done. And if I say to a wicked man, 'You will surely die,' but then he turns away from his sin and does what is just and right, if he gives back what he took in pledge for a loan, returns what he has stolen, follows the decrees that bring life, and does no evil, he will surely live; he will not die. None of the sins he sins he has committed will be remembered against him. He has done what is just and right; he will surely live.

Yet your countrymen say, 'The way of the Lord is not just.' But it is their way that is not just. If a righteous man, turns from his righteousness and does evil, he will die for it. And if a wicked man turns away from his wickedness and does what is just and right, he will live by doing so. Yet, O house of Israel, you say, 'The way of the Lord is not just!' But I will judge each of you by his own ways." (Ezekiel 33:1–20)

If we have listened carefully to these words of the watchman on the wall, we can hear everything we need to experience the next Great Awakening. One of the goals of this book is to improve our ability to listen carefully to what we are reading. To accomplish this goal, this book will ask several questions of the reader rather than simply stating the answers. This is important because it will deliberately slow the reader down, ensuring that he or she thinks about the answer to the question. Questions are very powerful, and our minds are created to answer all questions they encounter. We will understand the truth of God's word much better if information is offered to us in the form of a question rather than only as a statement of fact. To understand the meaning of a Scripture passage, pause to let yourself consider the passage that you have just read and then allow yourself time to answer the question before reading on to find the answer. This may seem cumbersome at first, but it is critical that we learn to listen carefully to God's Word, not simply to the opinions and interpretations of men, including those of the author of this book!

With this goal of a deeper understanding in mind, consider these questions with regard to the passage we just read from Ezekiel 33. Who is holding the sword that the watchman sees coming against the land? It is God who is bringing the sword against the land. And who is God speaking to? It is God's own people. This truth in itself should cause us to awaken. Does God want to destroy even one of His chosen people? Absolutely not! He clearly says, *I take no pleasure in the death of the wicked, but rather that they turn from their wicked ways and live.* So what is God asking His people to do? Will it do any good for the people to pray that God would not bring the sword against the land? Does God simply want His people to pray that the sword will not come? Will it do any good for the people to fast and pray for deliverance from the impending danger if they refuse to repent? Will God change His mind if enough people beg Him to stop? Or is there a reason that God is bringing the sword against His own people? Correctly answering these questions will lead us back to the ancient path that God is calling us to walk upon.

History tells us that revivals and awakenings must do more than touch our emotions. As stated earlier, there must be substance to any Great Awakening. We must awaken to something which has been lost. Most Christians today have a desire for the next Great Awakening in America, but they really do not know what it is that they are asking for. Many today are simply waiting for God to move, but they have no any idea what, if anything, they must do to prepare for the next Great Awakening. Yet there is one very obvious and necessary condition that the people must be in before there can be any kind of an awakening. This condition is so obvious that most people do not see it. The pre-awakening condition required of the people is that they must actually be asleep! If we are not asleep, we do not need an awakening. If we are not asleep, there can be no awakening!

Have today's Christians met this necessary condition? Have we fallen asleep? If we have fallen asleep, the problem we face is that we will not know that we have been asleep until after we wake up. If today's Christians have fallen asleep, then by definition we do not know it. This book is about identifying the specific condition of our state of sleep. It is about bringing us to an awareness of something that we are currently not aware of. This is a very challenging task, but the good news is that as soon as we acknowledge the issue upon which we have fallen asleep, the next Great Awakening will have begun!

Another cautionary warning should be given to those who are truly seeking the next Great Awakening. We should be warned that being awakened from our sleep is not always an enjoyable experience. The transition from darkness to light may be uncomfortable at first, as our eyes adjust to the light. If we really listen to the words of God's watchman on the wall, something is about to happen to us. We will experience a great collision between God's truth and our long-held traditional beliefs. Tragically, when this happens, many who have been praying for an awakening will instead run back into the darkness.

The first word that we will focus on from our foundational verse from Hebrews 2 is the word *drift*. Is it possible that today's Christians have drifted away from the truth and don't know it? What does it mean for a people to drift away from the truth, and could this even happen in this age of almost unlimited information that we live in today? We have more Bibles per capita than at any time in history. We have hundreds if not thousands of well-educated Christian authors who are writing more and more best-selling Christian books every day. We can now download these books to read without ever leaving our homes. We have the Internet, which allows us to instantly look at almost any translations of the Bible we choose. And while the percentage of Americans who are Christians may be on the decline, the actual number of professing Christians remains in the millions. So is it even possible that God's people in America today could have drifted away from God's truth? The answer is a resounding "*Yes!*"

Why have we not noticed this drift happening to us? It is because this drift has been gradual, so it has gone unnoticed by most believers, even by most Christian leaders. With all of the advantages we have as today's Christians, why are we drifting away from God? This drift has not been caused by a lack of information. The cause of this drift is again that we have a listening problem. To listen carefully to God's Word will require us to ask ourselves questions. God will not give us answers to questions we have not asked. Jesus taught his disciples:

> So I say to you: Ask and it will be given to you; seek and you will
> find; knock and the door will be opened to you. For everyone who
> asks receives; he who seeks finds; and to him who knocks, the door
> will be opened. (Luke 11:9–10)

One of the first questions we need to ask of God is for an understanding of what it is that we have drifted away from? The answer is in the substance of our faith, the truth about who God is, and what His great plan of salvation really is. In Hebrews 11:1 this *faith* is defined: "*Now faith is being sure of what we hope for and certain of what we do not see.*" What is it that today's Christians are hoping for? Are we hoping for what God wants for us, or for what we want from God? The Apostle Paul addressed this source of our faith in Romans 10:17, where he writes, "*So then faith cometh by hearing, and hearing by the word of God*" (KJB). God's Word is the source of our faith, and it alone provides the substance of what we should hope for. God's Word is the truth from which we have drifted. Jesus prayed for his disciples, "*Sanctify them by the truth, your word is truth*" (John 17:17). Today's Christians are not lacking in Bibles, so why are we drifting away from the truth? It is because we are not listening carefully to God's Word. We are reading what we already believe about God and about His plan of salvation rather than believing what we are reading. Acknowledging that this drift has taken place will not be easy. It will require great humility. In the familiar words of II Chronicles 7:14, God points his people in the direction of this humility as the first step back to Him, as He states: "*If my people, who are called by my name, will humble themselves and pray and seek my face and turn from their wicked ways, then will I hear from heaven and will forgive their sin and will heal their land."*

It is not fun to humble ourselves by admitting that we have been wrong about anything, especially with regard to the substance of our faith. History tells us that the Church is usually reluctant to accept a message that even suggests that a drift has taken place, and this is understandable. Good men, who have dedicated their lives to their teaching of God's Word, do not want to hear that their teachings have drifted away from the truth. To be told that we have been teaching the wrong message for the majority of our lives is not what we want to hear. But as we are warned in Proverbs 14:12, *"There is a way that seems right to a man, but in the end it leads to death."*

Great Awakenings are uncommon because people who have drifted off to sleep are not looking to be awakened. Everyone enjoys a good night's sleep. Nobody enjoys being abruptly awakened. In fact, the person who wakes us up will often receive a much less than grateful response from the person who has been awakened. For example our first response to being awakened by a fire alarm will probably be great displeasure, but when we come to realize what is at stake, we begin to appreciate the sound of the alarm that may have saved our lives. The same can be true on a spiritual level. As we drift away from the truth, and with the passage of time, our status quo becomes supported by our traditions. We become very comfortable with our traditions and will even become angry if those traditions are challenged. A Great Awakening will inevitably challenge our traditional beliefs, and it will function like a spiritual fire alarm, which is warning us of the great danger of remaining asleep.

Experiencing a Great Awakening is also like coming to a crossroads, which forces us to make a choice. The choice we must make is between *truth* and *tradition.* And because this is such a difficult decision, most awakenings are preceded only by conditions of pain, trouble, or fear. If we really know that we are in trouble, we are much more likely to accept the correction that takes place in an awakening. Many Christians are hoping that America is reaching this point of readiness, as it is becoming increasingly obvious that we are in trouble as a nation. But it is not only secular America that is at a crossroads; it is also the American Christian Church. Christianity's influence in our culture is in a great decline during a time when it is needed the most. At a time when the culture is living in fear of increasing crime, of economic collapse, of terrorism, of cancer and disease, and of global climate change, the Christian Church should have answers. The time is right for an awakening in the culture, but an awakening in the Church must happen first. When the world becomes dark, the Church is to be the light in that darkness. But light always requires a power source, and if we are honest, the Church is lacking this power at a time when the culture needs it the most.

The writer of Hebrews encourages us to listen very carefully to God's warnings, but many Christians today, like God's people in the past, will choose not to heed this warning. It is much easier to just keep listening casually to sermons each Sunday and to pick the next best-selling Christian devotional book rather than becoming a real student of God's Word. Reading our devotions each day is a good habit to have, but the time has come for much more. As the Apostle Paul writes, *"Do your*

best to present yourself to God as one approved, a workman who does not need
to be ashamed and who correctly handles the word of truth" (II Timothy 2:16). Paul
goes on to write, "*All Scripture is God breathed and is useful for teaching, rebuking,
correcting and training in righteousness, so that the man of God may be thoroughly
equipped for every good work*" (II Timothy 3:16–17).

Conclusion

The success of this book will not depend on its ability to persuade people to
believe something new. Neither the culture nor the Church is lacking in people who
will argue in favor of their own opinions. What we are in need of is the testimony
of God. As one of our foundational passages concludes, "*And God verified the
message through signs, wonders, various miracles, and by giving gifts of the Holy
Spirit whenever He chose to do so*" (Hebrews 2:4). The testimony of this book is not
directed only toward God's people; it is first and foremost directed toward God. This
book will succeed only if it has given God something to testify on behalf of, and that
something is called *truth*. Without God's testimony, no matter how persuasive of an
argument is made, there will be no Great Awakening, and nothing of eternal significance will take place. But when we rightly align our faith with God's truth, God's Word
tells us that He will testify on our behalf, and the next Great Awakening will begin!

A King, a People, and a Great Awakening

To better understand what will be needed for us to experience the next Great Awakening, it will be helpful to listen to a story. This is the story of a king, a people, and a Great Awakening. This was the fourteenth king in a long succession of kings who ruled over a great nation for a long time period that covered more than four hundred years. To put this four hundred year time period into perspective, it is approximately the same amount of time that has passed since the Pilgrims first came to America. At the time of this fourteenth king, the nation was in the midst of a great rebuilding project. Because this nation was very wealthy, they hired only the best workers to do the work, and they used only the best materials in the project. The project was very expensive, so one day the king called his top aide and said, *"Go to the keeper of the treasury and get enough money to pay the workers."* And that is what the aide did.

It should be pointed out that money at the time of this story was not the same as money is today. Money was not just numbers on a piece of paper or figures on a computer screen. Money at that time was actual tangible treasure, such as gold and silver coins, precious jewels, and other valuable commodities. Because this nation was very wealthy, the treasury was a very large vault, and on this particular day the keeper of the treasury decided to go all the way to the back of the treasury vault to gather the necessary money as the king had ordered. As he was gathering the treasure, his eyes fell upon something out of the ordinary. It wasn't gold, silver, precious stones, or jewels. It was leather, and it was covered with dust. It was tucked behind the piles of treasure. The keeper of the treasury carefully reached back and removed the object from its hiding place. He immediately recognized what he had found. It was an ancient scroll that had been written over one thousand years earlier, hundreds of years prior to even the first of the kings that had been ruling over this great nation.

As soon as he realized what he had found, the keeper of the treasury immediately brought the scroll to the king's aide and said, *"I have done what you have asked, and have gathered the money as requested, but look what I have found! It is an ancient scroll!"* We can only imagine the look on the aide's face as he carefully removed the ancient scroll from its container and began to read the words that appeared on it. *"We have to get this to the King at once!"* he said, and they rushed the scroll back to the king.

When they arrived back in the presence of the king, the aide said to the king, "*We have done what you asked, Your Majesty. We have gone to the treasury and gotten the money to pay the workers, but we have made a great discovery, for we have found something vastly more valuable than all the treasure in the treasury. We have found an ancient scroll that was written to our people over one thousand years ago.*" The king responded, "*Read this scroll to me.*" And as the aide read the words of this ancient scroll to the king, the king became so upset, and so convicted, that he literally tore his royal robe! He said, "*How could this have happened! How could the generations that have gone before us failed to follow the words of this scroll? And how could they have failed to pass the words of this scroll on to us? Now we are doomed to destruction unless drastic measures are taken. Call all of the people together, young and old, rich and poor, men, women and children, and we will read the words of this scroll to the people.*" And that is precisely what they did.

Not only did the king call all of the people of the land together to hear the words of the ancient scroll read to them, but the king stood before the people and vowed to return to again follow the words contained on that scroll. And not only did the king make this vow, but the people of the land did the same! What happened next can best be described as the greatest awakening this nation had ever experienced over its four-hundred year history. The changes that took place were far from easy changes. There was much pain in the process of the cultural transformation that took place. But the results were more than worth the effort, and this nation had the greatest celebration of its entire history!

This, as you may have already guessed, is not a fictitious story. This is a true story. This is history, or more accurately, His Story. This is an historical account of God's people as set forth in our Bibles at II Kings chapters 22 and 23. The purpose of telling this story is to encourage God's people to take the time to read the entire account upon which this story is based. This is the story of a king named Josiah, the king of Judah, which was a part of the nation of Israel. This is a story that needs to be studied by God's people today if we too want to experience the next Great Awakening. This is a story of real cultural change!

We can learn so much from this story if we will ask the right questions. What was this ancient scroll that had been written several hundred years prior to even the first of the kings of Israel? What words would cause a king to become so upset that he would literally rip his robe? And what words, when read to the people, would empower the people to transform their culture in ways it had not been transformed for four centuries? That ancient scroll was the Book of the Law, God's instructions for life, handed down to Moses on Mount Sinai. But what exactly is the Book of the Law? This is not a term that is used very often today, and it is not well understood by today's Christians. When most of us think of Moses and God's Law handed down on Mount Sinai, we think of the Ten Commandments. But would reading of the Ten Commandments alone make this king tear his robe? And would reading the Ten Commandments alone cause such a great awakening to take place?

It would probably take more than reading the Ten Commandments to cause this kind of reaction. The Book of the Law actually is more than the Ten Commandments. The Ten Commandments are the foundation of the Book of the Law, but the real heart of the Book of the Law, the words that if believed would cause a king to tear his robe and a people to transform their culture, can be found in Deuteronomy 28. Here we find words that will strike fear into the hearts of any man, woman or child who believes them to be true. The words of Deuteronomy 28, the heart of the Book of the Law, are some of the most difficult words to read in the entire Bible. But if we are going to experience the kind of cultural transformation that we need, we must not only read these words, but we must meditate on these words until we really understand why they carry such great power.

The first 14 verses of Deuteronomy 28 will bring us pleasure and put a smile on our faces, as God sets forth the many blessings that will come to His people, when they follow the words of the Book of the Law:

> If you fully obey the Lord your God and carefully follow all his commands I give you today, the Lord your God will set you high above all the nations on earth. All these blessings will come upon you and accompany you if you obey the Lord your God:
>
> You will be blessed in the city and blessed in the country.
>
> The fruit of your womb will be blessed, and the crops of your land and the young of your livestock—the calves of your herds and the lambs of your flocks.
>
> Your basket and your kneading trough will be blessed.
>
> You will be blessed when you come in and blessed when you go out.
>
> The Lord will grant that the enemies who rise up against you will be defeated before you. They will come at you from one direction but flee from you in seven.
>
> The Lord will send a blessing on your barns and on everything you put your hand to. The Lord your God will bless you in the land he is giving you.
>
> The Lord will establish you as his holy people, as he promised you on oath, if you keep the commands of the Lord your God and walk in his ways. Then all the peoples on earth will see that you are called by the name of the Lord, and they will fear you. The Lord will grant you abundant prosperity—in the fruit of your womb, the young of your livestock and the crops of your ground—in the land he swore to your forefathers to give you.

The Lord will open the heavens, the storehouse of his bounty, to send rain on your land in season and to bless all the work of your hands. You will lend to many nations but will borrow from none. The Lord will make you the head, not the tail. If you pay attention to the commands of the Lord your God that I give you this day and carefully follow them, you will always be at the top, never at the bottom. Do not turn aside from any of the commands I give you today, to the right or to the left, following other gods and serving them. (Deuteronomy 28:1–14)

It is truly a blessing to be the people of God, if we live in accordance with His Law, His directions for life! But a warning should be given before continuing on with the remainder of Deuteronomy 28. Just as the first 14 verses will bring us great joy and peace, the next 54 verses of Deuteronomy 28, almost four times as many verses, warn us of the consequences of disobeying of God's commands. These next 54 verses are some of the most difficult verses to read in the entire Bible. They begin with a list of the mirror image of curses that God will bring upon this same people if they choose to live in disobedience to His commands. Then in Deuteronomy 28:20, God declares: *"The Lord will send on you curses, confusion and rebuke in everything you put your hand to, until you are destroyed and come to sudden ruin because of the evil you have done in forsaking him."*

But it does not end there, it goes on to paint a picture that is so dark that it is almost beyond comprehension. Yet, as uncomfortable as it may be, it is necessary for God's people to read the entire chapter of Deuteronomy 28. As we will see, there is a reason that the Book of the Law paints this very dark picture of life that is not lived in accordance with God's directions! When we read these verses today, it is likely that we will simply read to get through them, reasoning that this is just what happened in the past to these wicked Israelites, and that God would never send such curses upon His people today. But Josiah and God's chosen people at the time of II Kings 22 and 23 believed that these words were true for them as well, and that these curses would be the consequences of failing to return to a life and culture of obedience to God's Law. It would be in these words that the people would find the power to change their culture.

As we consider the historical account of Josiah, the rediscovery of the Book of the Law, and the cultural transformation that followed, a question should be raised in our minds. If discovering the Book of the Law had this great of an impact on God's people then, would it have the same impact on God's people today? Could the spark for the next Great Awakening in America come simply through reading Deuteronomy 28 as our daily devotions, in our Bible studies, and from the Sunday morning pulpits? Would God's people today repent like they did at the time of King Josiah? The honest answer to this question is *probably not*. As much as we would like it to be that easy, we all know that even the words of Deuteronomy 28 are likely to be powerless in today's post-Christian culture.

But if we are determined to find the path to the next Great Awakening, we cannot stop here. We must listen more carefully to God's Word. We must become a people who continue to ask the next question until we find the answers we are looking for. So what is the next question? The next question is "Why not?" Why wouldn't these words have the same impact on God's people today that they had on God's people then? Has God changed? Has God's plan for His people changed? The answers to these questions will be addressed in great detail in later chapters, but for now the simple answer to both of these questions is "No, God has not changed" and "No, His plan for his people has not changed."

So where does that leave us? If God has not changed, and if His plan has not changed, then what has changed? Why wouldn't reading the Book of the Law change our Christian culture today? It is because God's people have changed. Our definition of God has changed. Our belief in His plan for us has changed. We no longer believe that God would actually curse His own people for failing to follow His directions. We have drifted away from the true God. We have fallen asleep and do not realize it. We have changed our understanding of who God is and what His standard of righteousness is. We no longer really believe that there will be disastrous and eternal consequences for our disobedience of God's Law. We too have lost the Book of the Law, just as God's people had lost it in the days of King Josiah. And our only hope is to rediscover the Book of the Law, just as they did. Rediscovering the Book of the Law will require more than just hanging the Ten Commandments back up on our walls, even though this would not be a bad start.

There is a deeper understanding that we can gain from looking at the history of God's people and the way they drifted away from God and from His Law. To receive this understanding, we must go back in time to the second king in the long succession of kings that ruled over God's people, Israel. This second king's name was Solomon. Solomon became king when he was still a very young man. And it pleased God greatly that when Solomon was given the opportunity to ask for anything he wanted, Solomon chose to ask God for wisdom to guide the great nation of Israel. And God favored Solomon with more than wisdom. God also allowed Solomon the favor of building the great temple in which God Himself would manifestly abide with His people. Shortly after Solomon had completed the building of this temple to God's exact specifications, but before God manifestly entered the temple, Solomon prayed to God. In his prayer, Solomon asked God to promise that if the people ever strayed away from God, but then repented, that God would forgive the people and take them back. You can read Solomon's entire prayer at II Chronicles 6:12–42. God's presence then filled the temple and shortly thereafter God answered Solomon's prayer and spoke words that are familiar to many Christians today:

> If my people, who are called by my name, will humble themselves
> and pray and seek my face and turn from their wicked ways, then
> will I hear from heaven and will forgive their sin and will heal their
> land. (II Chronicles 7:14)

These are words that have been the foundation of prayers across America for more than a decade, and it is these words of an unchanging God, with an unchanging plan, that give us confidence that it is not too late for the American Church to return to God. Yet, just three generations after God spoke these words to King Solomon, God spoke again, this time to Israel's King Asa, who was Solomon's great-grandson. Asa was a good king, and after God had given him great victory on the battlefield, God spoke these very important words of truth:

> The Lord is with you when you are with him. If you seek him, he will be found by you, but if you forsake him, he will forsake you. For a long time Israel was without the true God, without a priest to teach, and without the law. But in their distress they turned to the Lord, the God of Israel, and sought him, and he was found by them. (II Chronicles 15:2–4)

Did we listen carefully to these words? How could God's own people have been for a long time without Him? In today's Christian culture we are constantly told that God will never leave us or forsake us. This is a theme in countless contemporary Christian songs, and this is a point that is driven home from pulpits across this nation every Sunday. But God has clearly spoken the truth on this issue, which is that if we choose to remain with Him, He will never leave us, and if we choose to forsake Him, He will forsake us. Our label as *Christians* does not exempt us from this truth any more than it would have exempted those with the label of *Israelites* at the time these words were spoken to King Asa. We have drifted away from this truth because we too have for a long time been without a teaching priest and without the law.

It is unlikely that the religious leaders at the time of King Asa were happy to hear this Word of the Lord spoken to the king. A fictional illustration may help us see that this drift can really happen to God's people. Let us imagine that we were living at the time of King Asa. And let us pretend that we were journalists working for INN, the Israeli News Network. *Remember this is a fictional illustration.* We have heard the breaking news that God has just spoken to the king these surprising words, "*For a long time Israel was without the true God, without a teaching priest, and without the law.*" So we decide to get some expert commentary and analysis for a news story by interviewing the High Priest. When we get a chance to speak with the High Priest we ask him a series of questions. First we ask, "*Did you hear the breaking news? The Lord has told the king that for a long time we, the Nation of Israel, have been without the true God. Is this true?*" What would the High Priest's response have been? Is it likely that he would have admitted that God's presence had left them a long time ago? This type of an admission would have been very unlikely.

Being top notch journalists, we then we ask the follow-up question, "*The Lord said to the king that we have been for a long time without a teaching priest. Is that true?*" This question would likely get us into trouble. It would be again be very unlikely that the High Priest would acknowledge that they were not teaching God's Word properly. Then we ask the final question, "*The Lord has said to the king that we have for a long time been without the Law. Is that true?*" It is likely that the Priest would take us to the written scrolls to prove that they had not lost the Law. The High Priest might even respond by referring to the ever-increasing number of religious laws and regulations that were being written by the religious leaders as applications of God's Law. But does having possession of the scroll mean that you have maintained the Law?

The point of this fictitious illustration is in support of the proposition that it is likely that even the religious leaders of the time of King Asa would not have known, or at least would not have admitted, that these statements were true. It is likely that Israel had drifted away from God, and away from His truth, and they did not know it. They had stopped teaching the whole Law of God, and they were in great danger of the consequences. The question for the American Christian Church today is whether this could be true of us as well?

Conclusion

To experience the Next Great Awakening, we will need to become students of history, which is God's story about His people of the past. God is unchanging, and his plan and desire for His people is unchanging. Knowing how God has worked throughout history will prepare us for how He will work in the future. The historical account of King Josiah, and the rediscovery of the Book of the Law, is a wakeup call for God's people today. To lose the Law is a fatal flaw. The blessings of God come to a people who obey God's commands. The curses of God come upon a people who disobey God's commands. Deuteronomy 28, the heart of the Book of the Law, applies to God's people today just as it did at the time it was given by God to the people through Moses. The Law is more than the commands of God. The Law includes the consequences for disobeying those commands.

II Chronicles 7:14 gives us hope that God will restore us to the blessings He desires for us if we humble ourselves, and pray, and seek His face, and truly repent from our ways by following His commands. But God's people can drift away from God. Just as God spoke at the time of King Asa, God's people can be for a long time, without the true God, without a teaching priest, and without the law.

A Malachi Message

So if God does not change, and if His plan for His people does not change, then it is important for us to listen more carefully to the unchanging words God has spoken through His prophets. These words will help us to discover what is at the core of our problems today, and what we can do to change our culture. If it seems as though God has been silent for a long time, consider that after God spoke His final recorded words of the Old Testament to His people through the Prophet Malachi, there would be four hundred years of silence. At a time when many Christians are calling out to God for answers, it may be wise to change the way we are waiting for Him to answer our prayers. Rather than waiting like a man at a bus stop *waits* for the bus to arrive, maybe we should *wait upon* God like a waiter waits on a table. If we are to discern what the Lord is expecting from us, we will need to be much more active in our listening to what this unchanging God has already spoken to His people. Recall again the words that God spoke through the great Prophet Jeremiah:

> This is what the Lord says, "Stand at the crossroads and look. **Ask for the ancient paths.** Ask for the good way and walk in it, and you will find rest for your souls. But you said, 'We will not walk in it. I appointed watchmen over you and said, 'Listen to the sound of the trumpet' but you said, 'We will not listen.' Therefore hear O nations, observe O witnesses, what will happen to them. Hear O earth, for I am about to bring destruction upon this people, the fruit of their schemes, **because they have not listened to my words, and have rejected my law."** (Jeremiah 6:16–19) (emphasis added)

It is not too late to listen. It is not too late to hear the sound of the trumpet and to take warning. In fact, the first step toward the next Great Awakening will be to simply listen more carefully to what this unchanging God has already spoken to us throughout history, His Story.

During the two years prior to writing this book, the Lord gave me an almost endless desire to study the Book of Malachi. Until that time I had not given this book of the Bible much thought or attention. But that has changed. As I have continued to read and reread the words God has spoken through this last great prophet of the

Old Testament, I have come to see things in this book that I had never seen before. Everything we need to hear to move us into the next Great Awakening can be found in the words of the Lord spoken through Malachi. There is great significance in these last prophetic words of the Old Testament Scripture. This was God's final warning to His people then, and it may well be the final warning to God's people today!

In this chapter, we will go through these words God has spoken through Malachi, New Living Translation, with several brief observations and applications to consider as we stand at a critical crossroads in our culture today. If we are willing to really listen carefully to these words, we will gain the wisdom needed to choose wisely the path that will lead us back to the life and blessings that God desires for us. We will go through this powerful message of God delivered through Malachi verse by verse. The message takes the form of a dialogue between God and His people:

> This is the message that the Lord gave to Israel through the prophet, Malachi.
>
> "I have loved you deeply" says the Lord.
>
> But you retort, "Really, how have you loved us?"
>
> And the Lord replies, "I have shown my love for you by loving your ancestor, Jacob. Yet Esau was Jacob's brother, and I rejected Esau and devastated his hill country. I turned Esau's inheritance into a desert for jackals."
>
> And the descendants of Esau, in Edom, may say "We have been shattered but we will rebuild the ruins."
>
> But this is what the Lord Almighty says, "They may try to rebuild but I will demolish them again. Their country will be called the land of wickedness, and their people will be called the people with whom the Lord is forever angry. When you see the destruction for your-selves you will say, "Surely the Lord's great power extends far beyond our borders." (Malachi 1:1–5)

The goal in studying the words of Malachi is to not simply read them, but to listen very carefully to them. What is God really saying, and how do His words apply to us today? Today's Christians will have no problem with God reminding His people that, "*I have loved you deeply, says the Lord . . .*" We are very good at accepting the fact that God would love His people deeply. The focus of today's Christianity is primarily on the love of God. But then God says that while He loved Jacob, He has rejected Esau. The fact that God would reject anyone will be difficult for many Christians. Many today believe that God's love is universally given and completely unconditional to all who simply say "thank you." But if this is true, then why did God reject Esau? Esau was the grandson of Abraham, the first born son of Isaac. And not only did God reject Esau, but he rejected Esau's descendants. God said He would demolish them again when they tried to rebuild what God had destroyed. Is this a God who unconditionally loves all people, regardless of what they do? Do we really understand this God? Do we really understand the love of God?

The Lord then begins to bring indictment after indictment against His own people. As these words are read, listen carefully to the responses of the people to each of God's accusations. Listen especially to how the people had drifted off to sleep and were greatly surprised that God was bringing these indictments against them:

> The Lord almighty says to the priests, "A son honors his father, and a servant respects his master. I am your father and your master, but where are the honor and respect that I deserve? You have despised my name says the Lord."
>
> But you respond, "How have we despised your name?"
>
> And the Lord replies, "You have despised it by offering defiled sacrifices on my altar."
>
> But you ask, "How have we defiled the sacrifices?"
>
> You have defiled them by saying, "The Lord's altar deserves no respect. When you bring blind animals as sacrifices isn't that wrong. And isn't it wrong to offer animals that are crippled and diseased. Try giving gifts like that to your governor and see how pleased he is. Go ahead, beg God to be merciful to you, but when you bring that kind of offering why should He show you any favor at all says the Lord." (Malachi 1:6–9)

God is clearly telling His people that we are to give Him the honor and respect that He deserves. But are we doing this today? Do we honor God with the gifts we offer to Him? What do we offer to God? And what about His indictment against the sacrifices offered to Him on His altar? Does this have any application to us today? Obviously we no longer make animal sacrifices, because Jesus became the final Lamb who was slain for the payment of the penalty for our sins. So what application could this have for us today? Do we still offer sacrifices to God?

Consider the words of the Apostle Paul, who wrote, *"Therefore, I urge you brothers, in view of God's mercy, to offer your bodies as living sacrifices, holy and pleasing to God—this is your spiritual act of worship"* (Romans 12:1). Our sacrifice to God today is our living body, our very life! We are to be living sacrifices. Keeping this in mind, what was God's indictment against the animal sacrifices? They were offering less than their best! So what about the living sacrifices we offer God today? Do we give God the best of our lives or the left overs? And before we move on, what about the statement, ". . . *but when you bring that kind of offering why should he show you any favor at all* . . ." How would today's Christians respond to this question? Grace is the *unmerited favor* of God. Is it possible that God is saying to us that when we give Him less than the best of our lives, we should not expect Him to show us any *grace* at all? Is it possible that the receipt of God's favor today is still conditioned upon what we offer to God?

God's next statement is a shocking one. If you doubt that God is serious about the kind of sacrifices we offer Him, that doubt will be removed when you listen to these words:

> *"I wish that someone among you would shut the temple doors so that these worthless sacrifices could no longer be offered" says the Lord.* (Malachi 1:10)

Did we listen to what God just said? God would rather have the doors of His temple shut than accept these less-than-best sacrifices! Does this have any application to us today? We don't have temples, but we do have churches. We do not sacrifice animals, but we do offer our lives as living sacrifices. Could it be that God would rather have the doors to our churches closed than to accept the living sacrifices that are being produced in our churches today? What kind of *living sacrifices* are produced in today's churches? Are the lives of church-going people really any different than the lives of those who do not attend church? Is God pleased with the lives we are offering Him? Does He have the right to expect more from His people? Malachi continues:

> "I am not at all pleased with you," says the Lord, "and I will not accept your offerings. For my name is honored by people of other nations from morning until night. All around the world they offer sweet incense and pure offerings in honor of my name. But you dishonor my name with your actions. By bringing contemptible food you are saying 'It's too hard to serve the Lord' and you turn up your noses at His commandments.

> "Think of it, animals that are stolen and mutilated, crippled and sick, presented as offerings! Should I accept from you such offerings as these" says the Lord? "Cursed is the cheat, who promises to give a fine ram from his flock, but then offers a defective one to the Lord. For I am a great King, says the Lord, and my name is feared among the nations." (Malachi 1:10–14)

How might these words apply to us today? What are we offering to the Lord? One thing we offer up to God is our prayers. We can visualize our prayers rising to the Lord as incense. But are the prayers that we offer to God like a sweet incense to the Lord? If not, does God accept them anyway? What kind of prayer would make a sweet incense to the Lord? Are our prayers focused on what God desires from us or on what we desire from God? Remember that our lives are ultimately what we present as offerings God. Do we offer God the best of our lives or the leftovers? What does God think of leftovers?

God speaks of a cheat who promises to give a fine ram from his flock but then offers a defective one instead. Could this be applied to a man who says the sinner's prayer, promising to make Jesus his Savior and his Lord but then continues to live a self-centered life of sin? We tell nonbelievers that they should give their lives to Jesus, yet how many people who pray this prayer shortly thereafter take their lives back? Is a person who does this like the *cheat* who promises to give a fine ram from his flock but then offers a defective one to the Lord? How many people today promise to give their lives to the Lord but later offer Him only the leftovers? Will God settle for whatever we give Him and bless us anyway? Or would He actually curse a man for making this promise only to later change his mind? We have become so casual in our sinners' prayer conversions. We no longer see God as the Great King of the Universe. And we no longer fear His name.

In Malachi 2 the Lord shifts His focus onto the leaders of His people, the priests. Most Christians today do not have priests. But what if these words are directed at today's Christian leaders, such as pastors, teachers, and authors? As we listen to these next words, consider how they may be applied more broadly to today's Christian leaders:

> Listen you priests, this command is for you. Listen to me, and take it to heart. Honor my name, says the Lord, or I will bring a terrible curse against you. I will curse even the blessings you have received, indeed I have already cursed them because you have failed to take My warning seriously.
>
> I will rebuke your descendants and I will splatter your faces with the dung of your festival sacrifices, and I will add you to the dung heap. Then at last you will know that it was I who have sent you this warning, so that My covenant with the Levites may continue, says the Lord. (Malachi 2:1–4)

Few Christians today believe that God would actually bring a curse against His own people. But that is obviously not true. God has not changed. We do not serve a new and improved version of God, who now only blesses everyone, even when they have drifted away from Him. God is telling us that if we fail to honor His name, He will bring a terrible curse against us. Do we honor God's name? Do we even know God's name? We will address this issue in more detail in later chapters. God also says He will not accept his people's festival sacrifices. For many, if not most Christians today, our worship has turned into a casual holiday worship pattern in which we attend church only on the Christian holidays of Christmas and Easter, and these are not even the God-ordained festivals God has given to His people to ensure that they remember His story.

God continues to speak through Malachi:

> The purpose of my covenant with the Levites was to bring life and peace, and this is what I gave them. This called for reverence from

them, and they greatly revered me and stood in awe of my name. They passed on to the people all of the truth that they received from me. They did not lie or cheat, they walked with me, living good and righteous lives, and turning many from lives of sin.

The priests' lips should guard knowledge, and the people should go to them for instruction, for the priests are the messengers of the Lord God Almighty. But not you. You have left God's path. Your guidance has caused many to stumble into sin. You have corrupted my covenant with the Levites, says the Lord, so I have made you despised and humiliated in the eyes of all the people. For you have not obeyed me and you have shown partiality in your interpretation of the Law. (Malachi 2:5–9)

With these words, God is bringing a very great indictment against the leaders of His people. He begins by confirming His desire to bring life and peace to His people. But this life and peace is conditioned upon the people correctly exercising their free will, in reverent obedience to His commands. He then demands that the leaders be above reproach and that they teach all of the truth and that they live good and righteous lives, turning the people away from their sins. This is the responsibility of the leadership in God's Church. But then God accuses the leadership of doing the exact opposite by leading the people into sin rather than away from sin. God says that their guidance has not only failed to keep the people from sinning, it has actually caused many to stumble into sin. Why does God say this? It is because they have corrupted His covenant and not obeyed Him. God says that the leaders have left God's path and have shown partiality in their interpretation of the law. Could this be true of many of today's Christian leaders as well?

Many of today's pastors and teachers are actually causing the people to stumble into sin by failing to properly teach God's Law. We will be looking much more closely into this in later chapters, but for now consider the fact that today's Christian message has been evolving over time. Today's Christianity focuses primarily on receiving the forgiveness of our sins rather than on the need to turn away from our sins. We spend very little time teaching the people that to enter the Kingdom of God they must actually repent from their sins. For many this indictment will cause great discomfort. But as we will see more clearly later, when we remove repentance from sin as a necessary element of salvation, the power to actually overcome sin is also removed. And if the power to overcome sin is lost, we too have caused the people to stumble into sin.

Gods' final indictment against the leaders of His people in this section of Malachi is that they have not obeyed God and they have shown partiality in their interpretation of the law. Again, we will go much deeper into this issue later, but for now consider the contemporary teaching of God's Law. What percentage of teaching and preaching today is given to hearing and obeying God's Law? The answer is little or none. And on those rare occasions in which God's Law is taught, it is not taught as the Ten Commandments, but instead as the Ten Suggestions for Better Living. Why has this happened? And how will God respond to this interpretation of His Law? God continues to speak through Malachi:

> Are we not all children of the same Father? Are we not created by the same God? Then why are we faithless to each other, violating the covenant of our ancestors?
>
> In Judah, in Israel and in Jerusalem there is treachery, for the men of Judah have defiled the Lord's beloved sanctuary by marrying women who worship idols. May the Lord cut off from the nation of Israel every last man who has done this yet brings and offering to the Lord.
>
> Here is another thing you do. You cover the Lord's altar with tears, weeping and groaning because the Lord pays no attention to your offerings, and does not accept them with pleasure. You cry out, "Why has the Lord abandoned us?" I'll tell you why. Because the Lord witnessed the vows you and your wife made to each other on your wedding day, when you were young. But you have been disloyal to her, while she remained your faithful companion, the wife of your wedding vows.
>
> Didn't the Lord make you one with your wife? In body and spirit you are His. And what does He want? Godly children from your union. So guard yourselves, always remain loyal to the wife of your youth. For I hate divorce, says the Lord God of Israel, it is as cruel as putting on a victims bloodstained coat. So guard yourself, always remain loyal to your wife. Malachi 2:10–16

What does God think of the covenant of marriage? How many times in our Bibles do we hear God say that He hates something? But God hates divorce! And He hates divorce because His desire for marriage is so great. Marriage between one man and one woman, for life, is God's desire. God cannot tolerate man's destruction of this foundational institution. Why would He? Why should He? Why does God bring up the topic of marriage in this passage? It was in response to the cry of His people, *"Why has God abandoned us?"* So is it possible that the response of God to our destruction of His institution of marriage will be to abandon us to our own desires? What should God do when we offend Him? Should He just accept it as inevitable? Should He just tolerate the offense? Can God simply tolerate the sins of is people? The answer is a resounding *no!* God cannot tolerate any sin because He is absolutely righteous and absolutely just. There are only two possible responses that God can have when faced with sin: (1) God can render immediate judgment of the sin, or (2) God can pause by rebuking the sinner and giving him time to repent. But we must never forget that if He chooses to rebuke us, giving us time to repent before bringing judgment will not last forever.

Without the institution of marriage, as God has defined it, there is no hope for the generations to come. Marriage and family are the center of Godly life. A strong family institution means a strong community and a strong nation. A strong family is the only way to a strong education of our children. God deeply loves the institution of the family, and when even the leadership of His people abandons this institution, God will act. God must act. As we have seen in the words spoken by God to King Asa earlier, "*The Lord will be with you, if you are with Him. If you seek Him, He will be found by you. But if you forsake Him, He will forsake you.*" God is faithful to His Word. When we forsake marriage, we forsake God, and in time He will forsake us as well.

The closing words of chapter 2 of Malachi are a strong warning to the Church today:

You have wearied the Lord with your words.

But you ask, 'How have we wearied Him?'

You have wearied Him by saying that the Lord favors evildoers because He does not punish them. You have wearied Him by asking "Where is the God of justice?" (Malachi 2:17)

Are Christian's today wearying the Lord with our words? Could we be accused of saying, *the Lord favors evildoers because He does not punish them?* To listen carefully to what God is accusing His people of, we need to correctly define two of the words used in this passage: *favor* and *evildoers*. What is the favor of God? We do not use this word very often because it actually has a somewhat negative connotation today. Instead, we use the term *grace. Grace* is one of the most often-used words in our contemporary Christian prayers, songs, and sermons. When Christians today use the word *grace*, they are generally referring to the unmerited favor of God. Today's Christians are often quick to proclaim that we do not deserve God's favor, but yet God cover's us with His grace, or His favor, simply because He loves us unconditionally.

If the word *favor* and the word *grace* are interchangeable, then we too are guilty of saying the favor of God is upon evildoers. We do not use the word *evildoer* much anymore either. What is an evildoer? Obviously an evildoer is a person who does evil. This is another way of referring to a person who commits sin. An evildoer is a sinner. So do Christians today actually say that the Lord favors evildoers, when we say that the Lord shows grace to those who continue to walk in sin? This belief is actually foundational in today's Christian message. Today's Christianity is all about becoming a *sinner saved by grace*. We tell people that they should become Christians so that the Lord's grace will save them from the punishment of their sins. If we are honest with ourselves, we are just as guilty as God's people in the days of Malachi, when we say the Lord favors evildoers because He does not punish them so long as they are *Christian evildoers*.

The last word spoken in chapter 2 of Malachi is that the people have wearied Him by saying *"Where is the God of justice?"* This is the cry of many Christians today as well. They proclaim that Jesus is coming again soon, to bring justice back into the world by punishing those non-Christians who are causing all of the pain and suffering in this world. We hear people say that they are praying for the return of God's justice. But is this really what God wants to hear His people pray? And are God's people really ready for the return of the God of justice? Could it be that these words weary the Lord just as they did at the time of Malachi?

Malachi 3 begins:

> Look, I am sending you my messenger, and he will prepare the way before me. Then the Lord you are seeking will suddenly come to his temple. The messenger of the covenant whom you seek so eagerly is surely coming, says the Lord, but who will be able to endure it when he comes?
>
> Who will be able to stand and face him when he appears? For he will be like a blazing fire that refines metal, or like a strong soap that whitens clothes. He will sit and judge, as a refiner of silver, watching closely as the dross is burned away. He will purify the Levites, refining them as gold or silver, so that they may once again offer acceptable sacrifices to the Lord. Then once again the Lord will accept the offerings brought to him by the people of Judah and Jerusalem as he did in former times.
>
> At that time I will put you on trial, says the Lord. I will be a ready witness against all sorcerers, adulterers and liars. I will speak against those who cheat employees of their wages, who oppress widows and orphans, and who deprive the foreigners living among you of justice. For these people do not fear me, says the Lord. (Malachi 3:1–5)

Who is this messenger of the covenant God says He will send to His people? It is none other than Jesus. Consider that Jesus, the Son of Man, had not yet come to earth when God spoke these words through Malachi. So is God speaking of the first coming of Jesus here or the second coming? God asks who will be able to endure it when he comes and who will be able to stand and face him when he appears? Would this be true of the first coming of Jesus or the second coming? Jesus came first as the sacrificial Lamb of God, but his second coming will be as a Judge. Are Christians today really ready for Jesus to come as the righteous Judge? How many today will be ready to face him when he appears? What is the standard of readiness that will be required of us to endure it when he comes? How many Christians today will be able to stand and face Jesus when he comes?

The second coming of Christ will be in the form of a trial. The time will have come to separate the sheep from the goats, the righteous from the wicked. Who will be doing the testifying at this great day of judgment? It is God, Himself! And who will He testify against? He will testify against all sinners, including Christian sinners. What defense will a Christian who has continued to walk in sin have at the time of this great and dreadful day of judgment? What will the verdict be? Malachi then lists several of the sins which God will testify against, and then he makes a critically important observation. God identifies the real problem for those who have ears to hear. God says the problem is that these people do not fear me. God knows that a people who do not fear Him will be unable to overcome their sins and therefore will be unable to face Jesus when he comes.

Listen carefully to the next statement God makes through His Prophet, Malachi:

> I am the Lord your God, and I do not change. That is why you, O descendants of Jacob, are not already completely destroyed, says the Lord. Ever since the days of your ancestors you have scorned my laws and failed to obey them. Now, return to me, and I will return to you, says the Lord. (Malachi 3:6–7)

Many Christians today have come to embrace the theory of evolution as foundational to their understanding of life. This evolutionary worldview has greatly impacted our understanding of God, and of His great salvation plan. Many Christians believe that God is evolving over time. They seem to think that God is learning and growing just like us. Many Christians today view the God of the Old Testament as the God of wrath, who later takes the form of Jesus, who is the new and improved God of mercy and love they see in the New Testament. This belief in a changing God, who is learning as He tries new and improved methods to relate to His people, is a great error. Man changes; God does not change. In His own words, *I am the Lord, and I do not change.* The God of the Old Testament is no different than the God of the New Testament. The God of the twenty-first century is the same as the God that created the universe. The God of the future will be the same as the God of the past. God does not change! What changes is our belief about who God is and what God is doing.

God is calling His people to come back to Him. God does not change directions, but instead He calls His people to change their direction. This is what *repentance* is, returning to an unchanging God. We repent by moving from disobedience to obedience to God's commands. This is not an arrogant position for God to take because God is the source of all that is good, righteous, and just. God is always right. When man has a problem it is because he has strayed away from God's original intent. There is no exception to this rule. This is the truth. So when we have a problem, the root of that problem is sin, disobedience to God's directions for life. The root of every problem is that we have somehow drifted away from God's Law. And if we turn away from our ways and turn back to His ways we will be saved from the consequences of our disobedience. That is why God says, *Return to me, says the Lord, and I will return to you.*

Repentance is a simple solution to the problem of sin, but repentance is not easy. Repentance is always preceded first by conviction of sin and then by confession of sin. God's people at the time of Malachi were apparently no longer convicted of their sins because they had drifted off to sleep. They were unable to see the error of their ways. When God brought these indictments to the people through Malachi, the people continued to respond with disbelief that they had really drifted away from God's commands. Listen to the people's response to God's indictment that they had drifted away from Him:

> But you say, 'How can we return when we have never gone away?'
>
> And the Lord replies, "Should people cheat God, yet you have cheated me."
>
> Then you ask, "What do you mean? When did we ever cheat You?"
>
> And the Lord replies, 'You have cheated me of the tithes and offerings due to Me. You are under a curse because your whole nation has been cheating me. Bring all of the tithes into my storehouse so that there will be enough food in my temple. If you do this I will open the floodgates of heaven for you, says the Lord, 'I will pour out a blessing so great that you will not have enough room to take it in. Go ahead, try it. Let me prove it to you. Your crops will be abundant, for I will guard them from insects and disease. Your grapes will not shrivel before they are ripe. Then all nations will call you blessed, because your land will be such a delight, says the Lord. (Malachi 3:8–12)

After God calls His people to return to Him through repentance, the people respond with the either ignorant or arrogant reply that they have not strayed away from Him. The people are in denial. God then accuses His people of cheating Him. The people are again surprised at God's accusation. But as always, God is right, and the people are wrong. Yet God gives them hope and encouragement when He tells them that if they really listen, and repent, He will open the floodgates of heaven for them and pour down a blessing so great that they won't have enough room to receive it! If our grapes will not shrivel before they are ripe, will our bodies wear out with injury and illness before our time on earth has ended? We cannot even imagine the flood of blessings that God desires to pour out upon us if we will listen to Him and repent of our ways!

God then makes one last indictment against His people in Malachi 3, and it is a critically important one for us to hear if we are to experience the next Great Awakening:

> You have said terrible things against me, says the Lord, But you ask,
> 'What do you mean? How have we spoken against you?'

41

> You have said, 'What is the use of serving God? What have we
> gained by obeying His commands or by trying to show the Lord that
> we are sorry for our sins? From now on we will say, 'Blessed are the
> arrogant, for those who do evil get rich, and those who dare God to
> punish them go free from harm. (Malachi 3:13–15)

Could these words be true of today's Christians as well? Are we guilty of saying blessed are the arrogant for those who do evil get rich? To answer this question, we must look more closely at these words. A person who does evil is, again, a person who sins, because evil is sin, and sin is evil. So do we teach that evildoers—sinners—will get rich? If riches are material wealth, then this is an accurate statement, because many evil people do get rich. But as Christians we know that the greatest riches are not in our material possessions. Jesus said, "*What does it profit a man if he gains the whole world, but loses his soul?*" (Matthew 16:26) The greatest treasure we can receive, according to Jesus, is the salvation of our soul! So could today's Christians be guilty of saying that *those who do evil get rich?* The answer is yes! This is exactly what most Christians believe and teach today. This is what we too are saying when we proclaim that Christians who continue to walk in unrepentant sin will receive the greatest riches of all, eternity with God in His Kingdom.

The second part of this last indictment in Malachi 3 is that God's people were saying those who dare God to punish them will go free from harm. It would at first seem foolish for anyone to dare God to punish them. But upon closer consideration, this too is what many Christians today believe. We know that God punishes those who disobey His commands, not those who obey them. So this statement is clearly referring to a sinner, a disobedient man, who dares God to punish him for his sins. Many today believe that when a Christian sinner stands before God on the Day of Judgment and is faced with the eternal punishment for the sins which he has not overcome, he will go free from harm and not be punished because Jesus paid the penalty for him. In effect, this is a non-repentant sinner daring God to punish him! How many Christians, when they stand on the judgment seat, with sins from which they have not truly repented, will dare God to punish them? And what will God do? Will God repent from His ways? Will God change His mind and declare that sin will now be acceptable behavior in the Kingdom of Heaven?

Malachi 3 closes with a very important reference to the true people of God, those who fear Him:

> Then those who feared the Lord spoke with each other, and the
> Lord listened to what they said. In His presence a scroll of remem-
> brance was written to record the names of those who feared Him
> and loved to think about Him. 'They will be my people' says the Lord,
> 'On the day when I act they will be my own special treasure. I will
> spare them as a father spares an obedient and dutiful child. Then
> once again you will see the difference between the righteous and

the wicked, between those who serve God and those who do not. (Malachi 3:16–18)

Who is it that the Lord listens to in this passage? Whose names will be written on the scroll of remembrance? What is the scroll of remembrance? Why will only those who fear God be spared? Why will only those who fear God be His own special treasure? The fear of the Lord is the beginning of knowledge, the beginning of wisdom, and the key to living our lives in accordance with God's original intent for blessings and prosperity. We will come back to this point several times in the chapters to come, but for now consider carefully what the Lord is saying about those who fear Him.

God makes an important observation with regard to His people. He says, then once again you will see the difference between the righteous and the wicked. If there will come a time when God's people will once again see the difference between the righteous and the wicked, then there must also be a time when God's people will no longer be able to tell the difference between a righteous man and a wicked man. God is warning the people of such a time. If we are honest, we will acknowledge that we have come to such a time as this in today's Christian culture. People inside the Christian Church today do not live any differently than those living outside the Church. In a Christian culture that refuses to acknowledge and confront sin, many Christians cannot even tell whether they themselves are *righteous* or *wicked.* Many today will simply say, "*Who are we to judge between the righteous and the wicked; that is God's job.*" But the ability to differentiate between righteousness and wickedness is required of God's people!

God will one day make the final determination of who is righteous and who is wicked, but on that day it will be too late for those who have failed to make this distinction themselves. A reading of Psalm 1 will show us how critically important it is for us to know the difference between a righteous man and a wicked man:

> Blessed is the man who does not walk in the counsel of the wicked or stand in the way of sinners, or sit in the seat of mockers.

> But his delight is in the law of the Lord. And on this law he meditates, day and night.

> He is like a tree, planted by streams of water, which bears fruit in season and whose leaf does not whither.

> Whatever he does prospers. Not so the wicked!

> They are like chaff that the wind blows away.

> The wicked shall not stand in the judgment, nor sinners in the assembly of the righteous.

> For the Lord watches over the way of the righteous, but the way of the wicked will perish. (Psalm 1)

When we read this Psalm, it should compel us to ask the question, am I a righteous person, or am I a wicked person? Can we tell the difference between a righteous man and a wicked man? The ability to correctly identify and distinguish a righteous man from a wicked man will be foundational in the next Great Awakening.

So what is the difference between the righteous and the wicked. A righteous man is a man who lives in right alignment with God's commands, God's Law. A righteous man walks in obedience to God's commands. A wicked man is a man who walks in disobedience to God's commands, who walks in sin. We seldom use these terms today in fear of being considered judgmental or legalistic. We are very hesitant to call anybody a wicked person. And few Christians today believe that anyone can be a completely righteous person. Righteousness is often perceived as self-righteousness, and it carries a negative connotation. Being converted in today's Christianity is more about becoming a Christian than it is about becoming a righteous person.

Yet Jesus told the people to ". . . *seek first the Kingdom of God, and His righteousness*" (Matthew 6:33). Jesus also said, "*Blessed are those who hunger and thirst for righteousness, for they will be filled*" (Matthew 5:6). Jesus taught, "*Blessed are those who are persecuted because of righteousness, for theirs is the kingdom of heaven*" (Matthew 5:10). But how many Christians today truly seek to be righteous? According to the Apostle James being righteous is the key to an effective prayer life. James writes, "*The prayer of a righteous man is powerful and effective*" (James 5:16). Righteousness will be restored to God's people in the next Great Awakening!

The final chapter of the Book of Malachi is short and to the point, but its words are very important. These are the final words spoken by God to His people in the Old Testament. There would not be another prophetic word spoken by God to His people for the next four hundred years, so we must listen to them carefully:

> The Lord Almighty says, 'The day of judgment is coming, blazing like a furnace. The arrogant and the wicked will be burned up like straw on that day. They will be consumed like a tree, roots and all. But for you who fear my name, the sun of righteousness will rise, with healing in its wings, and you will be set free, leaping with joy, like a calf let out to the pasture. On the day when I act you will tread upon the wicked as though they were dust under your feet, says the Lord.
>
> Remember to obey the instructions of my servant Moses, all of the laws and regulations that I gave him on Mount Sinai, for all of Israel.
>
> Look, I am sending you my prophet Elijah, before that great and dreadful day of the Lord arrives. His preaching will turn the hearts of the fathers back to their children, and the hearts of the children back to their fathers. Otherwise, I will come and strike the land with a curse. (Malachi 4:1–6)

44

These are the words God chose to speak as a last warning and instruction to His people. They cannot be taken lightly. These are the words of an unchanging God, with an unchanging plan, spoken to an ever-changing people. God's people had drifted away from the truth. They had drifted away from God, and they did not realize that it had happened. God gave them a last warning that judgment was coming, and that only those who feared Him would survive it. He chose these last words to remind them to obey the instructions that He had given them through Moses. And he told them that before the great and dreadful judgment day arrives, He would send his Prophet Elijah to turn their hearts, or He would strike the land with a curse.

Everything we need for the next Great Awakening can be found in the word of the Lord, spoken through the Prophet Malachi. But we must listen carefully. This last chapter of Malachi gives us the vision of redemption we need. It is the vision of an awakening of God's people to the dawning of a new day, when the sun of righteousness will again rise with healing in its wings. A new day is about to dawn, and the sun of righteousness will shine the light of truth upon the earth again. But this light of truth from the sun of righteousness will only shine upon those who chose to learn to walk in the fear of the Lord. For those who are righteous, it will indeed be a very great day. But for those who are wicked, it will be a very dreadful day. We must choose which people we will be.

Conclusion

Everything we need to know to prepare ourselves for the next Great Awakening can be found in the last recorded Word of the Lord found in the Old Testament Scripture. When God's people reject God, He will reject them. God will not tolerate anything less than everything He desires from His people. When the leaders of God's people stop honoring God's name by teaching the people to obey the whole Law of God, the blessings of God become curses. God will return to His people only after the people return to Him. This will require the restoration of the fear of the Lord into the hearts of the people, for it is only those who fear God who will be His people, and who will see the sun of righteousness rising with healing in its wings.

The Road to Righteousness

"*Enter through the narrow gate. For wide is the gate, and broad is the road that leads to destruction, and many enter through it. But small is the gate, and narrow the road which leads to life, and only a few find it*" (Matthew 7:13–14).

"*I am the way, the truth and the life. No one comes to the Father except through me*" (John 14:6).

"*Whether you turn to the right or to the left your ears will hear a voice behind you saying, 'This is the way, walk in it*"(Isaiah 30:21).

"*This is what the Lord says, "Stand at the crossroads and look. Ask for the ancient path, ask where the good way is and walk in it, and you will find rest for your souls*" (Jeremiah 6:16).

"*Show me your ways O Lord, teach me your paths, guide me in your truth and teach me, for you are God, my Savior and my hope is in you all the day long*" (Psalm 25:4–5).

The Bible often refers to the life of God's people as a *walk*, a *road*, or a *way*. This analogy is used in both the Old and New Testaments in describing our path back into the Kingdom of Heaven. As we have already seen, the Prophet Jeremiah was used by God to call His people to ask for the *ancient path* and for the *good way*, and he warned the people to walk in it. Jesus called himself, *The Way* (John 14:6). Jesus said he is the only way to the Father. Early believers in Christ also referred to themselves as *The Way*. Some of the most powerful Psalms and Proverbs speak of the importance of staying on this narrow path, such as Psalm 37:23–24 which says: "*If the Lord delights in a man's way, He makes his steps firm; though he stumbles he will not fall, for the Lord upholds him in His grip.*"

But how do we know that we have entered through the narrow gate? How do we know if we have stayed on the narrow path that leads to life, which Jesus said only a few will find? These are some of the questions that will be addressed in this chapter.

God desires that His people walk on the ancient and narrow path that He has established for us from the beginning of time. God has given us everything we need to enter through this narrow gate and onto this narrow path, and he has also given us everything we need to stay on it. God has made this walk possible for us, and He has done it without taking away our free will! There is nothing that the powers of darkness can do to take us off this path against our will. The only way we leave this path is if we choose to leave it. And God also wants us to know whether we have left the narrow path. Psalm 119:105 tells us, "*Thy word is a lamp onto my feet and a light onto my path.*" This light, which is God's Word, is both the ability to see the path and the power to walk along this path. But this word of truth must be in our hearts and on our lips, or we are in danger of drifting away from God and of leaving this narrow path. God revealed this truth through Moses, who told the people:

> Now what I am commanding you today is not too difficult for you or beyond your reach. It is not up in heaven, so that you have to ask, "Who will ascend into heaven to get it and proclaim it to us so we may obey it?" Nor is it beyond the sea, so that you have to ask, "Who will cross the sea to get it and proclaim it to us so we may obey it?" No, the word is very near you, it is in your mouth and in your heart so you may obey it. (Deuteronomy 30:11–14)

There are five steps along this narrow path that leads to life, and knowing these five steps will give us confidence that we have not strayed off the narrow road. There may be other terminology or methods to communicate these same principles, but these are foundational to our walk back to God and into His Kingdom. This is the light of truth that must be carried to the highest hill. Our prayer for God's people should be like the prayer of King David who prayed, "*Send forth your light and your truth, let them guide me; let them bring me to your holy mountain, to the place where you dwell.*" (Psalm 43:3) May this light of truth, this power of God's Word, lead us to walk on this narrow path!

The five necessary steps along the ancient path that will lead us back to God are in a specific order. The first step on this path is to know God, because without God there is no truth. The second step on this path is to know the truth, because without the truth, there is no law. The third step on this path is to know the Law, because without the Law, there is no repentance. The fourth step on this path is to know what true repentance is, because without repentance there is no salvation. The fifth and final step is to know what salvation really is, because it is the God ordained point of destination of the Road to Righteousness. The summation of these five steps forms the narrow path: Without God, there is no Truth, without Truth there is no Law, without the Law there is no Repentance, and without Repentance there is no Salvation. God-Truth-Law-Repent-Salvation; this is the ancient path. This is the good way. Now we must choose to walk on it!

The Road to Righteousness

The True God

It is not a coincidence that the point of beginning on the road to righteousness is the same point of beginning as is set forth in Genesis 1:1, *"In the beginning, God . . ."* In the beginning was God. God is, was, and ever will be. He is self-existing, or in other words He did not come from anything else. God has always been. Everything that is seen and unseen comes from Him. He has no equal. God simply exists. This is more than just an academic conclusion. To know the true God, or to find the knowledge of God, is the point of beginning for all understanding. The New Testament also has an account of the beginning, which is found in John 1:1–14:

> In the beginning was the Word, and the Word was with God, and the Word was God. He was with God in the beginning.
>
> Through him all things were made; without Him nothing was made that has been made. In him was life, and that life was the light of men. The light shines into the darkness, but the darkness has not overcome it.
>
> There came a man who was sent by God; his name was John. He came as a witness to testify concerning that light, so that through him all might believe. He himself was not the light; he came only as a witness to the light. The true light that gives light to every man was coming into the world.
>
> He was in the world, and though the world was made through him, the world did not recognize him. He came to that which was his own, but his own did not receive him. **Yet to all who did receive him, to those who believed in his name, he gave the right to become children of God**—children born not of natural descent, nor of human decision, nor of a husband's will, but born of God.
>
> The Word became flesh, and made his dwelling among us. We have seen his glory, the glory of the One and Only, who came from the Father, full of grace and truth. (emphasis added)

The next Great Awakening will be a time when American Christians will move beyond acknowledging God, to again actually knowing the true God. This is a challenge because with each passing generation there seems to be a growing uncertainty of even the existence of God. We have allowed a battle to rage between science and religion that should not be taking place. Many of the greatest scientific minds in history properly grounded their understanding of science on their understanding of God and of His Word. The writer of Hebrews reminds us of the importance of knowing that God exists when he writes, *"Without faith it is impossible to please God, because anyone who comes to Him must believe that He exists, and that He rewards those who earnestly seek Him"* (Hebrews 11:6). The existence of God is not the issue that will be addressed in this book. This book presumes that the reader believes that there is a God. The purpose of this book is to *"Demolish arguments and every pre-tention that sets itself up against the knowledge of God, and ... take captive every thought to make it obedient to Christ"* (II Corinthians 10:5).

The point of beginning of this Road to Righteousness is to move beyond knowing that God exists to a place of knowing who the true God is. Jesus was once asked about eternal life, and his answer was profound. He said, *"Now this is eternal life: that they may know you, the only true God, and Jesus Christ, whom you have sent"* (John 17:3). God's people must know God! But do we really know Him? Is the God that we are worshiping today the true God, or have we created a false god, based upon who we want Him to be? We must accept God as He has defined Himself, and as He has revealed Himself to be through His Word. We were created in the image of God, and we must not redefine Him in our image. The consequences of redefining God are beyond disastrous.

God's words of wisdom, spoken through His Proverbs, call us onto this path which leads to the knowledge of God:

> My son, if you accept my words and store up my commands within you, turning your ear to wisdom and applying your heart to under-standing, and if you call out for insight and cry aloud for under-standing, and if you look for it as for silver and search for it as for hidden treasure, **then you will understand the fear of the Lord and find the knowledge of God.** (Proverbs 2:1–5) (emphasis added)

This first step on the Road to Righteousness, to know the true God, is not a casual step. It will require great effort, as though we were searching for a great treasure, because that is exactly what we are doing! Recall the Word of the Lord spoken to King Asa, with regard to the drift away from the true God that had taken place in His chosen people, Israel:

"For a long time, Israel was without the true God, without a priest to teach, and without the law. But in their distress they turned to the Lord, the God of Israel, and sought him, and he found by them" (II Chronicle 15:3–4).

Who is the true God? What are His attributes? What is His nature? What is His character? And why is it so important that we rightly define Him? It is actually more than important—it is critical to know the true God, because we will view everything in life through the lens of who we believe God is. Even God's Word will be understood only through the lens of who we believe God is. This cannot be overemphasized. When we seek to understand God's Word, we will do so through the lens of who we believe God is. If we interpret Scripture in a way that is not consistent with the true God, then we have erred, and we must change our interpretation. This is true even if we have held to that interpretation all of our lives. This is where truth and tradition will often collide. Traditions can be either good or bad, but they are always strong. Our traditions can either keep us in the truth, or they will keep us from the truth.

The only reason that we are able to know the true God is because He has made it possible to know Him. We are able to know God only because He has chosen to reveal Himself to us. God has made it possible for us to know who He is and God desires us to know who He is. When we come to know this God, we will see that when God desires something God requires it! This is worth repeating. What God desires, God requires!

Those who may doubt the importance of knowing God, should consider His words spoken through the Prophet Jeremiah in 9:23–24:

> This is what the Lord says: "Let not the wise man boast in his wisdom, let not the strong man boast in his strength, let not the rich man boast in his riches, but let him who boasts, boast in this: that he understands and knows Me, that I am the Lord, who exercises kindness, justice and righteousness on earth, for in these I delight," declares the Lord.

We know that God does not want us to be boastful but to instead be humble. But God clearly does want us to boast in one thing, that we know and understand Him! And what God desires of us, God requires of us. Knowing God is not optional; it is a requirement for God's people. Why would God ever settle for less than everything He desires? God sent His son, Jesus, to reveal Himself to His people. Jesus confirms God's desire for us to know Him when he said:

> You are my friend if you do what I command. I no longer call you servants, because a servant does not know his master's business. Instead, I have called you friends, for everything that I learned from my Father I have made known to you. (John 15:14–15)

There are two foundational precepts upon which we build our faith, the substance of what we believe to be true. The first precept is that God exists, and the second precept is that God has revealed Himself. We must be careful to build our understanding of who God is upon His own revelations and not upon the opinions of men. At the very middle verse of our Bibles, Psalm 118:8, we find this statement of truth, *"It is better to take refuge in the Lord than to trust in man."* There is nothing wrong with listening to the teachings and opinions of men, but our conclusions must always be consistent with the Word of God.

God is an absolute God, and there are five absolute characteristics of God that form a firm foundation in the building up of the knowledge of God. These five absolute attributes of God are as follows: (1) God is omnipotent, (2) God is omniscient, (3) God is absolutely righteous, (4) God is absolutely just, and (5) God is unchanging. Each of these absolute attributes deserves more consideration.

First, God is omnipotent. This means that He is all powerful. There is nothing that God cannot do because He lacks the power to do it. Nothing! When God speaks, power comes out of His mouth. When He spoke the very first words in Genesis 1:3, *"Let there be light,"* power came into the physical realm. In the physical realm, light always comes from power. Whenever we see light in the physical realm, we can confidently conclude that there is power at its source. Light is power. This is not true of darkness. Darkness is not power. Darkness is actually the absence of power, the absence of light. So when we are seeking to understand Scripture, we must do so through the lens of God's omnipotence, His unlimited power. If we ever interpret God's Word in a way which denies God's omnipotence we must change our interpretation.

Second, God is omniscient. This means that God knows all things. There is nothing that God cannot do because He lacks the intelligence to know what to do. God is not learning as time goes on. He has always been omniscient. He does not experiment with ideas. And because He is omniscient and omnipotent He cannot fail. God will always get what He wants, when He wants it. God cannot fail. If we ever interpret God's word in a way which denies God's omniscience, we must change our interpretation.

Third, God is absolutely righteous. Righteousness is His nature. His nature is righteous. In other words God is good all the time. He is never evil. There is no evil in God. God has no wickedness in Him. God's character defines what good is. God's will defines what good is. God has not arbitrarily defined good and evil. Good is that which reflects His nature and desire, and evil is that which does not reflect His nature and desire. The potential for good and evil have existed since God gave men and angels free will. God is the original source of righteousness. If we ever interpret Scripture in a way that would accuse God of being in any way wicked, we must change our interpretation of Scripture.

Fourth, God is absolutely just. This means that God cannot ever act unjustly. God must always do justice. God will always reward righteousness and He will always punish evil. God's justice is always perfectly measured. He will not reward righteousness beyond what justice requires and He will not punish wickedness beyond what justice requires. Within this absolute justice in God's nature there is room for mercy and grace, but God is first and foremost an absolutely just God. When God established that the wages of sin is death, He meant it. Without an understanding of God's justice, the cross makes no sense. Without an understanding of God's justice, grace makes no sense. If we interpret Scripture in a way which portrays God as being unjust, we must change our interpretation of Scripture.

Finally, God is immutable. This means that God does not change. God is eternally the same. God is not growing, and He is not diminishing. God is the self-sustaining One. There is not an Old Testament God and a New Testament God. There is only one God, and He is the same yesterday, today, and forever. And because God does not change, His will does not change. He does not change His mind. As we heard God speak through the Prophet Malachi, *I am the Lord your God, and I do not change.* God does not change. It is man who changes. That is why God cannot do the repenting for us. We must change our ways. We must repent. We must return to God and then God will return to us. Today's Christians must reject the evolutionary thinking that God is somehow evolving over time. And if our interpretation of Scripture is based upon an evolving or changing God, then we must change our interpretation of Scripture.

But truly knowing God goes beyond simply acknowledging His absolute character traits. To know God also requires us to know His name. Remember God's warning to His people through Malachi: *Honor My name, says the Lord, or I will bring a terrible curse against you* (Malachi 2:1–2). How many Christians today even know God's name? We casually refer to Him as *God*, but that is not His name. There are billions of people across the earth who would say that they worship *God,* but it is not the true God of Abraham, Isaac, and Jacob. To honor God's name we must first know what God's name is.

How did God get His name? The answer to this question is found in Exodus, where Moses was tending his flock when the Lord appeared to him in the flames of fire from a burning bush. Moses was told to take off his sandals because he was standing on holy ground. God then called Moses to return to Egypt to lead God's people out of the bondage of slavery. But Moses said to God,

> "Suppose I go to the Israelites and say to them, 'The God of your fathers has sent me to you,' and they ask me, 'What is his name?' Then what shall I tell them?' **God said to Moses, "I AM WHO I AM**. This is what you are to say to the Israelites: 'I AM has sent you.'" God also said to Moses, "Say to the Israelites, 'The Lord, the God of your fathers—The God of Abraham, the God of Isaac and the God of Jacob—has sent me to you.' **This is my name forever, the name by which I am to be remembered from generation to generation.** (Exodus 3:13–15) (emphasis added)

God specifically told Moses that His name is *I AM WHO I AM.* And then God said this shall be His name forever and that it is to be remembered *from generation to generation.* Recall the words spoken by God through Malachi:

> Listen you Priests, this command is for you. Listen to me, and take it to heart. Honor My name says the Lord, or I will bring a terrible curse against you. I will curse even the blessings that you have received, indeed, I have already cursed them, because you have failed to take my warning seriously (Malachi 2:1–2).

Can there be any doubt that knowing God's name is very, very important to God? But why did God choose this name, *I AM WHO I AM?* In Hebrew it is YHWH, a name that was so revered by the Jews that reverential caution was taken whenever it was spoken.

As we listen more carefully to this dialogue between Moses and God and as we recall the absolute character traits of God, it becomes clear that this is the only name that God could have used for Himself, *I AM WHO I AM.* Any other name would have compared God with something in creation, but God is the incomparable One. The only One to compare God to is Himself. Any other name would have somehow diminished Him in some way, and that is not possible. He is not simply the God of Abraham, because Allah is also the god of Abraham. Our Bibles often refer to Him as the God of Abraham, Isaac, and Jacob, or the God of Israel. God is the great I AM! And if we are wise, will we will honor His name for all generations.

Without God There is No Truth.

Truth is the second step on our Road to Righteousness. The truth of God is an absolute truth. We cannot live in a world without absolute truth, but that is precisely what the world today is trying to do. It should not come to us as a surprise that the world rejects absolute truth, because the world has rejected God, and without God there is no absolute truth! But God does exist, and therefore absolute truth must also exist. God's people are called to be defenders of this truth. Very few of God's people today are able to defend the truth, but this is a call upon each one of us. The Apostle Paul urges believers to *"Do your best to present yourself to God as one approved, a workman who does not need to be ashamed and who correctly handles the word of truth"* (2 Timothy 2:15).

Jesus was sent by God to testify to this truth of God and to show us how to do the same. After Jesus was taken into custody and brought before Pilate, he was asked whether he was the King of the Jews. Jesus responded; *"You are right in saying I am a king. In fact, for this reason I was born, and for this I came into the world, to testify to the truth. Everyone on the side of the truth listens to me"* (John 18:37). Jesus came into the world to testify to the truth! It is our responsibility to decide if we are going to be a people on the side of truth. Today's culture is asking the same question that Pilate asked, when he stood before the *Truth Incarnate,* and responded to Jesus, *"What is truth?"* (John 18:38) Today's culture is asking the very same question. Jesus had the answer, and we too are called to be defenders of absolute truth.

As believers, we can defend the existence of absolute truth against a world that rejects all truth. The next time someone proclaims to you that there is no absolute truth, simply respond to them with this question, "Are you sure?" If they say "Yes" then ask them the follow up question, "Are you absolutely sure?" If they say "No," they have admitted to you that they are just confused. But if they again say "Yes," then politely point out to them that they have disproven their own proposition, because they have admitted that they do believe in at least one absolute truth statement. They have acknowledged that at least one absolute truth statement does exist, and that statement is that absolute truth does not exist! The question is not whether or not absolute truth exists. It clearly does, and we cannot live in a world without absolute truth. It makes no intellectual sense to deny the existence of absolute truth. The real question is, How do we know what the truth is?

To become defenders of the truth, we must understand that there are two categories of truth: *particular truth* and *universal truth.* The first category of truth, *particular truth,* is the kind of truth which can be established through the scientific process. Particular truth is testable in the laboratory of physical science. An example of particular truth would be the temperature at which water freezes or the date of the next solar eclipse. The second category of truth, universal truth, cannot be determined through the scientific method, but it is absolute truth nonetheless. The absolute truth

Jesus came to testify on behalf of was this universal truth. Universal truth answers questions such as: Where does life come from? Does God exist? Is there life after death? What is the purpose of life? What is right, and what is wrong? What is good, and what is evil? These are questions regarding universal truth, and they have answers, but the source of the answers does not come from the mind of man, and they cannot be established with certainty through the scientific method. Universal truth has its source in God alone. Religion is man's attempt to discover this universal truth, but it is not the source of this truth. The best that man can do is to attempt to discover what the absolute universal truth is, but only God is the source or deter- miner of this truth.

In America it is tempting to think that absolute truth can be determined by the beliefs and desires of the people, but absolute truth is not determined by the vote of the majority in either a poll or a ballot box. Absolute truth is also not established by nine well-educated men and women who are seated on the Supreme Court. The best that even our highest courts can do is to give their opinions about what the truth is. This is why we call the decisions of our highest courts *opinions* not *truths.* Only God, through His Word, has established absolute truth. God has defined good and evil, and right and wrong, and man has no authority to change those definitions.

It is critical for those who desire to be defenders of the truth to understand that God has revealed His truth to man in two ways: (1) general revelation and (2) special revelation. Man can know what the truth is only because God has made knowing His truth possible. God has created us in a way that makes it possible for us to receive His revelation. This is a necessary element of being created in the image of God. General revelation comes to us through the creation itself. We are without excuse to conclude that there is no God, because the creation cries out that there is a God. Consider the words of the Apostle Paul in this regard:

> The wrath of God is being revealed from heaven against all the god- lessness and wickedness of men who suppress the truth by their wickedness, since what may be known about God is plain to them, because God has made it plain to them. For since the creation of the world God's invisible qualities—His eternal power and divine nature—-have been clearly seen, being understood from what has been made, so that men are without excuse. (Romans 1:18–20)

King David describes this general revelation of God in the Psalms:

> The heavens declare the glory of God; the skies proclaim the work of his hands.

> Day after day they pour forth speech; night after night they display knowledge.

> There is no speech or language where their voice is not heard.

Their voice goes out into all the earth, their words to the ends of the world. (Psalm 19:1–4)

God has also revealed Himself in a second way, through His special revelation, which is His written Word, or His Law. Again from Psalm 19:7–11, the great value and purpose of God's special revelation from his Word is expressed:

The law of the Lord is perfect, reviving the soul.

The statutes of the Lord are trustworthy, making wise the simple.

The precepts of the Lord are right, giving joy to the heart.

The commands of the Lord are radiant, giving light to the eyes.

The fear of the Lord is pure, enduring forever.

The ordinances of the Lord are sure and altogether righteous.

They are more precious than gold, than much pure gold; they are sweeter than honey, than honey from the comb. By them is your servant warned; in keeping them there is great reward.

The Apostle Paul tells us, "*All of scripture is inspired by God, profitable for teaching, for reproof, for correction and for training in righteousness, so that the man of God is prepared for every good work*" (II Timothy 3:16). To know the truth, we must know God's Word. Jesus prayed for his disciples in this regard when he asked his Father to, "*Sanctify them by the truth, your word is truth*" (John 17:17).

While absolute truth does exist, and God has made this truth known to us, history tells us that God's people have a tendency to drift away from the truth. There is a great battle raging in our culture today, and it is a battle that most Christians are not aware of. Yet, this battle is at the core of all of the great issues taking place in the areas of morality and politics. It is a battle between *absolute truth* and *absolute freedom*. This battle is currently being fought in the arenas of our state and federal Supreme Courts as they deal with the issues such as abortion, same-sex marriage, and religious liberty. This battle between absolute truth and absolute freedom is at the center of each of these great cultural issues. And because we do not see this battle for what it is, absolute truth is losing this battle both in our courts and in our culture. In pursuit of absolute freedom we have lost the absolute truth upon which those freedoms are built. The result is that we are losing both our freedoms and the truth.

Make no mistake here. Please do not misunderstand what you are about to read. Freedom is a very good thing! For generations Americans have given their lives for the freedoms we enjoy today. Freedom is a gift from God. Free will existed before the fall of man, and we will have a free will as we spend eternity in the Kingdom of Heaven. But freedom is not our highest purpose. God did not create us for the purpose of being free. God gave us freedom, the right to choose our own destiny, as a gift, but the ultimate and highest purpose for mankind is to use that gift of freedom wisely. Our highest purpose is to use the gift of freedom by choosing to be true to God's commands. Our highest purpose is to be true to God's desire for us! *Freedom* is the means, and *truth* is the end.

Jesus testified to this highest purpose of being *true* when he said, "*I am the way, the truth and the life. No one comes to the Father except through me*" (John 14:6). Our highest purpose is to be *the truth* like Jesus! God desires His people to live in accordance with His original intent and to have dominion over His creation, in accordance with His instructions. God created us with free will, but then He warned us to use our freedom wisely, in obedience to His Word. He gave us the gift of choice. We must now decide to either be obedient to His directions and to live in the light of His blessings or to be disobedient to his directions and to be cursed and die.

Jesus said, "Then y*ou will know the truth, and the truth will set you free*" (John 8:32). If we really desire to be free, then we must seek first to know the truth. And the truth that we should be striving for is a life of *liberty* rather than a life of absolute *freedom*. Absolute freedom is actually chaos, with every man doing what is right in his own mind. Absolute freedom will result in a world of survival of the fittest, which is not God's desire. Noah Webster's 1828 American English Dictionary defines *liberty* as "*freedom from undue restraints.*" The restraints placed upon us by the commands of God, His directions for life, are not *undue restraints* from which we should strive to be free. Liberty is the true gift of God. Liberty does not come from governments. Liberty does not come from our highest courts. Liberty does not even come from the Constitution. Liberty comes from God, and as Thomas Jefferson once observed:

> Can the liberties of a nation be thought secure, if we have removed their firm foundation, a conviction in the minds of the people that these liberties are a gift from God, that they cannot be violated but with His wrath. Indeed, I tremble for my country when I consider that God is just, and that his wrath cannot sleep forever. (Notes on State of Virginia (Philadelphia: Mathew Justice Carey, 1794), p.237, query XVII)

It is worthwhile to take a brief look at just two of the great freedom versus truth battles that are being fought both in our highest courts, and more importantly in today's court of public opinion. The first issue is abortion. The underlying freedom issue in this battle is the freedom of a woman to do with her body what she desires, without the government telling her what to do. This is a legitimate freedom concern. We do not want the government telling us what we can and can't do with our own bodies. But this freedom is not without limits, for in the case of an abortion, there is another life to consider, the life of the unborn child. There is a point when the freedom principle of a woman's right to decide what to do with her body runs into a truth principle, which is God's command, *Thou shalt not kill.* The killing of an unborn child is a direct violation of the Law of God. God will not tolerate the shedding of innocent blood. God has warned His people:

> They shed innocent blood, the blood of their sons and daughters,
> whom they sacrificed to the idols of Canaan and the land was des-
> ecrated by their blood . . . Therefore the Lord was angry with his
> people and abhorred his inheritance. (Psalm 106: 38, 40)

Yet, in the highest courts across this land, and more importantly in the court of public opinion, the people's desire for personal freedom appears to be winning the battle over the truth of God's Word on the issue of abortion.

A second area in which this battle between freedom and truth is raging is in the area of religious liberty. This is an issue which is causing great confusion in our culture. Most Americans will acknowledge that one of the great foundational principles of our nation has always been our religious liberty. Our U.S. Constitution guarantees this religious liberty in the First Amendment, which states in part, "*Congress shall make no law regarding the establishment of religion, or prohibiting the free exercise thereof . . .*" For the first two hundred years of American history we had a general consensus of the meaning of this statement in our Constitution. The founders did not want the federal government to establish a preferred Christian denomination. But today our judicial interpretation of these words is drifting away from the original intent of the Founding Fathers who drafted these words. Today we are wrongly applying this provision to remove our religious heritage and moral foundations from the public forum. We are doing this because we have a false understanding of the concept of separation of church and state, which will be addressed in more detail later.

The religious liberty issue can be framed as a battle between the freedom of a minority of individuals to not be exposed to any Christian references in the public forum, and the historical truth that this nation was founded upon Judeo-Christian principles. Yet, the atheists are now using the First Amendment as a weapon against religion, and more specifically, against Christianity. In many jurisdictions the atheists are winning the court battles due to the worldviews of some of the men and women who have been placed on our highest courts. A growing number of the justices on our highest courts view our Constitution as a living, breathing and evolving document. They view our Constitution as a sail that will take us anywhere the winds of public opinion may blow, rather than as an anchor that holds us in the safe harbor of truth. This will eventually require a total rejection of our nation's Christian heritage, and even the rejection of past decisions of our U.S. Supreme Court, which established the correct interpretation of religious liberty.

Until recently our United States Supreme Court recognized our nation's Christian heritage. The false concept of absolute freedom from religion is now winning many of the court battles. But even more dangerous is the fact that this evolving view of religious liberty has now been indoctrinated into generations of our children through the public education system. The majority of Americans today have been led to believe that it is possible to live in a culture without religious convictions, and they no longer understand that all people are religious. The only question is which religion's principles will govern our nation. We are again choosing absolute freedom from the religion of our forefathers over the absolute truth of our own history of religious liberty.

Without Truth There is No Law

The Law was not established by the Church; it was established by God. The Law, which has historically formed the foundation of the American civil society, is the Law of God, handed down to His people, through Moses, on Mount Sinai. The Hebrew word for the Law is *Torah*, which is defined by Vines Dictionary as *"the instruction of the sages of Israel, who were charged with the education of the youth, was intended to cultivate in the young a fear of the Lord so that they might live in accordance with God's expectations."* What a great definition! The Law is God's directions for life. Simply using this definition of God's Law could in itself spark a great awakening within the American Christian Church!

It is necessary to take a closer look at God's Law so that we can see why it is so critical to our life and survival. When God speaks, the Law comes forth from His mouth. The Law is sourced in absolute truth, which as we have seen, comes from God alone. God's Word is *Truth,* and God's Word is *Law.* When we rediscover the Law, we will rediscover why God's people must be lovers of the Law. We should be like the Psalmist, who wrote Psalm 119, the longest chapter of the Bible, with each and every verse referring to the power, purpose, and love of God's Law! The first 8 verses of Psalm 119 set the tone for this important Psalm:

> Blessed are they whose ways are blameless, who walk according to the law of the Lord.
> Blessed are they who keep his statutes and seek him with all their heart.
> They do nothing wrong; they walk in his ways.
> You have laid down precepts that are to be fully obeyed.
> Oh, that my ways were steadfast in obeying your decrees!
> Then I would not be put to shame when I consider all your commands.
> I will praise you with an upright heart as I learn your righteous laws.
> I will obey your decrees; do not utterly forsake me.

There is a great reward for those who truly delight in the Law of the Lord. As we are told in Psalm 112:1, *"Blessed is the man who fears the Lord, who finds delight in His commands."* It is more than worthwhile to read Psalm 119 in its entirety.

When most people think of the Law, they think of the Ten Commandments. But the Law is much more than the Ten Commandments. The Ten Commandments are a purposeful and powerful summary of the Law, but the Law of God was present before the Ten Commandments were given by God to the people on Mount Sinai. The Law was first given by God to Adam and Eve in the Garden of Eden, even before the fall of man. This, of course, makes sense when you consider that sin is disobedience to the Law. Therefore, without the Law, there could be no sin, and without the Law there could also be no righteousness. Without the Law there could be no free will, because freedom requires a choice, and the Law gives mankind the choice to obey God and live, or to disobey God and die.

God's Law was established by God when He planted the tree of the knowledge of good and evil in the Garden of Eden. God told Adam and Eve, *"You are free to eat from any tree in the garden; but you must not eat from the tree of the knowledge of good and evil, for when you eat of it you will surely die"* (Genesis 2:1). God had made it clear that only He has the authority to establish the Law, because only He has the authority to establish what is good and what is evil. The concept of *good* can only exist if there is also a concept of *evil*. The mirror image of the word *evil* is the word *live*. This is not a coincidence!

As we have seen, God's Law reflects His nature and His character. The Ten Commandments are not arbitrary rules God has established to see if man will be obedient. The Law is God's directions for life and blessings. But the Law is actually more than the commandments of God. The Law has two necessary components. The first component of the Law is the command, and the second necessary component of the Law is the consequence for obeying or disobeying the command. The Law is both precept and punishment. Without the second component, the consequence for disobedience, the Law becomes a mere set of suggestions for better living. But God does not make suggestions. When God speaks, it is Law that comes forth from his mouth. And because God's Law reflects His Nature, which is unchanging, the Law itself is also unchanging.

Understanding these two necessary components of the Law, the command and consequence, will help us to understand why the Old Testament Scripture is referred to as the Law and the Prophets. The commands of God were given to the people at the time of Moses on Mount Sinai. The prophets of God throughout the Old Testament then continued to warn the people of the consequences for disobedience of God's commands. As we have seen at the time of King Josiah, to lose the Law is a fatal flaw, and to rediscover the Law, the commands and the consequences for disobedience, leads to great revival and to restoration of the culture.

Moses understood and delivered the whole Law with both of its components, the commands and the consequences. Consider the reverence that was given by Moses to the Law that God had delivered to His people, as recorded in Deuteronomy 4:1–14:

> Hear now, O Israel, the decrees and laws I am about to teach you. Follow them so that you may live and may go in and take possession of the land that the Lord, the God of your fathers, is giving you. **Do not add to what I command you and do not subtract from it, but keep the commands of the Lord your God that I give you**.
>
> You saw with your own eyes what the Lord did at Baal Peor. The Lord your God, destroyed from among you everyone who followed the Baal of Peor, but all of you who held fast to the Lord your God are still alive today.
>
> See, I have taught you decrees and laws as the Lord my God commanded me, so that you may follow them in the land you are entering to take possession of it. Observe them carefully, for this

will show your wisdom and understanding to the nations, who will hear about all these decrees and say, "Surely this great nation is a wise and understanding people." **What other nation is so great as to have their gods near them the way the Lord our God is near us, whenever we pray to him? And what other nation is so great as to have such righteous decrees and laws as this body of laws I am setting before you today?**

Only be careful, and watch yourselves closely so that you do not forget the things your eyes have seen or let them slip from your heart as long as you live. **Teach them to your children and to their children after them.** Remember the day you stood before the Lord your God at Horeb, when he said to me, "Assemble the people before me to hear my words so that they may learn to revere me as long as they live in the land and may teach them to their children." You came near and stood at the foot of the mountain while it blazed with fire to the very heavens, with black clouds and deep darkness. **Then the Lord spoke to you out of the fire. You heard the sound of words but saw no form; there was only a voice. He declared to you his covenant, the Ten Commandments, which he commanded you to follow and then wrote them on two stone tablets.** And the Lord directed me at that time to teach you the decrees and laws you are to follow in the land that you are crossing the Jordan to possess. (emphasis added)

These words of Moses spoken in Deuteronomy 4:1–14 hold a key to unlocking the door to the next Great Awakening because they help us to understand what a blessing it is for God's people to have God's Law, His directions for life! But just as God later warned the people at the time of II Chronicles 15:3–4, it is possible for God's people to be without the true God, without a teaching priest, and without the Law.

Without the Law There is No Repentance

"Ever since the days of your ancestors you have scorned my laws and failed to obey them. Now, return to me, and I will return to you, says the Lord" (Malachi 3:7).

"Repent, for the kingdom of heaven is near" (Matthew 3:2).

"From that time on Jesus began to preach, "Repent, for the kingdom of heaven is near" (Matthew 4:17).

"Remember, therefore, what you have received and heard; obey it, and repent. But if you do not wake up, I will come like a thief, and you will not know at what time I will come to you" (Revelation 3:3).

It was the theme of both Moses and the Old Testament Prophets of God. John the Baptist proclaimed it in preparation for the Messiah. It summarizes the preaching of Jesus both while he walked with his disciples and again in the Book of Revelation. We have been praying for it when we pray II Chronicles 7:14, but are we really listening to the words that we are praying?

> If my people, who are called by my name, humble themselves and pray, and seek my face and turn from their wicked ways, then will I hear from heaven and will forgive their sin and will heal their land. (II Chronicles 7:14).

It is the step of true repentance!

Repentance is a complete change of direction. It is turning around and going in a completely opposite direction. Repentance is not making minor adjustments in our life as we proceed along our way. It is not adding Jesus to our lives. It is not taking ten steps to a better life. There is nothing wrong with doing these things, but they are not repentance. Repentance is a complete and total change in the way we live. Repentance is not easy. Repentance is more than saying a prayer. Repentance is not a onetime act, but instead it is a lifetime walk. Being convicted of sin is a good and necessary thing, but it is not repentance. Confessing our sins is a very good and necessary act, but it is not repentance. Repentance is more than talk; it is action. Repentance is not simply an emotion or feeling we have; it is a change of life. Repentance is more than taking a step in the right direction, as good and necessary as that may be. A person cannot take a walk without taking the first step, but one step does not constitute the true walk of repentance.

To understand what repentance really is, we must understand one little but powerful word. That word is the word *all.* Again, if we do not know who God is, we will never really understand what repentance really is. We will not understand true repentance until we come to a place of understanding that anything less than everything is nothing to God! We cannot add God to our lives any more than we can add the Pacific Ocean to our back yard swimming pool. It cannot be done. You just can't do it. Repentance is not adding God to our lives. True repentance is adding our lives to God's plan and purpose. We join Him in what He is doing, not the other way around.

Jesus was once asked "What is the greatest commandment?" and he responded,

> Love the Lord your God with *all* of your heart and with *all* your soul and with *all* your mind. This is the first and greatest commandment. And the second is like it: 'Love your neighbor as yourself.' All the Law and the Prophets hang on these two commandments. (Matthew 22:37–39) (emphasis added)

61

But have we really listened carefully to these words of Jesus? We have a tendency to ignore this little word *all*. Do we even believe that it is possible to love God with all of our hearts, with all of our minds, and with all of our strength, or do we simply ignore the word *all* as we apply this greatest of commands to our lives? The Apostle Paul understood the word *all* when he wrote; *"And whatever you do, whether in word or deed, do it all in the name of the Lord Jesus, giving thanks to God the Father through him"* (Colossians 3:17).

If we listen carefully to this verse, we will realize that Paul was calling us to a much higher standard of change than simply adding Jesus to our lives. This is a complete change in the way we live. Our words are not only our spoken words but the words that we think. Our deeds are the way we live out every moment of our lives. If we know the true God, then we know that anything less than everything is nothing to God. God desires everything from us, and therefore God also requires everything. God created us for His purpose, and that purpose was nothing less than complete submission to His directions. God would not require us to give him all of our lives unless He had also made it possible for us to do it!

Today's Christianity has removed the requirement of total surrender as a necessary element of repentance and as a requirement for salvation. Today we teach that repentance is accomplished by simply making a verbal statement of confession. But saying we are sorry is not repentance. True repentance happens when we come to a place where God is no longer our highest priority in life, but instead when God becomes our sole purpose in life. The Apostle Paul was referring to this total surrender when he wrote, *"As for me to live is Christ, and to die gain"* (Philippians 1:21). True repentance begins when God is removed from the top of our list of priorities and put on an entirely separate list. This new list has only one entry, and that entry is to hear and obey God.

Jesus spoke of this true repentance when he said, *"If you try to keep your life for yourself, you will lose it. But if you give up your life for me, you will find true life"* (Matthew 16:24). The time has come to listen carefully to what Jesus really taught us about true repentance. Jesus emphasized the need for true repentance when he was speaking to the people about some Galileans who had been killed, and he said,

> Do you think that these Galileans were worse sinners than all the other Galileans because they suffered this way? I tell you no! **But unless you repent, you too will all perish**. Or those eighteen who died when the tower in Siloam fell on them—do you think they were more guilty than all the others living in Jerusalem? I tell you no! **But unless you repent, you too will all perish.** (Luke 13:2–5) (emphasis added)

After his death and resurrection, Jesus told the Church in Ephesus, *"Remember the height from which you have fallen! Repent and do the things you did at first. If you do not repent, I will come to you and remove your lampstand from its place"* (Revelation 2:5). Jesus taught repentance as a prerequisite to entering the Kingdom of God. According to Matthew's Gospel, the focus of Jesus' ministry was on *repentance* from sin. Shortly after Jesus was baptized in the River Jordan, and after he overcame the temptations of Satan in the desert, Jesus preached *repentance!* Matthew writes, *"From that time on Jesus began to preach, "Repent, for the kingdom of heaven is near"* (Matthew 4:17).

There is another word that must be restored to the definition of true repentance. That word is *obedience.* Without obedience to God's commands we cannot claim to be walking on the path of repentance. God desires our emotions and our praises. He wants us to love Him with all our hearts, souls, and strength. But we must never forget that God desires and requires that we walk in total obedience to His commands. Without our obedience to His Law, we cannot say that we have repented. In fact, according to Jesus, we cannot say that we love him unless we walk in obedience to his commands! As Jesus said to his disciples, *"If you love me, you will obey what I command"* (John 14:15). He also went on to say, *"Whoever has my commands and obeys them, he is the one who loves me. He who loves me will be loved by my Father, and I too will love him and show myself to him"* (John 14:21).

The repentance that God requires from His people is more than a mental acknowledgment of God. Repentance is more than an emotional response to God's great love and mercy. True repentance is even more than a decision. True repentance is a walk of obedience to God's commands. It is a changed life! This truth can be seen from a short illustration of a man who went for a morning walk in the meadow. In this meadow was a small pond, and in the pond was a log. On this log sat three frogs, and as the morning sun began to shine down on the frogs, two of the frogs decided to jump off the log and into the water. How many frogs remained on the log? Most people will answer this question with simple math, and conclude that there was one frog left on the log. But the answer is that there were three frogs left on the log. This is true because deciding to jump off, and actually jumping off, are two different things. The same is true of repentance. We must not simply say we are going to repent, or even say that we have repented. We must actually repent by changing the way we live!

Without Repentance There is No Salvation

The final step on this road to righteousness, which is also the destination of our life's journey, is a place called *salvation.* Salvation is nothing less than our entry into the kingdom of heaven, and it is a destination which by God's design we are to reach before we die! Recall again that Jesus preaching was summarized in Matthew 4:14 as, *"Repent, for the kingdom of heaven is at hand."* Jesus also proclaimed, *"I tell you the truth, some who are standing here will not taste death before they see the kingdom of God come with power."* (Mark 9:38) But our understanding of salvation has drifted away from the truth of God's Word. So as we examine this final step on the road to righteousness we will focus on the complete picture of God's great salvation plan. As we build upon the foundation of the previous four steps, we will be able to better understand the great salvation plan of God. The purpose of this section is to make the case for *this great salvation* plan of God referred to in our foundational passage from Hebrews 2:1–4, which asks the question,

> So we must listen very carefully then to the truth that we have heard or we may drift away from it. The message God delivered through angels has always proved true, and the people were punished for every violation of the law, and every act of disobedience. What makes us think that we can escape, **if we are indifferent to this great salvation**, that was announced by the Lord Jesus, himself, it was passed on to us by those who heard him speak, and God verified the message through signs, wonders, various miracles, and by giving gifts of the Holy Spirit whenever he chose to do so. (NLT) (emphasis added)

Let us also recall our second foundational passage from the word of God, spoken through the Prophet, Jeremiah:

> This is what the Lord says, "**Stand at the crossroads and look. Ask for the ancient paths, ask where the good way is, and walk in it, and you will find rest for your souls**. But you said, 'We will not walk in it.' I appointed watchmen over you and said, 'Listen to the sound of the trumpet!' But you said, 'We will not listen.' Therefore hear O nations; observe O witnesses, what will happen to them. Hear O earth, for I am about to bring destruction upon this people, the fruit of their schemes, **because they have not listened to my words and have rejected my law**. (Jeremiah 6:16–19) (emphasis added)

The American Christian Church is at a crossroads today. We are faced with a choice between two paths, and our decision will determine our destiny as well as the destiny of generations to come. Whether we are aware of it or not, we are currently on a path that leads to destruction. We have been led down this path by our long held, but constantly evolving, traditional beliefs and by our emotions. It is not too late to change paths, but we will have to make the difficult decision of choosing *truth* over *tradition*. As spoken through the Prophet Jeremiah, God is warning us to ask for the ancient path, which represents truth, and then to walk in it. If we choose wisely, we can change our destination from one of destruction to one of blessings and salvation. Choosing the ancient path will mean that we choose to be led by God's unchanging truth and wisdom rather than by man's evolving traditions and by our emotions. To change our path we will need to be willing to ask some very bold questions with regard to the very foundations of our faith. Yet, this is how the next Great Awakening will begin.

There is no more foundational issue of our faith than to understand the destination point of this ancient path, a place called *salvation*. We need to open our eyes and look toward this destination, making sure that we are on the right path. The question we must ask ourselves is, Have we, as American Christians, become indifferent to this great salvation plan of God? To answer this question correctly, we will need a correct understanding of what God's great salvation plan is. God's plan of salvation is His response to something that first happened over 6,000 years ago. This event is known as the Fall. But to understand what happened at the Fall, we must first know what man and creation were like before the Fall occurred. This is true because the pre-Fall creation reflected God's original intent, and God's original intent for mankind and for creation forms the foundation of His great salvation plan.

Salvation is a Place of Original Intent

According to Genesis 1 and 2, God's original intent for His creation was *very good*. God had accomplished exactly what He desired at each step of creation. After each day of creation God said, "*It is good!*" And when God says that something is good, it is very good. God was not limited in any way from getting exactly what He desired. A God who is both omnipotent and omniscient has no limitations on what He can create! There was nothing in creation that was missing because God could not accomplish it. And nothing has happened since that time that will prevent God from getting exactly what He originally intended. Understanding this truth is critical in understanding God's plan of salvation. God's plan is to restore and redeem His creation to His original intent. Nothing can deny God what He desires, and the Fall is not an exception to this truth.

But if God's creation was exactly what He desired, then what went wrong? Why did all of creation fall? At first glance, it would appear that there must have been a flaw in God's original plan for creation, which caused the Fall to happen. But this cannot be true, because when we look at this issue through the lens of who God is, we know that God does not make mistakes. God is not learning as He goes. God does not operate by trial and error. It is true that creation, as it exists today, is not in every way good, but the Fall was not caused by a flaw in God's plan for creation. The Fall occurred because God created mankind with a free will, with the ability to choose to either obey or disobey His commands. And this was not a mistake. God chose to give mankind a free will, which required there to be the potential for a fall, the potential for sin. God created everything good, and He also intentionally made evil a possibility. This was the necessary cost of giving mankind free will. The potential for evil must therefore not be seen as a bad thing.

God also gave a free will to His angelic beings. In Genesis 3 God's word tells us the account of the fall of man, that the first fall came in the heavenly realm, when one of God's most powerful angels, Lucifer, chose to rebel against God. When Lucifer rebelled, he took with him one third of the angels. With this angelic fall, mankind was given an adversary to test his faith in God. Without being tested, faith is just a theory. Lucifer, now known as Satan, then successfully deceived Eve, and eventually Adam, into choosing to disobey God. And because God had given dominion over His creation to Adam before the fall, the entire creation then also came under the curse of sin. Since man's first disobedience to God, the creation has no longer properly reflected the original intent of God. Since that time all of creation has been groaning in anticipation of God's great salvation plan to unfold. This is what the Apostle Paul is referring to when he writes:

> The creation waits in eager expectation for the children of God to be revealed. For the creation was subjected to frustration, not by its own choice, but by the will of the one who subjected it in hope that the creation itself will be liberated from its bondage to decay and brought into the freedom and glory of the children of God. We know that the whole creation has been groaning as in the pains of childbirth right up to the present time. (Romans 8:19–22)

But God cannot be denied what He originally desired for either man or creation. God cannot fail to get what He desires. God was not taken by surprise by the fall of either angels or of mankind. God has always had a plan to return His creation, including mankind, to reflect His original intent. God's salvation plan had to be accomplished through the free will of man because, as the Psalmist has written, *"The highest heavens belong to the Lord, but the earth He has given to mankind"* (Psalm 115:16). When God gave mankind dominion over His creation, God ordained that the redemption of His creation must be done through man, not to man and not for man. God's salvation plan is not to save us in spite of ourselves, but it is instead a plan to make our salvation possible if we exercise our free will in accordance with His directions.

Salvation is the Solution to the Real Problem

God's plan of salvation, then, is His response to the problem of man's sin and the resulting curse upon the whole of creation. Sin is disobedience to God's commands, disobedience to God's directions for life. Prior to the fall of man, God had warned Adam and Eve that if they disobeyed His commands and ate from the tree of the knowledge of good and evil, they would die. With this command God established His unchanging Law. God established the Law by giving Adam and Eve both the command and the consequences for disobedience. God's word must never be doubted. Eve referred to this warning in Genesis 3:3, when she recalled that God had said, *"You must not eat fruit from the tree that is in the middle of the garden, and you must not touch it, or you will die."* She was referring to a statement God had made to Adam in Genesis 2:1 *"You are free to eat from any tree in the garden; but you must not eat from the tree of the knowledge of good and evil, for when you eat of it you will surely die."* Adam and Eve knew God's Law from the very beginning of time, and their disobedience was not one of ignorance, but of choice.

Before the fall took place, God had already established His unchanging Law, which states that the wages of sin is death. This Law was good. This Law was not flawed. This Law was not a mistake. This Law would not change. This Law was necessary because God had created mankind in His own image, an image of absolute righteousness. God is also absolutely just, and God warned Adam and Eve that there would be no tolerance of disobedience to His commands. To those who do not know God, this may seem extremely harsh, but by telling Adam and Eve not to eat the fruit of the tree of the knowledge of good and evil, God was warning them that only He defines what is good and what is evil, not man. God had given man dominion over creation, not sovereignty. Man was to take dominion over creation under God's Law, and only under God's Law. In other words, man was to live in liberty, not absolute freedom. God had established the consequences for man's disobedience before sin had been committed.

It is also critically important to understand that the Law, which established the consequence of sin to be death, was never the problem. The Law was established before the fall and was not given in response to the fall of man. The Law did not cause the fall. By establishing the Law, which says that the wages of sin is death, God actually made righteousness possible. Without a moral standard to govern man, there could be no virtue. God established that He would not accept anything less than everything He desired for His people! God's unchanging standard of righteousness was established, and for those who choose to walk within this standard, the blessings will be beyond our imagination. The Law was never the problem, for it reflected God's desire for man and creation to be absolutely good. The problem to be solved by the great salvation plan of God was not the Law, but instead was that man had disobeyed the Law. God's salvation plan is to bring man back into obedience to the Law, not to change the Law, or to save man from the Law.

It is necessary to gain a greater understanding of God's original intent for man. God chose to create man in His own image and therefore to give man free will. God created man to be a moral agent with dominion over His creation, not to be a preprogramed robot. God wanted mankind to reflect His image and to accomplish His desires for creation. Man could not live with free will if disobedience to God's commands was not a possibility. So God chose to give man the ability to choose to either obey Him or to disobey Him. Giving man free will was not a mistake, it was good. God's original intent was for man to have free will, yet to be empowered to exercise that free will by walking in righteousness, in complete obedience to His commands. This was God's original intent for man.

God's desire for mankind has not changed. It was God's desire for Adam to have free will, yet to walk in total obedience to His commands. God does not change, and therefore God's desire for man has not changed. God's original intent for the first Adam was the same as His intent for the second Adam, Jesus. Jesus, the Son of Man, walked in complete righteous obedience to God's Law. Jesus perfectly reflected God's will and this was and is God's purpose for all men. Jesus was the Word made flesh. The purpose of all of mankind is also to be the Word made flesh, the original intent of God manifested. Jesus testified to this purpose and plan not only by his words but also by His life. Jesus, the Son of Man, literally showed us the way to walk with God. Jesus' life was his greatest testimony. Jesus reestablished God's original standard for all men. Jesus truly is the way, the truth and the life.

The Apostle Paul understood that Jesus had come to re-establish this standard for all men when he wrote,

It was he (Jesus) who gave some to be apostles, some to be
prophets, some to be evangelists, and some to be pastors and
teachers, to prepare God's people for works of service, so that the
body of Christ may be built up until we all reach unity in the faith and
in the knowledge of the Son of God **and become mature, attaining
to the whole measure of the fullness of Christ.** (Ephesians 4:11–
13) (emphasis added)

The true purpose of God's great salvation plan is to redeem His people to the whole
measure of the fullness of Christ! With this truth in mind, there can be no question
that we have drifted away from this great salvation plan of God.

Salvation is from Sin

To understand the great salvation plan of God, it is necessary to look even more
closely at *sin.* Remember that sin is the problem which God's great salvation plan
addresses. Sin does not happen to us; it is a choice we make. Sin does not exist
outside of the free will of men and angels. The source of sin cannot be the flesh
because angels do not have flesh yet they sinned against God by walking in disobedience to His directions. Sin is disobedience of God's Law, and its source is within
the will of men and angels. The Law consists of both the precepts and the punishment, both the commands and consequences, for disobeying the commands. The
God-ordained consequence of sin is death. Death is not the real problem of man.
Death is a result of the real problem, which is sin. Without the consequences for disobedience, the Law is nothing more than a set of suggestions for better living. But
God does not make suggestions.

Sin, disobedience to God's Word, is the source of all of our problems. The consequence of sin is death because God cannot tolerate any sin. God's Word holds
the power of life itself. Jesus understood this when he proclaimed to Satan in the
desert, that "It is written: '*Man does not live on bread alone, but on every word that
comes from the mouth of God*" (Matthew 4:4). The Prophet Isaiah understood this
truth when He spoke these words from God to the people, ". . . *so shall my word be
that goes forth from my mouth: It shall not return to be empty, but will accomplish
what I desire and achieve the purpose for which I sent it*" (Isaiah 55:11).

The Old Testament is often referred to as being the Law and the Prophets. The
Law was given through Moses, and it included both the commands and the consequences for disobedience. At the very heart of the Book of the Law is Deuteronomy
28, which as we have seen, is a clear example of the consequences of obedience
and of disobedience to God's Law. History tells us that when the Law is in place,
the people live in the blessings of prosperity, but when it is lost or disregarded, the
people live under the curse of pain and despair. The consequences of disobedience to God's directions were restated from generation to generation by God's Old
Testament Prophets. It is critical for us to understand that the purpose and power

of Law and the Prophets did not end with the closing of the Old Testament. Jesus made this clear in Matthew 5:17–19 when he said,

> Do not think that I have come to abolish the Law or the Prophets; I have not come to abolish them but to fulfill them. I tell you the truth, until heaven and earth disappear, not the smallest letter, not the least stroke of a pen, will by any means disappear from the Law until everything is accomplished. Anyone who breaks one of the least of these commands and teaches others to do the same will be called least in the kingdom of heaven, but whoever practices and teaches theses commands will be called great in the kingdom of heaven.

Jesus said he did not come to abolish either the Law or the Prophets. Therefore he did not come to change either the commands or the consequences for disobedience of these commands. Instead, Jesus said that he has come to fulfill the Law and the Prophets. But what does this mean? If a man fulfills an obligation, he meets that obligation. If a man fulfills the law, he obeys the law. Jesus came in complete submission to the Law, in complete obedience to His Father's commands. He did not come to change the consequences for disobedience. Jesus did not come to obey the commands so that God's people would no longer be required to obey them. To conclude that Jesus fulfilled the Law so that we do not have to fulfill the Law would be in direct opposition to the original intent of God. Why would God send Jesus to die on the cross so that His people could keep on sinning and not be punished for their sins? Removing the punishment of sin, without removing the sins, would not serve the purpose or the intent of God and would be a change in the Law.

Many Christians today believe that they have been saved from the Law, but this is not true. The Law is God's directions for life. Vine's Dictionary defines the Law as: "*The 'instruction' of the sages of Israel, who were charged with the education of the young, was intended to cultivate in the young a fear of the Lord so that they might live in accordance with God's expectations.*" Why would God save us from His directions for life? Why would we want to be saved from God's directions for life? The Law is both the commands and the consequences for disobedience, so to take away the consequences of sin would be to abolish the Law. If God loves His people, He will not save them from the Law. If God really loves His people He will save them back to the Law! This salvation makes sense if we remember that sin is disobedience to God's directions for life. Salvation is the process of being brought back from disobedience to obedience to God's commands.

The Salvation Announcement

To better understand our drift away from God's great salvation plan, listen again to the writer of Hebrews in our foundational passage:

> So we must listen very carefully then, to the truth that we have heard, or me may drift away from it. **The message God delivered through angels has always proved true, and the people were punished for every violation of the law, and every act of disobedience.** What makes us think that we will escape if we are indifferent to this great salvation, which was announced by the Lord Jesus, himself. It was passed on to us by those who heard him speak. And God verified the message through signs, wonders, various miracles, and by giving gifts of the Holy Spirit, whenever He chose to do so. (Hebrews 2:1–4, NLT) (emphasis added)

What is it that the writer of Hebrews is telling us that we must listen to? It is the message God delivered through angels, which has always proved true. But what is this message delivered by angels? The answer can be found in the words of the angel of the Lord spoken to Joseph in Matthew 1:21, who said, "*She (Mary) will give birth to a son, and you are to give him the name Jesus, because he will save his people from their sins.*" Most Christians have read this verse many times over their lives. But have we listened carefully to what the angel of the Lord said? Why were Joseph and Mary to name their son Jesus? Understanding the answer to this question will be the first step toward rediscovering why there is such power in Jesus' name! This child was to be given the name *Jesus* because *he will save his people from their sins.* This was the angel's announcement of God's great salvation plan!

Most Christians today will say "*Amen!*" to this announcement of the angels in Matthew 1:21. But how many today will misinterpret what the angel of the Lord really said? While we read that Jesus will save the people from their sins, what we hear is that Jesus will save the people from the punishment of their sins. Many today may say, "What is the difference as long as we are saved?" There is a big difference! It is the difference between life and death; between the truth and deception; between walking in power and walking without power. It is the difference between the great salvation plan that honors God and a counterfeit salvation plan that dishonors God. The key to correctly understanding this announcement is to see the difference between being *saved from our sins* and being *saved from the punishment of our sins.* We need to ask ourselves which of these two salvation plans is the true salvation plan of God?

If we know who God is, then we can interpret His Word through the lens of that knowledge. Knowing that God is omnipotent, omniscient, absolutely righteous, absolutely just, and unchanging, we can then rightly determine which salvation plan He would choose. If God's salvation plan is from the punishment of our sins, without being saved from our sins, then salvation itself would by definition be an injustice because our continuing sins would not be punished. Salvation from the consequences of sin, without salvation from sins, would be a change in the Law, which states that the wages of sin is death. But we know that God does not change, and therefore His Law does not change. Salvation from our sins is really the only way that justice will allow us to be saved from the punishment of our sins. This is true because God is a God of absolute justice, which requires Him to punish sin and to reward righteousness.

Many Christians today may believe that understanding the plan of salvation is not necessary, so long as we put our faith in Jesus' death on the cross to save us. But the purpose of Jesus' death on the cross was to make salvation from sin possible, not to save us in our sins. Without the cross, as payment for the sins we have already committed, justice would not allow us to be saved from punishment. Justice requires that all sins must be punished, and the sentence established by God's Law is death. The cross opened the door to our salvation from sin, and from sin's consequences, by paying the price of punishment on our behalf. But this payment is only for the sins from which we have repented. The cross is an invitation to be saved from the punishment of the sins we have already committed. We accept this invitation by repenting, and we cannot repent today for sins that we will commit tomorrow. The cross is an invitation that is unmerited by anything we have done or could do. But the cross does not save us from the punishment of our sins unless we accept this unmerited invitation under God's terms.

Because God is holy, He cannot tolerate any sin. This is why approaching God is not a casual undertaking. When God is confronted with sin there are only two ways that He can respond: (1) He can immediately punish that sin, as justice requires, or (2) He can choose to pause before He executes judgment on that sin, giving the sinner time for repentance. Within God's perfect justice there is room for mercy and grace, but this mercy and this grace are not required of God, and they are not everlasting.

The great American thinker and Founding Father, Noah Webster, who felt called by God to write the 1828 American English Dictionary, understood these terms when he defined *The Days of Grace* that we live in as "... *a time of probation, in which an offer is made to sinners."* The true grace and mercy of God are really His undeserved and unwarranted decision to pause before He gives sinners what justice demands, giving us time to repent. A grace period to repent is not an injustice. But the days of grace are only for a period of time; they will not last forever!

A Parable about Salvation

The concept of the cross being an invitation to salvation, rather than salvation itself, will be foreign to many, and even offensive to some. But with this issue in mind, listen carefully to the teaching of Jesus on the issue of God's great salvation plan as recorded in Matthew 22:1–14, the parable of the wedding banquet:

> The kingdom of heaven is like a king who prepared a wedding banquet for his son. He sent his servants to those who had been invited to the banquet to tell them to come, but they refused to come.
>
> Then he sent some more servants and said, "Tell those who have been invited that I have prepared my dinner: My oxen and fattened

cattle have been butchered, and everything is ready. Come to the wedding banquet."

But they paid no attention and went off—one to his field, another to his business. The rest seized his servants, mistreated them and killed them. The king was enraged. He sent his army and destroyed those murderers and burned their city.

Then he said to his servants, "The wedding banquet is ready, but those I invited did not deserve to come. Go to the street corners and invite to the banquet anyone you find." So the servants went out into the streets and gathered all the people they could find, **both good and bad**, and the wedding hall was filled with guests.

But when the king came in to see the guests, he noticed a man there who was not wearing wedding clothes. "Friend" he asked, "how did you get in here without wedding clothes?" **The man was speechless**.

Then the king told the attendants, "Tie him hand and foot, and throw him outside, into the darkness, where there will be weeping and gnashing of teeth."

For many are invited, but few are chosen. (emphasis added)

If we have listened carefully to this teaching of Jesus, we can hear the great salvation message of God. Again, the invitation to this great banquet (salvation) was unmerited. The servants invited both the good and the bad to come, and apparently both the good and bad did come. But then something happened to one of the men who came to the banquet to which he was invited. When he was asked by the king how he had gotten into the banquet without the proper wedding clothes, the man was speechless. The king then sentenced this man to death! What are these wedding clothes that were so important to the king? Could they be the robe of righteousness required to be worn in the presence of the king? But if the king was merciful, loving, and full of grace, then why didn't he simply tell the servants to get the man some wedding clothes? Could it be that the man had to do this himself before He entered the banquet? Note that this parable ends with words that should make us think much more deeply about our salvation, as Jesus concludes this parable by saying that *many are called but few are chosen*.

How many Christians are going to hear these terrible words of condemnation when they come to the judgment seat and stand in the presence of the King? How many Christians are placing their confidence in a belief that they can put on the wedding clothes when they get to the banquet? How many will one day be as speechless as that poor man who was thrown out into eternal darkness? Did that man's ignorance help him avoid disaster? Will our ignorance of the truth about God's great salvation plan be a valid defense? Are we willing to listen and learn what we must do to accept this unmerited invitation to our salvation? Are we willing to put on our robes of righteousness before we meet the King?

Accepting this unmerited invitation is something that we must choose to do ourselves. God cannot accept the invitation for us. Jesus cannot accept the invitation for us. The Holy Spirit cannot accept this invitation for us. We must choose to accept this invitation, and our acceptance is not simply saying "Thank you for the invitation." The only way that we can accept this unmerited invitation is to repent from our sins. We must choose to turn away from our sins. We must submit our will to God's Law. Being convicted of sin is a very good and necessary element of repentance, but it is not repentance. Confessing our sins is a very good and necessary element of repentance, but it is not repentance. If we are not convicted of sin and if we do not confess our sins, we will not repent of our sins. But simply being convicted of sins, then confessing our sins, and finally saying thank you to God that He has forgiven our sins is not repentance, and therefore it is not acceptance of the unmerited invitation to salvation.

So why do so many Christians today believe that conviction of sin, confession of sin, and a thank you to God is enough? It is because we have wrongly defined what salvation is! We have changed the focus of salvation from repentance to forgiveness. If the sole purpose of God's plan of salvation is to unconditionally forgive us for all of our past, present and future sins, then there is no need for repentance. Repentance becomes an option for those who want to be *serious Christians*. But if God's plan of salvation is to save us from our disobedience and to obedience, then repentance is actually the first step into salvation! Repentance is our only way of accepting God's invitation. We must choose to submit our will to God's will by the initial step of repentance from our disobedience. We then begin the walk of obedience that God desires and requires of us. Repentance is a choice that we must make for ourselves, but it is not a one-time decision; it is a lifetime walk.

There is no better illustration of repentance and salvation than the one used by Jesus in Matthew 7:13–14:

> Enter through the narrow gate. For wide is the gate, and broad is the road, that leads to destruction, and many enter through it. But small is the gate and narrow the road, that leads to life, and only a few find it.

The narrow gate is the gate of repentance. The narrow path is the path of obedience to God's commands. It seems right in today's Christian culture to attempt to widen this gate by telling people that all they must do to enter into salvation is to say a simple prayer. It seems loving and kind to then tell people that once they have entered through the narrow gate by this prayer, there is nothing that they could ever do to lose their salvation. It seems right to tell the new believer that once he has said the sinner's prayer all he needs to do is believe in Jesus. We have attempted to change the narrow gate into a wide gate, and we have almost completely ignored what it means to walk the narrow path of repentance, which is a walk of obedience.

Proverbs 14:12 warns us, *"There is a way that seems right to a man, but in the end it leads to death."* While the primary focus on evangelism within today's Christian Church is on getting as many people *saved* as we can, the truth of God, as announced by Jesus, is that few will find this salvation. God desires *quality* of salvation over *quantity* of salvation. Nothing can prevent God from getting exactly what He desires. So if God had desired salvation to be a wide gate, it would have been a wide gate. But God chose to make this gate a narrow gate because He desires His people to have free will, and that only those who truly chose to come will be saved. There is great power in this truth.

God's plan of salvation must bring honor to God. God would never settle for a second-rate salvation plan. God's plan of salvation must therefore solve the real problem, which is that man has chosen to sin, to walk in disobedience to His directions for life. If God's Law were the problem, then God's plan of salvation could be to change the Law by saving us from the punishment of our sins, without saving us from our sins. But if sinning against God is the real problem, then the plan of salvation must empower us to actually overcome our sins, which means we must be saved from sinning. The problem that God's great plan of salvation solved was the problem of our disobedience, not that our disobedience would be punished. God's solution to this problem, His plan of salvation, was not to simply take away the consequences of our sins, but instead it was to empower us to go and sin no more!

Three Reasons we have Drifted Away from the Truth

There are three primary misconceptions that have led many of today's Christians to drift away from this ancient path and toward a new salvation path, which is salvation from the punishment of our sins, rather than salvation from our sins. These three misconceptions are deeply imbedded into today's Christian traditions. And because traditions are so strong, we have come to believe in them simply because we have always believed them. Many will become offended at even the suggestion that we have drifted away from the truth about God's salvation plan. This drift away from truth and toward traditions has been happening for generations, and many Christians today will not be interested in listening to the evidence from God's Word that will awaken them to this drift. Many today are totally satisfied with this new salvation plan, which saves them from the punishment of their sins but not from sinning. This drift has happened because we have been listening to the opinions of men and not to the Word of God.

The first and most powerful traditional misconception is that overcoming our sins is impossible. It seems humble to confess that we are all sinners saved by grace. Many will quote Romans 3:10–12 in support of their belief that overcoming all of our sins is not possible: *"As it is written: 'There is no one righteous, not even one; there is no one who understands, no one who seeks God. All have turned away, they have together become worthless; there is no one who is good, not even one."* But in this letter the Apostle Paul is quoting from the Old Testament Book of Psalms, and these words were clearly intended to identify the problem of sin, not to suggest that overcoming sins is not possible. The Psalmist was speaking of the fool who does not believe God, not the true believer. The Psalmist writes,

> The fool says in his heart, "There is no God." They are corrupt, their deeds are vile; there is no one who does good. The Lord looks down from heaven on the sons of men to see if there are any who understand, any who seek God. All have turned aside, they have together become corrupt; there is no one who does good, not even one. (Psalm 14:1–3)

Many will also quote the Apostle Paul in Romans 3:23, where he writes, ". . . *for all have sinned and fall short of the glory of God. . . .*" But this again is not what God desires of all men. It is instead a statement of the problem, not the solution. If we choose to interpret the writings of the Apostle Paul, without reading his words through the lens of knowing who God is and what Jesus taught, some will conclude that Paul believed that we are saved in our sins, rather than from our sins. But in the same letter to the Romans Paul later writes, "*What shall we say then? Shall we go on sinning so that grace may increase? By no means! We died to sin; how can we live in it any longer?*" (Romans 6:1–2) Paul goes on to write,

> What then? Shall we sin because we are not under law but under grace? By no means! Don't you know that when you offer your-selves to someone to obey him as slaves, you are slaved to the one whom you obey—whether you are slaves to sin, which leads to death, or to obedience, which leads to righteousness? But thanks be to God that, though you used to be slaves to sin, you wholeheart-edly obeyed the form of teaching to which you were entrusted. You have been set free from sin and have become slaves to righteous-ness. (Romans 6:15–18)

The Apostle Paul understood God's salvation plan, but many of today's Christians are misinterpreting what Paul was saying about salvation and sin. We must inter-pret Paul's teachings in a way that honors God by being consistent with who God is, with what was taught by the Law and the Prophets, and finally with what Jesus taught. This one false foundational belief, that overcoming our sins is impossible, is the seed of deception that has been planted and has been growing within the Church for generations upon generations. It has now become our traditional Christian belief, and as a tradition, it has great power over us. But is overcoming all of our sins really impossible, even for the great plan of salvation authored by God, Himself?

Who decides what is possible for mankind? It is God, not man, who has estab-lished what is possible for man. This is a very important truth to understand if we are to rediscover the great salvation message of God. God is self-existing and self-sus-taining; man is not. God has no limits on what He can do. This is not true of mankind.

God created mankind with the potential to be everything He desires us to be, but we will never be God. That is impossible! As stated earlier, God created us with the original intent and purpose to walk with free will, yet to walk in complete obedience to His directions. God would not make it impossible for us to fulfill His desire for us.

If God has not made complete obedience possible for man, then our disobedience would not be our fault; it would be God's fault! Many today do not understand that this is the ramification of a belief that overcoming our sins is impossible. When we hold to this belief, we are actually bringing an indictment against God. This false belief that overcoming all sin is impossible leads to a great drift away from God's salvation plan. It inevitably leads to the belief in a salvation from the punishment of our sins rather than a salvation from our sins. If God, who is absolutely just, did not make it possible for man to overcome his sins, then God would be unjust to punish us for our sins. God cannot require us to do something that He has not ordained it possible for us to do! Yet in today's Christian culture, whether it is expressed through sermons, books, or music, we are reminded time and time again that we are all destined to remain sinners saved by grace, and that our righteousness is as filthy rags in God's eyes. But this false belief does not honor God.

It honors God when man walks in complete righteousness, absolute obedience to His Law. True and complete righteousness is a good thing. Absolute obedience is a good thing. This is what God desires of man. Yet many today believe that walking in total obedience to God would actually lead us to self-righteousness and pride. Not only do many Christians reject a completely righteous walk as being possible, but many Christians do not believe that it is possible to be righteous for even a whole day, for an entire hour, or even for a full minute. We have come to accept sin as an inevitable and constant part of our lives. As a result, we have surrendered to the power of sin in our lives before we even commit the sin. We have been deceived. This happens when we fail to see the difference between temptation and sin.

God's Word tells us that overcoming all sin is good and that it is also possible. God's word does not tell us that we will be able to avoid all temptations. When faced with temptations we have access to the power to overcome those temptations and to not sin. Sin does not happen to us, it is something we choose to do. It is a matter of the will. God has given us a way to overcome all temptations, if we choose to walk in the light of this truth. But if we wrongly believe that temptation is sin and that sin is something that happens to us, then we will be led to believe that overcoming all sin is not possible. Temptation cannot be sin because Jesus was tempted in all ways, yet he did not sin. If temptation is sin, then Jesus would have been guilty of sin. But Jesus overcame all temptations, and He was without sin! Jesus showed us *the way* God requires us to live.

To determine whether overcoming our sins is possible we must look to the word of God, as spoken through the Prophets, through the teachings of Jesus, and through the writings of the Apostles. First, consider two statements God made to His people through His Prophet and servant, Moses. God had manifested His presence to the people in the form of a great cloud of smoke that had descended upon Mount Sinai with thunder, lightning, and the sounds of trumpets. God then delivered the Ten Commandments directly to the people through the sound of His own voice. The people trembled in fear, and then Moses said to them, *"Do not be afraid. God has come to test you, so that the fear of God will be with you to keep you from sinning"* (Exodus 20:20). God had delivered His commands in a way in which the people would fear Him and therefore be empowered to obey His commands, and to overcome all of their sins!

Later, Moses recalled what the Lord had spoken to Him: *"Oh, that their hearts would be inclined to fear me and keep all my commands always, so that it might go well with them and their children forever"* (Deuteronomy 5:29). Did we listen carefully to what God said? God expected his people to obey all of his commands always. In this statement God revealed a great truth which we have lost. The fear of the Lord in our hearts is the power to overcome all of our sins! God has established that it is possible to overcome all of our sins if we fear Him. The only remaining issue is whether we believe what God has said.

What did Jesus teach with regard to the possibility of actually overcoming our sins? On at least two occasions, in John 5:14 and John 8:11, Jesus commanded people to *go and sin no more.* Jesus did not tell the people to sin less, or to do the best that you can. Jesus told them to go and sin no more! Would Jesus say this if it were not possible to actually go and sin no more? On another occasion, when teaching the disciples about God's salvation plan, Jesus said, *"With God all things are possible"* (Matthew 19:26). If we conclude that overcoming sins is not possible, then we would be changing the plain meaning of this statement. It makes no sense to interpret this Scripture passage to mean that all things are possible with God, except overcoming our sins. And in His most famous message, the Sermon on the Mount, Jesus told the people to *"Be perfect, therefore, as your heavenly Father is perfect"* (Matthew 5:48). Would Jesus say this if overcoming our sins is not possible? If we walk in disobedience to God's commands, we are not perfect. Yet many Christians today continue to view perfection as their enemy because they believe that over-coming their sins is not possible.

Consider the words of the Apostle John, who was called to carry God's great salvation message into all of the world. John writes,

> Everyone who sins breaks the law; in fact, sin is lawlessness. But you know that he appeared so that he might take away our sins. And in him is no sin. **No one who lives in him keeps on sinning. No one who continues to sin has either seen him or known him.** (I John 3:4–6) (emphasis added)

Has Jesus taken away our sins if we continue to sin? John goes on to write, *"No one who is born of God will continue to sin, because God's seed remains in him; he cannot go on sinning, because he has been born of God"* (I John 3:9). Would John make this statement if he did not believe that overcoming our sins is possible?

The Apostle Paul, in his letter to the Philippians, wrote *"I can do everything through him who gives me strength"* (Philippians 4:13). Why would we choose to interpret this statement as meaning I can do all things, except overcoming all of my sins, through him who gives me strength? We have become a double-minded people.

While overcoming our sins is possible with God's great salvation plan, He has not predetermined obedience or disobedience for us. Each individual must make this choice for himself. God has given each of us everything we need to walk, with free will yet in total submission to His Law. It is God who has defined what is and is not possible for us. And it is man who must choose whether he will submit to God's Law. God created us with potential and also with limitations. Complete righteous obedience to God's commands is within these limits. If overcoming our sins were not possible, then God would be denied what He desires. But this conclusion would deny God's sovereignty. For God to be denied what He desires would mean that there is a power above God. But when we look through the lens of knowing who God is, then we know that this cannot be true. God has made a way for us to actually overcome all of our sins!

There is a second reason why so many of today's Christians have chosen to change God's great salvation plan from a plan to save us from our sins to a plan to save us from the punishment of our sins. It is because of our traditional Christian belief that says that salvation is easy. For generations Christians have come to almost cherish how easy it is to be saved. We often wonder why more people don't get saved when it is as easy as saying the sinner's prayer. But is the great salvation plan of God really that easy? If salvation is obtained by simply telling God that we are sorry for our sins and then saying thank you that our sins are forgiven, then it is easy. But if salvation is about a daily walk of righteousness, of overcoming sin and walking in complete obedience to God's commands, then salvation is not easy.

So is salvation easy? Listen carefully again to what Jesus taught, rather than to the opinions of men and our traditional teachings. In Matthew 7:13–14, Jesus answers this question with great clarity. He said,

> Enter through the narrow gate, for wide is the gate and broad is the
> path that leads to destruction and many enter through it. But small
> is the gate and narrow the path that leads to life, and few find it.

If salvation is really easy, would Jesus refer to it as a narrow gate, and a narrow path, that few will find? Jesus also told his disciples, "*I tell you the truth, it is hard for a rich man to enter the kingdom of heaven. Again I tell you, it is easier for a camel to go through the eye of a needle than for a rich man to enter the kingdom of God*" (Matthew 19:23–24). Does this sound like an easy plan of salvation? The disciples concluded that this standard of salvation was actually too difficult, but Jesus responded, "*With man this is impossible, but with God all things are possible*" (Matthew 19:26). The great salvation plan of God is not impossible, but it is also not easy!

Did the Apostles teach that salvation is easy? In his letter to the Philippians, Paul stressed the requirement of the hard work of obedience in God's plan of salvation when he said,

> Therefore, my dear friends, as you have always obeyed—not only
> in my presence, but now much more in my absence—continue

> to work out your salvation with fear and trembling, for it is God
> who works in you to will and to act according to his good purpose.
> (Philippians 2:12–13)

If Paul believed salvation is easy to obtain would he have stressed that it must be worked out with fear and trembling?

A third reason that many Christians today do not believe in a salvation from our sins is their belief that we are saved by *grace* through *faith,* and not by works, and that actually overcoming our sins would be *works.* This statement of salvation by grace through faith is true, but its truth is dependent upon a correct understanding of both the word *grace* and the word *faith.* The counterfeit belief in a salvation by grace through faith does not come from the Word of God spoken through the Prophets or from the teachings of Jesus. If we correctly understand *grace* to be the power unto righteousness and *faith* to be the substance of what we believe, then we are clearly saved by grace through faith. But a misunderstanding of grace as God's decision to overlook our sins so long as we are *Christian sinners* and faith as a simple acknowledgement that Jesus is our Savior and Lord has led many Christians to fear being considered *legalistic* more than they fear sinning against God.

This should not be a surprise to those who study God's Word, which warns us time and again that at the end times the problem of even God's people will be *lawlessness,* not *legalism.* And those who fear legalism more than they fear sinning against God are destined to become a lawless people. People who seek complete obedience to God's Law are not legalistic. Obedience is not legalism; it is righteousness. Repentance is not legalism; it is turning away from our disobedience and turning toward obedience. Again, there is nothing that one must do to earn the invitation to be saved through Jesus' death on the cross. But when *legalism* is wrongly defined as obedience to God's Law, then a false doctrine of salvation has been created. If we remove the requirement of obedience to God's commands from the plan of salvation, we have drifted away from the truth. God's plan of salvation is to obedience of God's commands, not from obedience to them.

When we teach that the foundation of our salvation is that God has decided not to punish our sins because of His unconditional love for Christians, we have become indifferent to His great salvation plan. When we replace the need for true repentance with a simple sinner's prayer of confession and forgiveness, we have left the ancient path that leads back to God. Remember what Jesus said to those who professed to love him. "*If you love me, keep my commands*" (John 14:15) and "*Whoever has my commands, and obeys them, he is the one who loves me. And he who loves me, will be loved by my Father, and I too will love him, and show myself to him*" (John 14:21). Jesus was not preaching legalism; he was preaching righteousness!

If we truly desire the next Great Awakening to take place, then it is time to rediscover the true grace of God, which is the power unto righteousness, and the true faith in God, which is the truth that our faith must be evidenced by the good fruit of obedience to His commands. Yes, we are sinners saved by grace, but grace is not God's unilateral decision to overlook our sins because He loves us too much to punish us. And yes, we are saved through faith, but this faith must be in the truth of God's Word. We are not saved by our good works, but we are saved unto good works. The Apostle Paul wrote, *"For we are God's workmanship, created in Christ Jesus to do good works, which God prepared in advance for use to do"* (Ephesians 2:10). We are at a crossroads where we must choose the real *grace* of God and the real *faith* in God. *Grace* is God's plan to empower us to actually overcome our sins. And *faith* is the substance of the truth of God's Word, which must be evidenced by our words and deeds. This is the grace and the faith which will save us and will bring honor and pleasure to God!

Our faith is the substance of what we believe. God's Word is not true because we believe it. We believe God's Word because it is true! God's Word tells us *"Faith comes by hearing, and hearing by the word of God"* (Romans 10:17, NKJV). To understand any aspect of our faith, the best place to begin is with the teachings of Jesus. If anyone would understand what *grace* really is it would be Jesus, whom we are told in Hebrews 12:2 is the author and finisher of our faith. Jesus is the greatest teacher of the faith that ever walked the earth. So what did Jesus teach his disciples with regard to salvation by *grace?* The answer to this question will surprise most Christians. The recorded teachings of Jesus do not use the term *grace*. While the majority of Jesus' teaching was about salvation and entering the kingdom of heaven, Jesus' teachings did not refer to *grace* when he taught these concepts. Jesus did not teach that God would forgive the sins of His people simply because He loved them too much to punish them. Jesus did not teach that salvation comes through being labeled as a *Christian.* Jesus did not preach that salvation comes through reciting a *sinner's prayer.* Jesus preaching was instead summarized in Matthew 4:17 as, *"Repent, for the kingdom of heaven is near."*

While Jesus did not teach that salvation was based upon grace, he did regularly teach about the necessity of overcoming our sins. One of his most clear and focused teaching in this regard came when he had been teaching the Jews, who believed in him, about salvation. He said, *"If you hold to my teachings then you are really my disciples. Then you will know the truth, and the truth will set you free"* (John 8:31–32). This teaching offended some of the Jews, who responded that they were not slaves to anyone because they were the descendants of Abraham. In other words they felt that their status as God's chosen people entitled them to God's unmerited favor, to God's grace. But Jesus boldly confronted their traditional beliefs when he said, *"I tell you the truth, everyone who sins is a slave to sin. Now we know that a slave has no permanent place in the family, but a son belongs to it forever. So if the son sets you free, then you will be free indeed"* (John 8:34–35).

Have we listened carefully to this teaching of Jesus with regard to the necessity of overcoming sin? Who did Jesus say was a slave to sin? He said, *I tell you the truth, everyone who sins is a slave to sin.* But what about Christian sinners? Is a Christian sinner any different than a descendant of Abraham who sinned? What happened to wicked Israelites in the Old Testament? What will happen to wicked Christians today? Is our salvation based upon our label as Christians saved by grace, or is it based upon the way we choose to live our lives? God's grace is real. The grace of God comes to us in the form of an unmerited invitation to be forgiven, along with the God-given power to walk in obedience to His commands. Jesus boldly says that if the Son sets you free, then you will be free indeed. Jesus came to set us free from our sins, not simply to free us from the punishment for our sins. The *grace* Jesus taught was in the form of power to go and sin no more!

The Apostle James stressed the importance of proper teaching when he said, *"Not many of you should presume to be teachers, my brothers, because you know that we who teach will be judged more strictly"* (James 3:1). How we teach God's great salvation plan may be the greatest way we either honor or dishonor God. We dishonor God if we change His great salvation plan. God desires nothing but the best for His people. God never settles for less than the best. To teach God's great salvation plan as a plan that takes away the consequences of our sins but does not empower us to walk in actual righteousness does not honor God. We correctly teach that Jesus died on the cross to pay the penalty for our sins, but we have failed to warn sinners that to receive God's forgiveness, they must be willing to let go of their sins and actually stop sinning.

At the time of the Protestant Reformation, Martin Luther was highly critical of the teaching of the doctrine of indulgences, which was the payment of money to receive the forgiveness of sins. But isn't this what we teach as well when we say that salvation is from the punishment of our sins rather from our sins? The focus of the message of salvation today is upon God's forgiveness of our sins rather than on our repentance from our sins. Today's Christians are grateful to God for His forgiveness of our sins, but very few of us are interested in obeying all of God's commands all of the time.

We must be careful not to treat the cross as the *great indulgence* price paid so that we can keep on sinning and not be punished for our sins. While the cross was the price that was paid to make the way of salvation possible, the cross is only a part of the great salvation plan. The cross is the invitation. The cross has made repentance possible. The cross says it is not too late to repent from our sins. But the cross is the beginning point of salvation, not the end. The end is what we do with the cross. The end goal of God's great salvation plan is not that His people could continue to sin without any consequences. The end of God's great salvation plan is the redemption of His people and of all of His creation. This means that His people, with their free will intact, must again walk in total obedience to all of God's commands.

God's great salvation plan is not a great indulgence plan. God's great salvation plan is worthy of God's righteous and just nature. God's great salvation plan is the solution to the real problem, man's sins. God's great salvation plan must be worthy of God. God's great salvation plan must honor God. A plan which saves us from the punishment of sins, but leaves us powerless to overcome sin, is not worthy of God and it is not honoring to God. A salvation plan which leaves us sinning is neither a loving plan nor a great plan. God's great plan of salvation is better than that!

There is only one salvation plan that is worthy of God. There is only one salvation plan that is honoring to God. There is only one salvation plan which is true. It is God's plan to save us from our sins. The only salvation plan worthy of God is a plan which empowers us to overcome our sins. The cross is about opening the door to allow us to choose to walk through that door. The cross does not save us; the cross invites us to be saved. This statement may shock many, but God's desire is not that all men be saved. If He wanted all men to be saved then He would not have given man free will. What God desires is that all men, who choose to walk in obedience to His commands, be saved. And God has made a way for everyone who chooses righteousness, to be righteous! God has given us the key to the door to our salvation. He has also given us the wisdom, knowledge, and power to stay on the narrow path of salvation.

Consider this Word of the Lord spoken through the Prophet, Isaiah:

> The Lord is exalted for He dwells on high. He will fill Zion with justice and righteousness. He will be the sure foundation for your times, a rich store of salvation, and wisdom, and knowledge; the fear of the Lord is the key to this treasure." (Isaiah 33:5–6)

There is actually another reason why people do not believe that overcoming all of our sins is possible. It is because we have lost the key to the door of salvation. We have lost the power to overcome sin. We have lost the fear of the Lord, and without the fear of the Lord in our hearts, overcoming our sins is impossible!

The great salvation plan of God is a plan to empower us to overcome our sins by walking through the narrow gate of repentance, and then by walking on the narrow path of righteousness. Does this mean one slip and we die? Absolutely not! Remember Psalm 37:23–24: *"If the Lord delights in a man's way, he makes his steps firm; though he stumble, he will not fall, for the Lord upholds him with his hand."* The only way we fall is if we choose to stay off the narrow path and continue in our sins. If we stumble into sin, we must repent. The walk is a walk of repentance. But true repentance is not a game to be played. A person who chooses to sin, to leave the narrow path, planning to repent later, is fooling himself. He is not walking in repentance. He has not turned away from his sins. He is a slave to his sin, and he will surely die!

If this great salvation plan of God puts the fear of God in you, praise the Lord! You are on the ancient path. You are walking on the Road to Righteousness. God has placed the key in the door to your salvation. God has placed the seed of faith in you which will empower you to overcome the sins in your life. As God has spoken through the Prophet, Malachi, the sun of righteousness will rise in your life, with healing in its wings, and the kingdom of heaven is at hand!

Conclusion

There is a narrow gate and a narrow path which leads to the Kingdom of Heaven, and only a few will find it. It is an ancient path, which was established by God, not by man's religion. While walking this path will not be easy, God has made a way for us to stay on this path until we reach the God ordained point of destination, salvation itself. But this walk is a lifelong choice me must make. There are five steps that must be understood if we are to successfully navigate this Road to Righteousness that leads back to God.

The first step along this path is to know the true God. This knowledge of God includes knowing His absolute character traits. God is omnipotent, omniscient, absolutely righteous, absolutely just, and unchanging. We will understand God's Word only through the lens of this knowledge of God.

Without God there is no Truth. Absolute truth exists, and its only source is God. God has revealed His absolute truth to us through both general revelation (His creation) and special revelation (His Word). God has given mankind free will, but His purpose for mankind is not to be free to do whatever he pleases. God's purpose for man is to use this gift of freedom wisely by choosing to be true to God's commands. In pursuit of freedom, God's people have often lost the truth upon which this freedom is built.

Without truth there is no Law. God's Word is Law. God's Word is truth. The Law is God's directions for life. The Law reflects the nature and character of God. When the Law is not grounded in truth, it becomes nothing more than a set of rules for manipulation by those in power. The Law is more than the commands of God. The Law has two necessary components: (1) the commands and (2) the consequences for disobedience of the commands. Without the consequences for disobedience the Law becomes nothing more than suggestions for better living.

Without the Law there is no repentance. Repentance is more than conviction of sin. Repentance is more than confession of sin. Repentance is the actual turning away from sin. Sin is disobedience to God's commands; therefore, repentance is turning from disobedience to the Law to obedience to the Law. Repentance is not a onetime prayer; it is a lifetime walk. Repentance must be complete, not partial. Anything less than everything is nothing to God. Repentance is not easy, but it is not impossible, and God has given us everything we need to do it.

Without repentance there is no salvation. Salvation is the place of destination of the Road to Righteousness. Salvation is life in the Kingdom of Heaven. Salvation begins before our bodies physically die. Salvation is the return to God's original intent for mankind. Salvation is from disobedience to obedience. Salvation is not simply from the punishment for our sins; it is from our sins. Sin is the problem God's great salvation plan addresses. Salvation is not from God's Law; it is back to God's Law, His unchanging directions for life.

A Vision of this Great Salvation

---- ❊ ----

"Without a vision, the people perish: but he that keepeth the law, happy is he."
(Proverbs 29:18, KJV)

A More Abundant Life

In our foundational Scripture passage from the Prophet Jeremiah, we are told to stand at the crossroads and look! When we look at something with our eyes, we get a vision of it in our minds. It will be helpful to see a vision of the great salvation plan of God we are seeking to understand. This chapter will use a series of illustrations to paint a visual image of God's great salvation plan. The first illustration begins with two points, point A and point B.

A More Abundant LIfe

●

B

Life Today

●

A

Point A represents the life of a person who has not yet become a believer in the true and living God, and in His great salvation plan. Point A is the life that most people are living today, including most Christians. Point A represents everything that we are and everything that we believe at a given point in time in our life, before we come to the knowledge of the truth of who God is and what His purpose and plan is. Point A

84

is the point at which most people, regardless of their age, are living at the present time, and it is the life that most people will continue to live for their entire lives.

Point B is the life that we all know, deep down in our souls, that we were created to live. It is the life that we hope to someday live. Point B is a more abundant life. It is a life with more power, with more purpose, with more peace, and with more joy than we now have. Jesus referred to this Point B life when he said, "*I came that they may have life, and have it abundantly*" (John 10:10, New American Standard). God has a purpose and plan for every man, woman and child, and point B is that life. Point B is the life that God desires that we live today, and it is the life that we were created to continue to live for all of eternity. Point B is a life which we must choose to live. Point B is a life lived in accordance with God's original intent, a life lived in accordance with God's directions, and it is exceedingly and abundantly greater than anything that we can imagine.

Point A is the life that most Christians are living today, and Point B is the life that God desires all Christians to be living today. Life's challenge is how to move from Point A to Point B, but before we look for the way from Point A to Point B, we need to first have a better understanding of the Point B life God desires for us. It is very important to understand that the Point B is not life after we die and go to heaven. Point B is not a life we can live only after we leave these physical bodies behind. Point B is a life in which we have a physical body, a soul, and a spirit, and it is a life we are to live right now!

Point B is the life that God intends all of us to live, and it is the life we would be living today if not for sin. Point B is the life that Adam and Eve lived before the fall, before they chose to disobey God's directions for life. Point B is a life of physical health and a life in which our minds have been renewed in accordance with God's Word. It is a life in which we have the free will to choose to obey or disobey God's commands but where we also have the power to choose a life of obedience and blessings and to reject a life of disobedience and curses. Point B is a life in which we exercise our free will by submitting to the power of God's directions. Point B is the life that Jesus taught his disciples to live and the life that Jesus made a way for us to live.

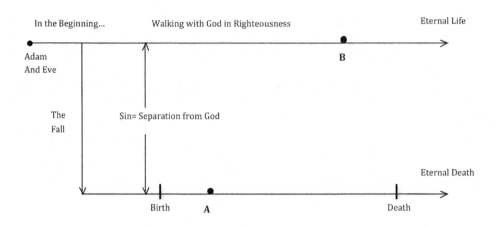

The second illustration puts Point A and Point B in a broader context. Before the fall, Adam and Eve lived their lives on the higher level of the Point B life. They walked in righteous obedience to God's directions for life. They walked with God. They had physical bodies which were healthy and strong. They had minds and wills that were in perfect alignment with God's directions for life. And they were filled with the Holy Spirit. Yet they lived on earth, not in heaven like the angels. The Point B life is a life on earth! When Adam and Eve disobeyed God's Law, sin entered the world, and they fell from the level of a Point B life to the level of Point A life. They continued to reside in physical bodies, but these bodies were now subject to infirmities. Their souls, which are made up of their minds, their emotions, and their wills, were no longer aligned with God's directions for life. And they were no longer filled with God's presence in the form of His Holy Spirit. Their sin separated them from God, and from that point in time forward all people have been born on the level of the Point A life. Sin, man's disobedience to God's Law, caused this fall from level B to level A, and sin has now separated us from God. This separation from God is the great problem of mankind. This separation is the problem which God's great plan of salvation has addressed.

Whether we are living on the level of point A or on the higher level of Point B, we are experiencing the passage of time. However, the mere passage of time will not move us from Point A to Point B. We move from Point A to Point B only through the decisions we make. The path from Point A to Point B is a path we must choose to walk on. It is actually a series of choices we make, minute by minute, hour by hour, day by day, year by year, and God has given us everything we need to arrive at the destination of our choice. If we choose to stay at Point A for our entire lives, the end of our journey will also be exactly what we have chosen, a life without God, which is actually called *death*. Physical death, however, is not the end of existence. Death is the eternal separation from God, but it is not the end of our existence. This is a critical point of understanding, which has been lost in much of today's Christianity.

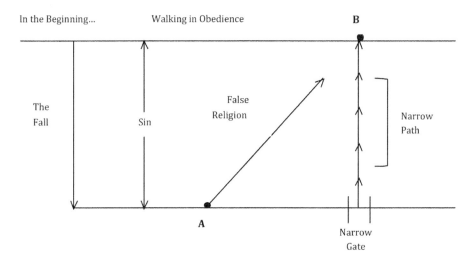

The third illustration is of the two paths that people can choose to take in their attempt to move from Point A to Point B. Most, if not all, people will at some time in their lives set out on a journey from Point A to Point B, because we all know that there is more to life than what we are currently living. This is not unique to Christians. All people, even secular humanists and self-proclaimed atheists, are religious people. The direct path from Point A to Point B represents man's search for a greater truth, which is religion. We all have a desire to set out in a search for meaning and truth about our life and purpose. But there is a problem. As man sets out to move from Point A to Point B, he inevitably creates a false religion. Psalm 14:12 warns us that *"There is a way that seems right to a man, but in the end it leads to death."* Mankind is not capable of creating a way back to God, a way from Point A to Point B. All religions, except for the great plan of salvation of the true God, are false religions and will end in destruction. There is only one way back to God, and it is requires that we enter through a narrow gate and that we then walk upon a narrow path. The only way to cross over this great divide between God and Man is the ancient path that God has ordained for us to walk from the beginning of time.

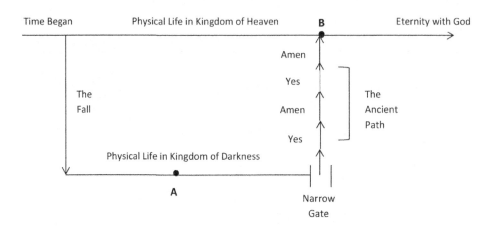

The fourth illustration is of the narrow gate and the narrow path God has established through His great salvation plan. As a person lives their life on the level of Point A, there will come a point in time when they will be faced with a choice. They must make a decision in response to their exposure to the *Good News* that God has made a way for them to return to Him, and to reenter the Kingdom of Heaven. The presentation of this Good News is true evangelism. It is the same message that both John the Baptist and Jesus proclaimed: "*Repent, for the Kingdom of Heaven is near*" (Matthew 3:2 and 4:17). This Good News invitation is freely offered to everyone, and it cannot be earned. But this invitation must be accepted on God's terms, not on the terms of man's religion. And God has ordained that the only way to accept this invitation is to repent of our sins and to then walk in obedience to God's commands. In the Kingdom of Heaven, which Jesus came to reestablish on earth, the people must obey the commands of the King! Therefore, as God begins to reveal Himself and His plan to the new believer, the only acceptable response will be *yes* and *amen*.

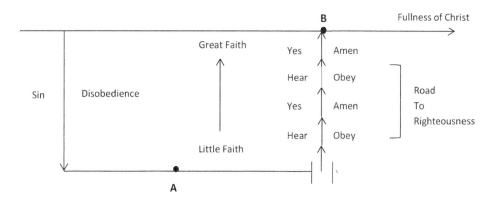

When we choose to accept this invitation back into the Kingdom of Heaven, we do not immediately die and go to heaven. We continue to live in physical bodies, but we no longer live on the level of Point A. Instead, we now live on a higher level in which we hear and obey God's commands, His directions for life. The fifth illustration is of the walk on this narrow path as we seek to know God, to know His commands, and to obey His directions. We begin a life of hearing and obeying God's directions for life. God reveals truth to us, and we say *yes* and then walk in obedience to that truth. This is a path of ever-increasing faith. God continues to reveal Himself to us, and so long as we respond with *yes* and *amen,* we grow in our faith. With the passage of time we continue to climb higher and higher toward the Point B life that God has planned for us. We grow from being *children* of God to becoming *manifest sons and daughters* of God. And as we grow in our faith, we also grow in the power of righteousness that comes from that faith. Our entire purpose in life is to grow up ". . . *until we all reach unity in the faith and in the knowledge of the Son of God and become mature, attaining to the whole measure of the fullness of Christ"* just as the Apostle Paul writes in Ephesians 4:13.

As we continue to walk on this Road to Righteousness, seeking the face of God and obeying all that He tells us, we begin to fulfill the purpose for which God created us. The whole purpose of our life becomes to know God as He manifests Himself to us and then to be used by God as an instrument through whom He manifests Himself to others. This is the life that Paul spoke of in Romans 8:19, when he wrote that all of creation is waiting for God to reveal His sons and daughters. This is the more abundant life that God desires for us and that He also requires of us. This is a life in which we become a blessing to God by serving His redemptive purpose rather than living to simply be blessed by God for our purposes. Life's purpose changes in the Kingdom of Heaven from the life of Point A, where we lived for ourselves, to a Point B, life lived for the glory of the King. The sole purpose in life on this narrow path is to press on toward the goal of being everything God desires us to be. Our prayers become increasingly bold as we realize that we are made in the image of God, a God who does not settle for anything less than everything from us. We approach God with this same standard of righteousness that He has shown to us. We approach God with this same attitude that anything less than everything He has for us is not satisfactory!

This new life on the narrow path, the ancient path, is not a life of seclusion, lived in a monastery on a mountaintop. It is a life lived as a husband or a wife, as a parent or a child, as an employer or an employee, just as it was before we entered into this new life. But the life we now live is for the sole purpose of hearing and obeying God. God is no longer an item on our list of priorities, but instead He has become our sole purpose. Everything we are and everything we do is now simply how we live out that purpose in this lifespan God has given us on the earth. We are now ambassadors of the Kingdom of Heaven on earth. This is what we were created to be, and this is what we were created to do! We have become agents of God's great plan to redeem His creation. And because we belong to God, not to ourselves, God is able to use us for His purpose. Because we are truly His sons and daughters, living in accordance with His Law, then everything we have actually is His. As God gives us dominion over His creation, He is actually redeeming that part of creation back into His Kingdom!

God's plan of salvation can be summarized with the following statement of affirmation: *If I am His, and it is mine, then it is His.* This is God's ordained plan to redeem His creation. It begins with a life of total surrender to His will and commands. God then redeems the creation through this surrendered life by giving the redeemed person authority to bring everything given to that person back into the Kingdom of God. Whatever God has given us, including our possessions, our sphere of influence, and even our relationships, is redeemed because whatever we have actually belongs to God. This is God's plan to redeem His creation through His people.

This walk on the ancient path begins by first going through the narrow gate called *repentance.* The first step is to turn away from our sins and to hear and obey God. Every time we say *yes* to God's Word, by our words and our deeds, we discover that God has more for us to know about Him and about His Kingdom purposes. As we continue to grow in our knowledge and understanding of God and continue to say *yes* and *amen* to His directions, God leads us on to a walk of ever-increasing faith. And as our faith increases, so does our power to do that which God has ordained us to do. The walk up this ancient path is also a walk of ever-increasing power and purpose, and it is the process of moving from being the children of God to becoming the manifest sons and daughters of God! All of creation is waiting for us to walk up this path and become God's agents of redemption.

The goal of each and every man, woman, and child who enters through this narrow gate and begins walking up this narrow path is to reach the point of maturity that God desires for us before our time on earth has ended. Just as a family rejoices in the birth of a new baby, the heavens rejoice when we enter through this narrow gate and become a child of God! But just as a new born baby is destined to grow into a healthy and happy adult, the newly born again believer is destined to grow into a manifest son or daughter of God. While the birth of a new born baby is a reason to celebrate, if that baby does not grow and mature over time, the celebration turns to tragedy. The same is true of a born-again believer. The purpose of the new birth is not to stay a baby believer. The purpose of every person who is born again into the Kingdom of Heaven is to become a mature manifest son or daughter of God, no less than the whole measure of the fullness of Christ. Anything less than this transformation is a tragedy in the eyes of God! Our sole purpose in life should be to grow in our faith. Everything we do in our lives should simply be how we live God's purpose for us. And if this Point B life is not incentive enough, how we spend eternity will be determined by how far we travel up this Road to Righteousness during our lifetime!

God is waiting for us to come to this Point B life of great rewards and blessings, as the writer of Hebrews states: "*And without faith it is impossible to please God, because anyone who comes to Him, must believe that He exists, and that He rewards those who earnestly seek Him*" I(Hebrews 11:6). Jesus urged his followers to walk on this *ancient path* when he said, "*Seek ye first the Kingdom of God, and His righteousness, and all these things will be added onto you*" (Matthew 6:33, King James Version).

Tragically, today's Christian culture is more focused on getting our sins forgiven than it is about becoming God's manifest sons and daughters, mature men and women who know the true God and obey His commands. Most Christians today view the narrow gate simply as a ticket to heaven when they die. Today many believe that our purpose in life is to simply thank Jesus that we are not going to hell. Should we be eternally thankful to God for sending Jesus to the cross to pay the price of salvation? Of course we should! But saying that we are sorry for our sins and thanking God for forgiving our sins is not repentance, and it is not an acceptance of God's great plan of salvation. God's redemptive purpose for His creation will be accomplished only through mature manifest sons and daughters of God. These are men and women who have chosen to move from Point A to Point B. The Apostle Paul understood this purpose and plan as evidenced by his words: "*I consider that our present sufferings are not worth comparing with the glory that will be revealed in us. The creation waits in eager expectation for the sons of God to be revealed.*" (Romans 8:18–19)

The whole creation is waiting for God's people to move from point A to point B! While Point B is the point of destination for the individual, it is actually the point of beginning of God's great plan to redeem His creation!

The Plumb Line Restored

There is another visual illustration which will help us to regain the vision of redemption which is God's great salvation plan. It begins with a simple vertical line, which we will refer to as the *plumb line*. This plumb line will not only help us to better understand God's great salvation plan, it will also help us to walk on the ancient path that leads from point A to point B.

The Plumb Line

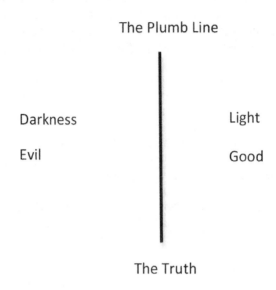

| Darkness | Light |
| Evil | Good |

The Truth

To understand this illustration we need to again begin at the beginning of time. In Genesis 1:1–2 we are told, *"In the beginning God created the heavens and the earth. Now the earth was formless and empty, darkness was over the surface of the deep, and the Spirit of God was hovering over the waters."* At this point, God had not yet formed the creation. The three basic elements of the universe, *time* (in the beginning), *space* (the heavens), and *matter* (the earth) were present, but there was something missing. That something was energy, or *power.* The creative force, the power, that would come from the spoken Word of God, was about to begin the creation process. And it is interesting that the words God chose to speak were *"Let there be light . . ."* in Genesis 1:3.

The word God spoke to describe the power of His purpose and will was the word *light.* Light is power. In the physical world, whenever we see light, we can always conclude that behind that light there is power. Without power, there is no light. Even reflected light originates only with a power source. This is not the case with darkness. When we experience darkness in the physical world, the correct conclusion to be made is that there is an absence of power. Darkness is the absence of power. Light is the presence of power. Light always overcomes darkness in the physical realm, and the same is true in the spiritual realm. We will come back to this point again later.

When God spoke the words, "*Let there be light,*" He could have just as well said "*Let there be truth.*" It was at that point in time, in the beginning, that God established *absolute truth.* According to Noah Webster's 1828 American Dictionary of English Language, *truth* is defined as *"conformity to fact or reality; exact accordance with that which is, or has been, or shall be."* God had just established *reality.* That reality was and continues to be God's original intent for all of creation, including mankind. Noah Webster goes on to comment that this *truth* is God's revealed will. And remember, God always gets exactly what He desires. God cannot be denied what He wants because there is nothing that can prevent God from getting exactly what He desires. And when God spoke the creation into existence, the first thing He did was to draw a line. In the next verse we are told, "*God saw that the light was good, and he separated the light from the darkness*" (Genesis 1:4). On one side of the line was power and light. On the other side of the line was the absence of power and darkness. On one side of the line was *good,* and on the other side of the line was *evil.* When God established this line, He actually established the Law, which defines good and evil.

When God later created man, He created him to live on the right side of this line. God created Adam with the purpose and plan of spending all of eternity on the right side of this line. God had created Adam in His own image, an image that was only good, not evil. God also created Adam with free will, with the ability to choose to either obey or disobey His commands. With this free will, God also created the potential for evil, as well as the consequences for disobedience to His commands. But God gave Adam everything he would need to live eternally with God, walking in righteous obedience and power, with dominion over the entire creation. From the beginning of time, man was given a choice as to which side of the line he would choose to live. This line, also known as the Law, gave mankind the directions for life.

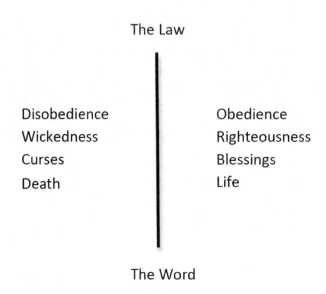

It is important to give further consideration as to what this line represents. This line is the Word of God! On the right side of this line is obedience to God's commands, which is righteousness. On the left side of this line is disobedience to God's commands, which is sin, or wickedness. On the right side of this line we find blessings and life. On the left side of this line we find curses and death. On the right side of this line we live with God in the kingdom of light. On the left side of this line we live in the kingdom of darkness, separated from God. This line of truth defines everything. This line will never change because it reflects the nature of a God who never changes. There can be no improvements to this line, because God is perfect, and therefore the line is also perfect. As written in Psalm 18:30 "*As for God, His way is perfect; the word of the Lord is flawless.*" To understand this line is to understand the difference between life and death, and between blessings and curses.

The Word of God is the most powerful force in the universe. It is the creative force of behind the universe. There are no other powers that rival the power of the Word of God. As God spoke through the Prophet Isaiah, "*So is my word, that goes forth from my mouth: it will not return to me empty, but will accomplish what I desire, and achieve the purpose for which I sent it*" (Isaiah 55:11). But what is the second most powerful force in the universe? It is not the power of Satan, because Satan is the father of darkness, which is actually the absence of power. The second greatest power in the universe is the choice or the free will of man! It is the decisions made by those to whom God has given both dominion and free will. This is by God's design, and it is what God desires. We are told in Psalm 115:16, "*The highest heavens belong to the Lord, but the earth He has given to man.*" God has chosen to give man this great authority, as stewards over His creation. God continues to be sovereign over all of creation, but He has chosen to delegate authority to mankind to accomplish His purpose and His plan!

So while God established this plumb line called *absolute truth,* which will never change, He also gave mankind the ability to choose which side of this line we would live on. This line was established by the commands of God, and it also established the unchanging consequences for disobedience to those commands. God told Adam that only He had the authority to establish this line, and that man had no authority to change it. This is clear from Genesis 2:16–17: "*And the Lord commanded the man, "You are free to eat from any tree in the garden; but you must not eat from the tree of the knowledge of good and evil, for when you eat of it you will surely die.*"

This plumb line, which is the Law, was established before sin was ever committed. This Law established both the command and the consequences for disobedience. Adam later choose to disobey God, and from that time forward every man, women and child who has been born, with the exception of the second Adam, Jesus, has been born on the left side of this line.

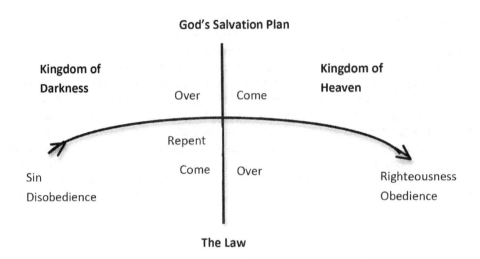

God was not taken by surprise by man's disobedience. God established His great salvation plan for man before man ever committed a sin. This great salvation plan would restore us to the place of God's original intent, to a life on the right side of the line. God did not predestine Adam to sin. Adam had a choice, and God had given him everything he needed to walk, with free will, in righteous obedience to all of God's commands. God's original and unchanging intent for man was to live on the right side of the line, not the left. This line did establish the potential for sin, but it did not cause sin. Sin is man's choice to disobey God's commands, and sin is man's fault, not God's fault. God did not want man to sin, nor did man have to sin in order to accomplish what God wanted in creation. Sin will not prevent God from getting exactly what He wants from both mankind and creation. God's original and ongoing intent is that His people are to live on the right side of the line, with free will, and also with dominion over His creation.

This dominion mandate is set forth in Genesis 1:26: *"Then God said, 'Let us make man in our image, in our likeness, and let them rule over the fish of the sea and the birds of the air, over the livestock, over all the earth, and over all the crea-tures that move along the ground.'"* It should be noted that man was not given dominion over other men. Each man was to live under the directions of God's Law, which was to be written on his own heart. Each man was to be self-governing from within, not under the dominion of other men. External government of men over other men was not God's original intent, but instead is a result of man's disobedience to God's directions for life. When internal government was lost, external government became necessary.

If we know the true God, we know that God does not have problems. When you are both omnipotent and omniscient, it is not possible to have a problem that can't be solved. Man is made in the image of God, but he is not God, and man does have problems. The primary problem of every man, woman, and child born after Adam, with the exception of Jesus, is that we are born on the wrong side of God's line. If something does not happen within our life span to move us from the left side of this line to the right side of this line before we die, then our end will be separation from God and eternal destruction. Contrary to what many people may believe, God will not transform a wicked man who is living on the left side of the line into a righteous man on the right side of this line after the man dies. We must cross this line before we die, because God will not do this for us! There is no exception to this rule.

God's great plan of salvation is man's only hope. God's plan empowers us to come over from the left side of this line to the right side of this line. God's plan empowers us to come over from a life of disobedience to a life of obedience to His commands. God's plan empowers us to change from being wicked people to becoming righteous people, and God's word tells us that this transformation must take place before we die. While God clearly does not lack the power to force any man to come over this line against his will, that is not God's desire, because forcing man to obey His commands would not be consistent with God's original purpose of giving mankind free will. God's purpose and plan has always been to empower us to overcome sin by our own choice, and God will not revoke his gift of free will. God's plan of salvation will succeed, but only for those who choose to seek it, believe it, and walk in it!

God's great plan of salvation is a plan to empower us to *come over* to His side of the line, by *overcoming* our sins. The only way to come over the line is to overcome sin. And the only way to overcome sin, which is disobedience to the Law, is to obey the Law. God's great salvation plan is a plan to empower us to repent, to turn away from our sins, and to walk in righteousness, as God has originally intended for us. God's plan of salvation does not delay this righteousness until after we die. Delayed righteousness would not serve God's purpose of having us walk in righteousness and in dominion over His creation. This conversion must take place while we are still alive or it is too late for God's purpose to be accomplished through us. We cannot be agents of God's redemption of the physical creation after we have physically died. Righteousness is not a gift that we will get when we reach heaven; it is a choice we must make before we die. Repentance is not something we can do after we die. The great salvation plan of God is better than that. Our salvation must begin now, and then it is to continue for all of eternity!

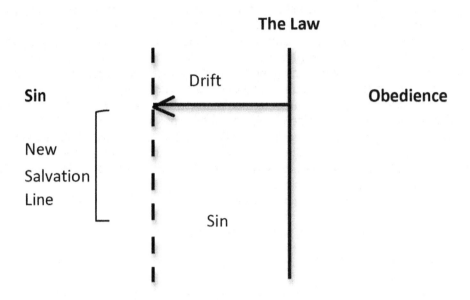

But there is a problem, which is depicted in the illustration above. It is not a problem with God's line, and it is not a problem with God's plan of salvation. The problem is that man has a tendency to drift away from the line. History tells us that God's people drift away from the line because we lose our understanding of God's Law. Remember the words spoken by God to King Asa:

> The Lord is with you if you are with Him. If you seek Him He will be found by you. But if you forsake Him, he will forsake you. For a long time Israel was without the true God, without a priest to teach and without the Law. But in their distress, they turned to the Lord, the God of Israel, and sought him, and he was found by them. (II Chronicles 15:2–4)

How could it be that God's people could lose the Law? How could they drift away from the line God has established for their own good? It happens when we allow our religious opinions, which over time become our traditions, to change the line. It is not possible to actually change the line, but what happens is that we change what we believe the line to be. We actually lose the Law when we try to change the Law. This happens when we begin to teach a new salvation plan by failing to teach the whole Law. The drift takes place when we teach a plan of salvation that eliminates the consequences for disobedience to God's Law. When we do this, we dishonor God, and we drift away from the truth. This has happened to God's people throughout history. And this is what has happened to the Christian Church in America today. We too have become a people, who have been for a long time without the true God, without a teaching priest, and without the Law!

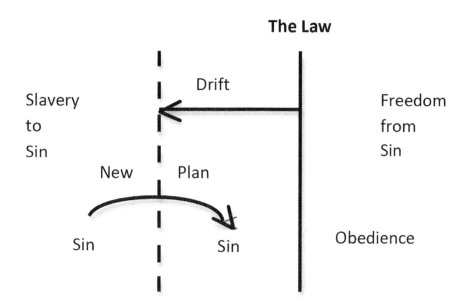

The illustration above will help us to see this drift away from the Law, away from the line, and the creation of a new line. This new line is a counterfeit line. The plumb line of God's truth does not actually drift. This new line is the result of teaching a new salvation plan rather than God's great salvation plan. This new salvation plan is a plan that says that we do not have to actually cross over from the left side of God's original line to the right side of His line. This new salvation plan says that we do not have to actually obey God's commands in order to be viewed as righteous in God's eyes. This new plan says that actual repentance from all of our sins is only in theory, not reality, and that actually turning away from all sin is not a requirement of salvation. This new plan says that God has made a way for us to be saved from the punishment of our sins, without actually being saved from committing sins.

As illustrated above, this new salvation plan has a new line we must cross in order to be saved from the punishment of our sins. This new salvation plan says that the way to salvation is by simply acknowledging how wonderful and loving Jesus is, because he went to the cross to pay the penalty for our sins. This new salvation plan teaches that because of what Jesus did for us we no longer need to worry about being punished for our sins. This new salvation plan says that salvation from the punishment of our sins is as easy as believing that Jesus died on the cross for us. This new salvation plan denies the ability to actually overcome our sins by walking in obedience to God's Law. This new salvation plan says that actual and complete repentance from our sins is impossible here on earth because we have a sin nature that rules over our lives. This new salvation plan treats sin as an incurable disease, rather than a choice we make. And while this new salvation plan does not directly encourage sinning, it proclaims that the only sinners who will be punished for their sins are the non-Christian sinners.

If this new salvation plan sounds too good to be true, that is because it is neither a good plan nor is it a true plan. This new salvation plan requires a change in the unchangeable plumb line God has drawn. This new salvation is a plan that empha-sizes forgiveness over repentance. This new salvation plan serves the people's pur-pose of escaping the punishment for our sins, but it does not serve God's purpose of redeeming His creation through His people, and to His original intent. This new salvation plan changes God's Law into God's suggestions for better living. This new salvation plan rejects God's Law by eliminating a necessary element of the Law, the consequences for disobedience. This new salvation plan is really a plan that should be called *lawlessness*.

With this visual illustration of God's plumb line in mind, let us again consider the words of Jesus as he was teaching the Jews about God's great salvation plan. He said, "*If you hold to my teaching you are really my disciples. Then you will know the truth, and the truth will set you free*" (John 8:31). This offended many of the Jews who considered themselves to be God's chosen people because they were the descendants of Abraham. They said that they were not slaves to anyone! Then Jesus responded; "*I tell you the truth, everyone who sins is a slave to sin. Now we know that a slave has no permanent place in the family. But a son belongs to it forever. So if the Son sets you free, then you will be free indeed*" (John 8:31–35).

Jesus is the greatest teacher of God's great plan of salvation that has ever walked the earth. Jesus understood God's salvation plan. So, referring to our illus-tration, is a person who sins living on the left side of God's plumb line or on the right side of this line? Obviously a sinner is on the left side of the line. And what does Jesus say about *everyone* who is on the left side of this line? He says that they are a slave to sin. And what does Jesus say about the salvation of those who are slaves to sin? He says they have no permanent place in the family; they will not be saved! Jesus then says that if the Son sets us free, we will be free indeed. But what is it that the Son sets us free from? Is it freedom from the punishment of our sins, while we live on the left side of this line, or is it actual freedom from the sins? If the Son does not set us free from our sins, then we remain on the wrong side of the line, and we will not be saved from the punishment of our sins! To be *free indeed* we must move from the left side of this line and to the right side of the line!

Many Christian's today believe that Jesus came to change the line and that sal-vation is about changing our label from a *non-Christian sinner* to a *Christian sinner.* This belief is grounded in a false understanding of the concept of *salvation by grace* because it does not define *grace* as the power to overcome sin. Did Jesus come to change the line that God had established from the beginning of time? What did Jesus say in this regard? And remember that this line is really the Law, God's stan-dard of righteousness. The line therefore consists of the two necessary elements of the Law: (1) the commands of God and (2) the consequences for disobediences of the commands. As we have seen earlier, this line was established through the Old Testament Law and the Prophets. So did Jesus come to change the Law and the Prophets? Listen again to Jesus' own words in this regard:

> Do not think that I have come to abolish the Law or the Prophets; I have not come to abolish them but to fulfill them. I tell you the truth, until heaven and earth disappear, not the smallest letter, not the least stroke of a pen, will by any means disappear from the Law until everything is accomplished. Anyone who breaks one of the least of these commands and teaches others to do the same will be called least in the kingdom of heaven, but whoever practices and teaches theses commands will be called great in the kingdom of heaven. (Matthew 5:17–19)

Jesus did not come to change the line! Jesus came to make a way for us to cross over the line, by turning away from our sins so that we could be restored to the more abundant life that he speaks of in John 10:10 ". . . *I have come that they may have life, and have it to the full."* Can this abundant life be found on the left side of God's unchanging line? No, the great salvation plan of God is to move us from the left side of the line to the right side of the Line. When man's religion, regardless of the intentions of those who create it, moves the line God has established, the results are disastrous. When we drift away from God's unchanging line, we drift away from the true God!

Just as a man who crosses the counterfeit line of salvation lacks the power to overcome the sins in his life, a Church that teaches and functions on the left side of God's plumb line has no power to overcome the trends in the culture. Until the Church repents from its teaching a false line of salvation, God cannot empower it to influence and redeem the culture. The Church that Jesus is returning to will be a pure and spotless bride, which teaches and operates on the right side of God's line, the side of true righteousness and obedience to God's commands. The men and women of God are the Body of Christ through whom God will manifest Himself. God will accomplish His redeeming purposes only through those who have crossed over the line of truth and are living in righteous obedience to His Law. This Body of Christ, which is the Church, must be made up of men and women who have overcome sin by the power of the truth written on their hearts. They are not free from all temptations, and they may even stumble into sin from time to time, but they are people who walk in the fear of the Lord, which empowers them to overcome all sins. They are the people who are God's own special treasure, as spoken of through the Prophet Malachi:

> Then those who feared the Lord spoke with each other, and the Lord listened to what they said. In His presence a Scroll of Remembrance was written to record the names of those who feared the Lord and loved to think about Him. They will be my people, says the Lord. On the day when I act, they will be my own special treasure. I will spare them as a father spares an obedient and dutiful child. Then once again you will see the difference between the righteous and the wicked, between those who serve God and those who do not. (Malachi 3:16–18, NLT)

101

The time has come for God's people to cross over this line and into the Kingdom of Heaven. It is time for the Church to become the pure and spotless bride that will receive Jesus when he comes again. As Jesus said, "*This, then, is how you should pray: "'Our Father in heaven, hallowed be your name, your kingdom come, your will be done on earth as it is in heaven'*" (Matthew 6:9–10). Jesus was teaching us to pray that God would draw us across this plumb line into His kingdom, a place where God's Law is obeyed and His purpose is accomplished on earth as it is in heaven!

Conclusion

Without a vision the people perish. Today's Christians need our vision of salvation to be restored to God's original intent. Jesus came that we would have a more abundant life, which is to begin now, and is to continue forever more. Seeking this more abundant life must be our sole purpose in life. Salvation comes only by entering a narrow gate of repentance, and then walking a narrow path of obedience. This walk on the ancient path ordained by God is a series of steps we take as we hear and obey God's commands, His directions for life. It is a walk of ever-increasing faith and power, and our goal is to reach a faith and a life of attaining to the whole measure of the fullness of Christ. We must not simply be satisfied with seeking forgiveness; we must first seek righteousness.

In the very beginning of time God established a plumb line of absolute truth. This line defines good and evil, and this line will never change. This line separated the light from the darkness, righteousness from wickedness, and it also established the foundation for blessings and curses. God's original intent for mankind was to live on the right side of this line, in total and complete obedience to God's commands. God has given us everything we need to live our entire lives on the right side of this line. Salvation is the process of coming over from the left side of this line to the right side of this line, by overcoming our sins, our disobedience to God's Word. Jesus said that everyone on the left side of this line is a slave to sin and will not enter the Kingdom of Heaven. When we change the plan of salvation, we drift away from the truth of God.

An Announcement by the Angels, by Jesus, and by the Apostles

The Salvation Message of Angels

> So we must listen very carefully then, to the truth that we have heard, or we may drift away from it. **The message God delivered through angels has always proved true, and the people were punished for every violation of the law, and for every act of disobedience. What makes us think that we can escape if we are indifferent to this great salvation, which was announced by the Lord Jesus himself, it was passed on to us by those who heard him speak,** and God verified the message through signs, wonders, various miracles, and by giving gifts of the Holy Spirit whenever He chose to do so. (Hebrews 2:1–4 NLT) (emphasis added)

The writer of Hebrews, in this foundational passage, is telling us how to avoid drifting away from the plumb line of truth we have just seen. In this chapter we will listen very carefully to this great salvation message first announced by the angels, then announced by Jesus, and finally passed on to us by the Apostles. What is the message God delivered through angels? What was this great salvation that was announced by the Lord, Jesus, himself? What did the Apostles believe about this salvation message? As Christians we all profess to believe in Jesus, because this is the foundation of our Christian faith. But is it possible that we have been taught to believe in Jesus without believing what Jesus actually taught about God's salvation plan? We have already considered the standard of salvation set forth through the Law and the Prophets in the Old Testament Scriptures. We also know that Jesus studied the Scriptures, and that he stood upon the foundation of God's Word when he was tempted by Satan in the desert. So what exactly did Jesus teach about God's great salvation plan?

Before listening to what Jesus taught about salvation, we must first consider the message delivered by angels with regard to Jesus, which tells us what Jesus was sent to do. This message was delivered by an Angel of the Lord to Joseph regarding the upcoming birth of his son. The Angel's message was this: "**She (Mary) will give birth to a son, and you are to give him the name Jesus, because he will save his people from their sins**" (Matthew 1:21). The Amplified Bible adds these words to the end of this passage: ". . . *that is, prevent them from failing and missing the true end and scope of life, which is God.*" This is the message of God's great salvation plan, delivered by His angels. And there is great power available to those who seek to understand and believe this message!

Most Christians today believe that there is power in the name of Jesus, but do we understand why there is such power in his name? In John 1 we are told,

> In the beginning was the Word, and the Word was with God, and the Word was God. He was with God in the beginning. Through him all things were made; without him nothing was made that has been made. **In** him was life, and that life was the light of men. The light shines in the darkness, but the darkness has not understood it. There came a man, sent by God; his name was John. He came as a witness to testify concerning that light, so that through him all men might believe. He himself was not the light; he came only as a witness to the light. The true light that gives light to every man was coming into the world. He was in the world, and though the world was made through him, the world did not recognize him. He came to that which was his own, but his own did not receive him. **Yet to all who received him, to those who believed in his name, he gave the right to become children of God**—children born not of natural descent, nor of human decision or a husband's will, but born of God. The Word became flesh and made his dwelling amount us. We have seen his glory, the glory of the one and only, who came from the Father, full of grace and truth. (John 1: 1–14) (emphasis added)

Jesus was the *light* which came into the world, and as we have seen, light is power. The King James Version of John 1:12 says, "*But as many as received him, to them he gave power to become the sons of God, even to them that believe on his name . . .*" To really believe in Jesus' name and to receive that *power* to become God's sons and daughters, we must understand why he was given the name, *Jesus*. According to the angels, he was to be given the name *Jesus* because he would *save the people from their sins*. In other words, he would bring the people back to a righteous relationship with God, where we could walk in the power and purpose for which we were created. Jesus did not come to simply make things better for us; he came to redeem us. Jesus came to restore us to righteousness, which requires power! This is more than a salvation from the punishment of our sins; it is the power to actually overcome our sins. This was the salvation message God delivered through angels, which has always proved true.

The Salvation Message of Jesus

As we listen carefully to the following teachings of Jesus on salvation, we must again remember to view these teachings through the lens of who God is. Remember that God is omnipotent, omniscient, absolutely righteous, absolutely just, and unchanging. When we listen to Jesus' teachings, we must not interpret them in a way that is inconsistent with God's nature. Jesus submitted entirely to his Father. Jesus said, *"I tell you the truth, the Son can do nothing by himself; he can do only what he sees his Father doing, because whatever the Father does the Son also does"*(John 5:19). Jesus never taught anything different than what he had learned from his Father. Jesus is not a new and improved version of God, as many today seem to think he is. Jesus was the Word made flesh, the will and mind of God in human form. He was the second Adam, and He was everything that God the Father intended him to be.

After Jesus had been baptized in the Jordan River, the Holy Spirit descended upon him like a dove. He was then led into the wilderness where we are told that he was tempted in every way by Satan. Jesus overcame all of Satan's temptations by standing on the Word of God. Jesus could not stand upon the New Testament writings of the Apostles, because they had not yet been written. Jesus stood upon the Word of God, the Law, and the Prophets as set forth in the Old Testament. From that time forward Jesus began to preach, *"Repent, for the Kingdom of Heaven is near"* (Matthew 4:17). In other words, the key word in summarizing Jesus preaching of salvation was the word *"Repent."* Jesus preached that to enter the Kingdom of Heaven a person must repent from their sins. Jesus taught that the people must actually turn from their sins, just as had been proclaimed through the Law and the Prophets before him. Jesus' preaching was consistent with his name! He came to save the people from their sins.

Once again, in John chapter 8, recall that Jesus had been teaching the Jews, and many of them believed in him. Then Jesus made a statement about salvation from sin we must listen carefully to until we understand it. He said, *"If you hold to my teachings, you are really my disciples. Then you shall know the truth, and the truth shall set you free"* (John 8:31–32). These words offended some of the Jews who were listening, who responded that they were the descendants of Abraham and that they were not slaves to anyone. But Jesus then responded, with great focus and emphasis, *"I tell you the truth, everyone who sins is a slave to sin. Now we know that a slave has no permanent place in the family, but a son belongs to it forever. So if the Son sets you free, then you will be free indeed."* There is no other passage in the Gospels in which Jesus more clearly announces the great salvation message he was sent to deliver to God's people.

In considering this passage more closely, we must again listen to what Jesus is teaching here. First, consider who Jesus was speaking to. It was to God's own people, the Jews, whom we are told *believed* in Jesus. Jesus is telling his own people that we must hold to his teachings if we are to be his disciples. We must therefore also hold to Jesus' teaching about what it means to be saved. He then says that we shall know the truth and the truth shall set us free. What was the truth he was speaking of? It was the substance of his teachings. And what is it that his teachings would set them free from? It was from their sins!

Jesus' teaching of salvation from sins is confirmed by his next statement in explanation and response to the objections of some of the Jews. He begins with the bold words, "*I tell you the truth . . .*" If we are to ever listen very carefully to Jesus teachings it is when he says, "*I tell you the truth.*" And then he announces the message of the great salvation message that we are looking for. He says, "*I tell you the truth, everyone who sins is a slave to sin.*" Did we hear what Jesus taught? Who is a slave to sin? Everyone who sins! Would this include nonbelievers who sin? Would this include believers who sin? Would this include descendants of Abraham who sin? Would this include Christians who sin? The answer to each of these questions is *yes!* There is no category or class of people who sin, who are not slaves to sin!

Many Christians today will respond to this teaching the same way that some of these Jews responded. Many today believe that if we are *Christian sinners,* we will spend eternity with God, even if we continue to walk in sin. But what did Jesus say next? He said that we all know that a slave has no permanent place in the family. What is Jesus really getting at here? Is he saying that a slave to sin has no permanent place in the family of God? What else could he be referring to? The answer is nothing else! Jesus is teaching that every person who sins, including a Christian sinner, is a slave to sin, and therefore a Christian sinner is not going to spend eternity with God! Jesus clearly taught that we need to be saved from our sins, not simply from the punishment of our sins.

But what do we do with this teaching of Jesus? This is a very hard teaching. It is tempting to read this teaching with the lens of what we already believe, rather than to believe what Jesus is actually teaching. It is tempting to exclude the *born again* Christians from this teaching. It is tempting to simply fall back on our traditional belief that this would all change after the cross, after God poured out his grace upon all believers. But why would Jesus make this statement if he believed that his death on the cross would change this truth? Why would Jesus teach this way if he knew that one day God's grace would be poured out on all Christian sinners so that they could spend eternity with God even though they continued to be slaves to sin? The answer is that Jesus would not teach this if the cross was intended to save us from the punishment of our sins and not from our sins.

Are we willing to be Jesus' disciples, and actually hold to his teachings? Jesus concluded this teaching by saying, "*If the Son sets you free, then you will be free indeed.*" What will we be set free from? The answer should be obvious to us by now. We are set free from our sins. And when we are set free from our sins, we are also set free from the punishment of our sins. We are not holding to his teaching if we conclude that Jesus taught that we would be set free from the punishment of our sins while we continue to walk in sin. It is easy to say that we *believe* in Jesus, but the real question is whether we *believe* what Jesus taught?

It is important to build our faith on a foundation of truth, which means we must build our understanding on the whole body of Jesus teachings, not just one passage. Some may conclude that Jesus' teaching in John 8:31–35 is confusing and may not mean what it appears to say. So let us study more of Jesus' teachings on salvation. We will limit our study in the remainder of this chapter to the teachings of Jesus as recorded in the Book of Matthew. Remember that we are seeking to find the great salvation message announced by the Lord Jesus, himself as referred to in Hebrews 2:1–4.

As we have seen, God has drawn a plumb line called the Law, which separates the righteous from the wicked and which separates the Kingdom of Heaven from the Kingdom of Darkness. And again, our salvation is the process of crossing over from the left side of this line to the right side of this line. We must *overcome* sin in order to be saved from sin. God has made a way for us to come over the line, to live in obedience to His commands. This way is the *ancient path* God has established, and it is the way we must walk if we are to enter the Kingdom of Heaven. It is important to therefore listen to Jesus' teachings about this plumb line called the Law. Did Jesus come to change or abolish this line? Jesus could not have more clearly answered this question than through these words:

> Do not think that I have come to abolish the Law or the Prophets; I have not come to abolish them but to fulfill them. I tell you the truth, until heaven and earth disappear, not the smallest letter, not the least stroke of a pen, will by any means disappear from the Law until everything is accomplished. (Matthew 5:17–18)

Jesus did not come to abolish the Law or the Prophets, the commands or the consequences for disobedience of the commands, as spoken through the Prophets. Instead, he came to fulfill them. But what does it mean to fulfill the Law and the Prophets? Many Christians today will interpret this statement to mean that Jesus fulfilled the requirements of the Law, so that we do not have to fulfill them. But does this make sense? Does this interpretation of the *fulfilling* of the Law honor God? Would this interpretation serve God's purpose for mankind? And is this interpretation consistent with what Jesus taught about salvation from sin? The answer to each of these questions is a resounding "*No!*"

To understand the teachings of Jesus it is again critical to always interpret what Jesus taught through the lens of who God is. If we study the teachings of Jesus with this definition in mind, we will know the truth of Jesus' teachings. Would God send Jesus into the world so that God's people would no longer be required to obey His commands, His directions for life? To conclude that this was God's purpose and plan for sending Jesus into the world would be to conclude that God had given up on His original desire for His people to walk in complete obedience to His commands. To come to this conclusion would be like saying that God failed in His original plan for man, so now He had to pay the price for man's sins to avoid having to punish them. This would be a confession by God that it is impossible for man to overcome his sins. This would suggest that God had to resort to a backup plan to deal with man's sins. But God did not have to lower the standard of righteousness for man because His original standard was too high, and that is not what Jesus taught.

In Jesus' most famous message, the *Sermon on the Mount,* Jesus makes this statement: "*For I tell you that unless your righteousness surpasses that of the*

Pharisees and teachers of the law, you will certainly not enter the kingdom of heaven" (Matthew 5:20). Jesus was teaching about salvation, which is entering the Kingdom of Heaven. Jesus was telling us that the standard of righteousness for salvation is very high. Whatever the Pharisees and teachers of the law were doing and teaching on righteousness was evidently not up to God's standard. The question for us today is whether our teachings on righteousness, and even more importantly, whether our lives themselves are up to the standard required for entry into the Kingdom of Heaven?

Jesus then goes on to teach a higher righteousness in the *Sermon on the Mount.* He says that not only must we not commit murder, but that anyone who says *'You fool'* will be in danger of the fire of hell. Then he raises the standard of the Law regarding adultery by saying that anyone who looks at a woman lustfully has already committed adultery with her in his heart. He continues to raise the standard by saying,

> If your right eye causes you to sin, gouge it out and throw it away.
> It is better for you to lose one part of your body than for your whole
> body to be thrown into hell. And if your right hand causes you to sin,
> cut it off and throw it away. It is better for you to lose one part of your
> body than for your whole body to go into hell. (Matthew 5: 29–30)

Many Christians today will consider this teaching of Jesus to simply be hyperbole. They may think he was just trying to make a point and that he certainly did not mean that anyone should actually consider cutting off their arm or gouging out their eye. But was Jesus applying hyperbole here? Or was he warning the people about how painful it will be to experience eternity in hell? Is it hyperbole to say that being thrown into hell for eternity will be more painful than gouging out an eye or cutting off an arm? Is it possible that Jesus was actually emphasizing the necessity of overcoming our sins? Was he saying that we must do everything necessary to overcome sin, including gouging out an eye, if that is the only way we can avoid lusting over a women? Does Jesus want us to gouge out our eye? No. But if that is the only way one can avoid sin, then it is better than sinning and then experiencing the eternal pain and anguish in hell. In other words, as painful as it would be to cut off an arm or to gouge out an eye, that pain is nothing compared to the pain of spending eternity in hell!

Before leaving Matthew 5:27–30, we should ask one more question. If the great salvation plan that Jesus taught was that he would fulfill the Law so that we do not have to, then why would Jesus make such shocking statements about the need to take these extreme steps to overcome our sins? Would these statements of Jesus make sense if he knew that one day all of the people's sins, including the lusts of the eyes, would be covered by his blood? Why would Jesus teach the people to take such drastic steps to overcome sin if he knew that he was going to the cross to cover up all of their sins so that God would no longer see them? Would Jesus have taught like this if eventually salvation would come to all who simply say *thank you* to God for forgiving their sins?

Jesus continues to increase the people's understanding of the required standard of righteous in his *Sermon on the Mount,* when he tells them to "*Be perfect, therefore, as your heavenly father is perfect*" (Matthew 5:48). Was this just hyperbole again, or was Jesus serious? Was Jesus saying that it is possible to *be perfect* as God, Himself, is perfect? The answer is *yes.* Jesus is acknowledging that God's original intent for man is to walk in perfect righteousness. This is consistent with God's command to His people in Leviticus 19:2 and 37, where the Lord spoke to Moses, and said, "*Speak to the entire assembly of Israel, and say to them "Be holy, because I, the Lord your God, am holy." and "Keep all my decrees and all my laws and follow them. I am the Lord."* Remember that Jesus never taught anything inconsistent with the Law and the Prophets.

Later in his *Sermon on the Mount,* Jesus taught the people to "*Seek first the kingdom of God, and His righteousness, and all these things will be added onto you*" (Matthew 6:33). Whose righteousness are we to seek? What is God's standard of righteousness? Is His standard of righteousness perfect obedience or something less? Jesus goes on to teach them to "*Ask and it will be given to you; seek and you will find; knock and the door will be opened to you. For he who asks receives; he who seeks finds; and to him who knocks, the door will be opened*" (Matthew 7:7–8).

What would Jesus have us ask for? What if we were so bold as to ask for the power to overcome all sins, all of the time? Would asking for this level of righteousness please God, or anger Him? What will God do with this kind of request? On the other hand, will it please God if we ask for a lesser form of righteousness or a lesser form of salvation? What if we ask Him to save us from the punishment of our sins but not for the power to actually overcome our sins? Will God grant a request for a lower standard of righteousness?

So far the teachings of Jesus have set the standard of salvation very high. This is consistent with Jesus' statement in Matthew 7:13–14: "*Enter through the narrow gate, for wide is the gate and broad is the road that leads to destruction, and many enter through it. But small is the gate, and narrow the road that leads to life, and few find it.*" Is the salvation message of today's Christianity really a small gate and a narrow path? Is a salvation obtained through a simple sinner's prayer really like a small gate and narrow path that few will find? If repentance from sin is removed as a condition of the salvation message, the gate then becomes a wide gate, not a narrow gate. Yet today's Christianity consistently attempts to widen this gate that Jesus has said is narrow, a gate that Jesus says only a few will find.

After referring to the great salvation as a narrow gate and a narrow path, Jesus then uses the analogy of a good tree and a bad tree in teaching about this great salvation plan of God. The following words of Jesus should send shivers down the spines of today's casual Christians:

> Watch out for false prophets. They come to you in sheep's clothing, but inwardly they are ferocious wolves. By their fruit you will recognize them. Do people pick grapes from thorn bushes, or figs from thistles? Likewise every good tree bears good fruit, but a bad tree bears bad fruit. A good tree cannot bear bad fruit, and a bad tree

cannot bear good fruit. Every tree that does not bear good fruit is cut down and thrown into the fire. Thus, by their fruit you will recognize them. Not everyone who says to me, 'Lord, Lord,' will enter the kingdom of heaven, but only he who does the will of my Father who is in heaven. Many will say to me on that day, "Lord, Lord, did we not prophesy in your name, and in your name drive out demons and perform many miracles?" Then I will tell them plainly, "I never knew you. Away from me you evildoers." (Matthew 7:15–23).

Are we ready to really listen carefully to these words of Jesus? What is this telling us about the great salvation message that Jesus was announcing? Does this sound like today's salvation message? We have changed the great salvation message into a simple prayer with a polite *thank you* to God for forgiving our sins. We then tell the new Christian to go and spread this *good news* to others, so that they can get their sins forgiven as well. We think it is kind and loving to have made it so easy to become a *Christian sinner* saved by grace. We often wonder why everyone doesn't do it!

But what was Jesus really teaching in Matthew 7:15–23? What is good fruit? What is bad fruit? Is it reasonable to interpret a good tree as being a true believer and the fruit on the tree his actions? If so, Jesus is saying that a true believer will not sin, and a nonbeliever will. But how does this teaching align with the sinner saved by grace theology of today's Christianity? If I am a sinner saved by grace, am I a good tree or a bad tree? Is a believer who continues to sin actually a good tree that continues to bear bad fruit? Would this interpretation make sense?

To emphasize that bearing good fruit is a necessary element of salvation, Jesus then makes a statement that should put the fear of the Lord back into the hearts of all of God's people. He says,

> *"Not everyone who says to me, 'Lord, Lord,' will enter the kingdom of heaven, but only he who **does** the will of my Father who is in heaven."* (Matthew 7:21) (emphasis added)

These words should make us take a closer examination of salvation obtained simply through making a statement in a prayer that Jesus is our Lord. A Christian is a person who has accepted Jesus as their Lord and their Savior. But we have become so casual in our use of these terms *Savior* and *Lord* that Christianity has become a mere label. Jesus is warning us that *salvation* is much more than a label. It is also more than the words we speak. True Christianity must be reflected in the acts of obedience that we live. So was Jesus teaching that a Christian who bears bad fruit will also enter the kingdom of heaven? No, Jesus said that good trees cannot bear bad fruit; they bear only good fruit. This teaching about salvation being like a fruit tree is repeated in Matthew 12:33, and it is further evidence that Jesus taught God's great salvation plan as salvation from our sins, not a salvation simply from the punishment of our sins.

In Matthew 10, we are told that Jesus sent out his twelve disciples with specific instructions to carry the good news of salvation to the people. Within these instructions, Jesus warns his disciples, "*Do not be afraid of those who kill the body but cannot kill the soul. Rather, be afraid of the One who can destroy both the soul and body in hell*" (Matthew 10:28). If the good news of salvation Jesus had taught the disciples was a salvation from the punishment of their sins, regardless of their actions, this warning would make no sense at all. If the disciples had their salvation securely in their pockets and hell was not a possibility, then why would Jesus make this statement to them? Jesus understood that the fear of sinning against God was the power unto righteousness that the disciples would need as they were sent out into the world. Jesus wanted to ensure that the disciples feared God more than they feared anything else that they may have encountered on their journey.

Jesus was later specifically teaching about who exactly will be saved at the end of the age. He said,

> The Son of Man will send out his angels, and they will weed out of his kingdom everything that causes sin and all who do evil. They will throw them into the fiery furnace, where there will be weeping and gnashing of teeth. Then the righteous will shine like the sun in the kingdom of their Father. He who has ears, let him hear. (Matthew 13:41–43)

Do we have ears to hear what Jesus was teaching? He says that those who do evil will be thrown into hell. Is there any room here for Christians who do evil? To do evil is to sin. So what about Christian sinners saved by grace?

We live in a culture in which labels are very powerful. We want certain labels and we don't want other labels. Because Christians are afraid of being labeled as *legalistic* we focus our faith almost entirely upon what we *believe* rather than on how we live. Today's Christian faith tells us that all we must do is believe and be saved, and that anything more than a salvation by this *belief* is a salvation by works, which is *legalism.* But do we ever really tell people exactly what it is we must believe? Consider Jesus' teaching in Matthew 16:27, where he specifically addresses the great and dreadful day of his return; "*For the Son of Man is going to come in his Father's glory with his angels, and then he will reward each person according to what he has done.*" Is Jesus announcing a great salvation based upon what we *believe,* or upon what we do in response to what we believe?

If we reject salvation as being based upon overcoming sins, what sense do we make of Jesus words in Matthew 19:17, when he was specifically asked what we must do to receive eternal life. He responded, "*If you want to enter life, obey the commandments.*" With such a clear and concise response from Jesus, why are today's Christians so opposed to a salvation from sin message? Jesus taught a salvation plan that empowers us to actually overcome our sins rather than a plan which allows us to simply avoid the punishment of our sins.

Jesus continued to address the man who had asked him what he must do to enter the kingdom of heaven. Jesus said, "*If you want to be perfect, go, sell your possessions and give to the poor, and you will have treasure in heaven. Then come, follow me.*" We are then told that the man went away sad, because he had great wealth. Jesus used this experience to teach the disciples about the great salvation message, and he said, "*I tell you the truth, it is hard for a rich man to enter the kingdom of heaven. Again I tell you, it is easier for a camel to go through the eye of a needle than for a rich man to enter the kingdom of God.*" This was a hard teaching, and the disciples were greatly astonished and asked, "*Who then can be saved?*" (Matthew 19:16–25) After having heard Jesus teach them about the great salvation plan of God, the disciples concluded that the standard of salvation seems too high! But Jesus responded to their concerns with these words, "*With man this is impossible, but with God all things are possible*" (Matthew 19:26).

Are we listening carefully to what Jesus said? Will we accept his words as truth, or will we twist his words to support our traditional beliefs about salvation? What did Jesus teach about the standard of righteousness required to enter the Kingdom of Heaven? Some today will interpret this passage to mean that this young man, who went away sad because he was very rich, will still enter the Kingdom of Heaven because God will do the impossible for him. But does this make sense? Was Jesus saying that the standard of righteousness seems high, but it really isn't that high? No, Jesus was stressing that the standard of righteousness to enter the Kingdom of Heaven is total surrender and nothing less. This is why having great material wealth on earth makes it so difficult for a rich man to meet the standard of giving up everything he has. The more we have, the more we must surrender. When Jesus says that with God all things are possible, he is saying that God has a plan to empower us to do what seems to us to be impossible! God is not going to make it possible to enter the Kingdom of Heaven by lowering the standard, but instead He will make it possible by empowering us to walk in complete righteous obedience to His commands.

Jesus continued to teach this extremely high standard of righteousness required to enter the Kingdom of Heaven as he taught through a parable in Matthew 22:1–14. While we have considered this parable previously, it is worthwhile to hear it again:

> The kingdom of heaven is like a king who prepared a wedding banquet for his son. He sent his servants to those who had been invited to the banquet to tell them to come, but they refused to come.
>
> Then he sent some more servants and said, 'Tell those who have been invited that I have prepared my dinner: My oxen and fattened cattle have been butchered, and everything is ready. Come to the wedding banquet.'
>
> But they paid no attention and went off—one to his field, another to his business. The rest seized his servants, mistreated them and killed them. The king was enraged. He sent his army and destroyed those murderers and burned their city.
>
> Then he said to his servant, 'The wedding banquet is ready, but those I invited did not deserve to come. Go to the street corners and invite to the banquet anyone you find. So the servants went out into

the streets and gathered all the people they could find, both good and bad, and the wedding hall was filled with guests.

But when the king came in to see the guests, he noticed a man there who was not wearing wedding clothes. 'Friend,' he asked, how did you get in here without wedding clothes?' The man was speechless.

Then the king told the attendants, 'Tie him hand and foot, and throw him outside, into the darkness, where there will be weeping and gnashing of teeth.'

For many are invited, but few are chosen.

There is much to learn about God's great salvation plan in this parable. Note that after the initial invitees had rejected the King's invitation, the servants were told to invite everyone they see to the banquet, including both the good and the bad. This confirms that we do not have to stop sinning to get the invitation. The invitation to the great salvation gathering is unmerited. But then something goes very wrong for one of the men who had accepted the invitation, and was present when the King makes his arrival. This man was not wearing the necessary wedding clothes. Could these wedding clothes be the required robe of righteousness that must be worn when we arrive at the judgment seat? Could it be that this man came to the banquet without repenting of his sins, without putting on the required white robe of righteousness?

Many of today's Christians will have a difficult time with this part of the wedding banquet parable. They picture God as a loving and merciful King, who, when he arrived at the banquet and saw the man without the proper wedding clothes, would have called to His servants and ordered them to get the man the proper wedding clothes. But this is not what the King did. It was too late for this poor sinner to put on the proper garment after the King arrived. This man needed to have the proper clothes on before he entered the banquet room. Could it be that Jesus was teaching that in God's great salvation plan we must repent of our sins before the great and dreadful Day of Judgment arrives?

Jesus concludes this parable with words that many of today's Christians will ignore. He said, "*For many are invited but few are chosen.*" This is consistent with Jesus earlier words, "*Enter through the narrow gate, for wide is the gate and broad is the road that leads to destruction, and many enter through it. But small is the gate and narrow the road that leads to life, and few find it*" (Matthew 7:13–14). There is much pressure within the Christian community today to tell people that salvation is easy and that all it takes is a simple prayer and you will have eternal life with God. But Jesus did not teach an easy salvation plan. Jesus taught the truth, which is that salvation is a long and challenging lifetime journey, one which God has empowered us to walk, but one we must also choose to walk every day of our lives.

Jesus' Message After His Resurrection

Jesus' announcement of the good news of God's great salvation plan did not change after his death and resurrection. Just before he ascended into heaven Jesus gave us his Great Commission:

> All authority in heaven and on earth has been given to me. Therefore go and make disciples of all nations, baptizing them in the name of the Father, and of the Son, and of the Holy Spirit, and **teaching them to obey everything I have commanded you**. And surely I am with you always, to the very end of the age. (Matthew 28:19) (emphasis added)

We are to baptize the nations in the name of the Father, of the Son, and of the Holy Spirit, but we are also to teach them to obey everything Jesus commanded us. And the commandments of Jesus were always the same as the commandments of his Father, which are grounded in God's unchanging Law. In other words, Jesus told his disciples to teach the people to be righteous, that they may obey God's directions for life, and to go and sin no more.

There is one more announcement by Jesus of this *great salvation plan* of God that we should consider before moving on to the writings of the Apostles, those who heard Jesus speak. It comes from the last book of the Bible, the Book of Revelation. These are the red letter words spoken by Jesus, and recorded by John, with regard to who will be saved. They are found in Revelation chapters 2 and 3, within the seven letters to the seven churches. In each of these letters Jesus again announces the great salvation message of God, as he emphasizes in each letter that it is only those who *overcome* their sins who will be saved.

To the Church in Ephesus Jesus says; *"Remember the height from which you have fallen! Repent and do the things you did at first. If you do not repent, I will come to you and remove your lampstand from its place . . . He who has an ear, let him hear what the Spirit says to the churches. To him who **overcomes**, I will give the right to eat from the tree of life, which is in the paradise of God."* (Revelation 2:5,7) (emphasis added)

To the Church in Smyrna, Jesus says; *"He who has an ear, let him hear what the Spirit says to the churches. He who **overcomes** will not be hurt at all by the second death."* (Revelation 2:11) (emphasis added)

To the Church in Pergamum Jesus says, *"**Repent** therefore! Otherwise I will soon come to you and will fight against them with the sword of my mouth. He who has an ear, let him hear what the Spirit says to the churches. **To him who overcomes**, I will give some of the hidden manna. I will also give him a white stone with a new name written on it, known only to him who receives it."* (Revelation 2:16–17) (emphasis added)

To the Church in Thyatira, Jesus says, *"**To him who overcomes and does my will to the end**, I will give authority over the nations—'He will rule them with an iron scepter; he will dash them to pieces like pottery' just as I have received authority* *from my Father, I will also give him the morning star. He who has an ear, let him hear what the Spirit says to the churches."* (Revelation 2:26–29) (emphasis added)

To the Church in Sardis, Jesus says, *"Yet you have a few people in Sardis who have not soiled their clothes. They will walk with me, dressed in white for they are worthy. **He who overcomes will, like them, be dressed in white.** I will never blot out his name from the book of life, but will acknowledge his name before my Father and his angels. He who has an ear, let him hear what the Spirit says to the churches."* (Revelation 3:4–6) (emphasis added)

To the Church in Philadelphia, Jesus says, *"I am coming soon. Hold on to what you have, so that no one will take your crown. **Him who overcomes** I will make a pillar in the temple of my God. Never again will he leave it. I will write on him the name of my God and the name of the city of my God, the new Jerusalem, which is coming down out of heaven from my God; and I will also write on him my new name. He who has an ear, let him hear what the Spirit says to the churches."* (Revelation 3:11–13) (emphasis added)

And to the Church in Laodicea, Jesus says, *"Those whom I love I rebuke and discipline. **So be earnest, and repent**. Here I am! I stand at the door and knock. If anyone hears my voice and opens the door, I will come in and eat with him, and he with me. **To him who overcomes**, I will give the right to sit with me on my throne, **just as I overcame** and sat down with my Father on his throne. He who has an ear, let him hear what the Spirit says to the churches."* (Revelation 3:19–22) (emphasis added)

This is the great salvation plan of God, which was *announced by the Lord Jesus, himself* as set forth in our foundation passage from Hebrews 2:1–4. We must listen very carefully to these words spoken by Jesus about who will be saved. It is only those who *overcome* who will receive the blessings of salvation! And what is it that we must overcome, if not our sins? It is not the punishment from our sins that we are to overcome. It is our sins we must overcome. This is the great salvation plan announced by the Lord Jesus. This is the great plan of salvation that the Apostles, *who heard him speak,* then passed on to us in their New Testament writings.

The Message Passed on by the Apostles

Before moving on to look at the great salvation message as passed on to us by those who heard Jesus speak, we must again remember to put on the proper lens that is necessary to understand these writings. This lens is the knowledge of who God is. It is in knowing the very nature of God that we can gain confidence in our understanding of these teachings. Our interpretation of these writings must be worthy of and honoring to a God who is omniscient, omnipotent, absolutely righteous, absolutely just, and unchanging. This lens is the only hope that we have in restoring the unity of the faith that God desires in the Church. When we consider the New Testament writings, we must presume that these writers are speaking of the true God and that their understanding of His great salvation plan is consistent with His nature. To interpret the New Testament writings in a way which is inconsistent with God's nature, as expressed through the Law and the Prophets, and then as announced by Jesus, would be to change God's great salvation plan, which would dishonor God.

As we begin to look at this great salvation plan of God, as passed on to us by those who heard Jesus speak, we have come to a critically important point in reaching the unity of understanding that we all desire. And more importantly, this is the unity which God desires for His people. To come to this unity of understanding the writings of the Apostles, we must begin with the acknowledgement that the Apostles are not the authors of this great salvation plan. It was God who established this unchanging plan of salvation, and it was first announced through the Law and the Prophets of the Old Testament. Jesus then announced the same great salvation message through his teachings and through his life's example. God sent His only begotten Son to testify to the truth of His plan. Then the Apostles were given the charge of passing on this same plan to future generations, including to God's people today.

If we took nothing else into consideration in seeking to understand the great salvation plan of God, other than the Old Testament Scriptures and the four Gospels of Jesus, we would have a much greater unity in our understanding of God's plan of salvation than exists in today's Christian Church. Many Christians today will not accept the plan of salvation that was so clearly established and announced by God through the Law, the Prophets and the teachings and life of Jesus. The Old Testament Scriptures and the red letter teachings of Jesus leave very little room for discrepancy when it comes to the plan of salvation. This should come as no surprise to those who understand that Jesus could do nothing except what he saw his Father doing. Yet, when presented with the evidence of the plan of salvation from these two sources alone, many Christians today will become defensive and even angry. And the reason for this rejection can be found in the way we read our Bibles.

There are two very different approaches that we can take in reading the Bible. The approach by many, if not most Christians today, is to interpret the Bible by viewing it from the back to the front. In other words, they begin with the New Testament writings, and after interpreting the meaning of the Apostles writings, they then go back and interpret the Gospels, and finally the Old Testament, in a way that is consistent with their interpretation of the Apostles writings. Many today take this approach because they believe that the writers of the New Testament had the greatest understanding of God's plan of salvation. But interpreting Scripture in this way has led us to our current place of great divisions within the doctrinal interpretations of the Church. This is true because the writings of the Apostles are not always consistent with each other.

While the Old Testament Law and Prophets and the teachings of Jesus are not always easy to accept, they are always consistent with each other. The writings of the New Testament Apostles, however, at times appear to be in opposition to each other when it comes to understanding the plan of salvation. This is true from writer to writer, and it is even true at times within the writings of the same Apostle. There are times when we read the writings of the great Apostle Paul, when he seems to say two completely opposite things within the same letter. This observation is not meant to discredit the understandings of the Apostles, but rather to acknowledge that two Christians today can also come to two different conclusions about very important issues of the faith when they each interpret those writings as they look through their differing preconceived beliefs. This has led the Church to its current state of great confusion and division.

Recall that we just heard Jesus teach that all things are possible with God, so bringing His Church into a place of unity in understanding Scripture is not impossible. In fact, knowing the desire of God for this unity will leave us no choice but to conclude that this unity in the Body of Christ is necessary in God's eyes. What God desires, God requires, and what God requires will be accomplished! But this unity will only take place when we all look at Scripture through the same lens. The lens that we must use to interpret the New Testament writings is the lens of who God is and what He has spoken through His Old Testament Prophets and through Jesus. Only after this lens is in place will we be able to understand and learn from the teachings of the New Testament Apostles. In other words, we must begin by understanding the Old Testament, which defines who God is and what His original intent is, was, and will always be. Next we must listen to the testimony of Jesus, God's manifest Son, through his teachings and through his example. Only then can we properly understand the writings of those who heard Jesus speak.

Again, consider what the writer of Hebrews is warning us to do in our foundational verse from Hebrews 2:1–4:

> So we must **listen very carefully** then, to the truth that we have heard, or we may drift away from it. The message God delivered through angels has always proven true, and the people were punished for every violation of the law, and every act of disobedience. **What makes us think that we can escape if we are indifferent to this great salvation, that was announced by the Lord, Jesus himself, it was passed on to us by those who heard him speak**. And God verified the message through signs, wonders, various miracles, and by giving gifts of the Holy Spirit, whenever He chose to do so. (NLT) (emphasis added)

To change our interpretation of the Law and the Prophets or of the teachings of Jesus based upon our interpretations of the writings of the Apostles will inevitably lead to discrepancies and divisions. We must not come to the conclusion that the Apostles had a greater understanding and revelation of God's salvation plan than Jesus had. And we certainly cannot reinterpret what Jesus referred to as the Scriptures, the Old Testament writings of the Law and the Prophets, based upon a belief that the Apostles had a greater revelation of God's plan than God Himself had. To take this approach to interpreting scripture, by viewing Scripture from the back to the front of our Bibles, will erode our acceptance of Scripture as inerrant. The time has come to believe what we are reading, rather than to read what we already believe!

Let us consider the message of salvation that was passed on to us by those who heard Jesus speak. How did the disciples, who heard Jesus teach about this great salvation message, present God's salvation plan to the people? It would take several books to consider all of the disciples' teachings on this subject, so we will limit our observations to a few of the statements of John, James, and Peter, the three disciples who appear to have been the closest to Jesus. We will then also look briefly at two statements made in the Book of Jude.

It should be noted that Jesus' teachings on salvation were not always easy for even the disciples to accept. Consider what happened when Jesus was teaching about being the *bread of life*. Jesus had been teaching the disciples that to have eternal life they must ". . . *eat the flesh of the Son of Man and drink his blood.*" In John 6:60 we are told that, *"On hearing it, many of his disciples said, 'This is hard teaching. Who can accept it?' Jesus then responded, "Does this offend you? What if you see the Son of Man ascend to where he was before! The Spirit gives life; the flesh counts for nothing. The words I have spoken to you are spirit and they are life. Yet there are some of you who do not believe."* Then from John 6:61, we are told, *"From this time many of his disciples turned back and no longer followed him."*

Jesus, God's only begotten Son, was teaching the truth about the great salvation message, yet many of his disciples stopped following him! Does this suggest to us that the message Jesus was teaching about salvation was an easy message or a very difficult message to accept? Would Jesus disciples have left him if he had taught that salvation was received through a simple prayer of *thank you* to God? Jesus told them that his words are spirit and life, y*et there are some of you who do not believe.* This should stir us to reconsider our casual belief today that we will be saved from the punishment of our sins if we simply *believe* in Jesus, and do not believe what Jesus actually taught. It is time for us to *listen carefully* to exactly what it is that we are to believe. We need to awaken to this great salvation from sin message that Jesus taught, and that was passed on to us by those who heard him speak.

The Message of John

So let us start with the message passed on to us by John:

> This is the message we have heard from him and declare to you: God is light; in him there is no darkness at all. If we claim to have fellowship with him yet walk in the darkness, we lie and do not live by the truth. But if we walk in the light, as he is in the light, we have fellowship with one another, and the blood of Jesus, his Son, purifies us from all sin. (I John 1:5–7)

This verse says so much about the true God, and who His true people are. The *light* is the power of righteousness, and God is absolute righteousness. God is this light. And if we are His true people then we too must walk in this *light* of righteousness, just as He is righteous! If we walk in sin we are not walking in the light. John says that if we claim to be His people, then we cannot go on sinning. Darkness is sin, which is disobedience to God's Law. Light is righteousness, which is obedience to God's Law.

John goes on to write,

> If we claim to be without sin, we deceive ourselves and the truth is
> not in us. If we confess our sins, he is faithful and just and will for-
> give us our sins and purify us from all unrighteousness. If we claim
> we have not sinned, we make him out to be a liar and his word has
> no place in our lives. (I John 1:8–9)

This is a very important passage because it is often used in support of today's pre-
vailing Christian belief that sinning is inevitable, and that we are all destined to continue to walk in sin, at least until we get to heaven. But is this what John is saying?
Did John write this passage as a statement in support of the belief that actual salvation from sins is not possible? The first reason we must reject this interpretation
of John's writings is because, as we have seen, it is not consistent with what was
taught by the Law and the Prophets, and it is not consistent with the teachings of
Jesus. The correct interpretation of this passage, which would be consistent with
Scripture, would be that if you are sinning, yet deny that you are sinning, you are
deceiving yourselves. Instead, if we sin, we must confess our sins and then choose
to turn away from those sins. This interpretation of John's writings would also be
consistent with the final words of this passage, where we are told that we will be
purified from all unrighteousness. We clearly are not purified from all unrighteousness if we continue to walk in the darkness of sin.

   This interpretation of John's message of salvation is supported further by his
later statement:

> My dear children, **I write this to you so that you will not sin**. But
> if anybody does sin, we have one who speaks to the Father in our
> defense-Jesus Christ, the Righteous One. He is the atoning sac-
> rifice for our sins, and not only for ours but also for the sins of the
> whole world. (I John 2:1–2) (emphasis added)

John would not write these words if he believed that overcoming all of our sins is
impossible. John was passing on the teachings of Jesus here, that we must *go and
sin no more,* but in case we do sin, we must immediately repent and receive the
forgiveness that was purchased for us on the cross. John specifically says that he
is writing these words so that you will not sin!

   The Apostle John understood the great salvation plan of God, and he wanted
God's people to also not only understand this plan, but to have confidence in their
salvation. John makes it clear that this confidence will come with the evidence of a
life lived in obedience to God's Law. He also warns those who profess to be believers,
yet who continue to walk in sin, as he writes:

> We know that we have come to know him if we obey his com-
> mands. The man who says, "I know him," but does not do what he
> commands is a liar, and the truth is not in him. But if anyone obeys
> his word, God's love is truly made complete in him. This is how we

know we are in him: Whoever claims to live in him must walk as
Jesus did. (I John 2:3–6)

These words of John should eliminate any doubt about the salvation plan that John preached. It was the same message that Jesus preached. John says that in order to be saved we must walk as Jesus walked. Could the standard of salvation be any higher than this? How much sin did Jesus walk in? Yet most Christians today have come to believe that walking in sin is inevitable. So today's Christians continue to walk in their sins, relying on God's mercy and grace to save us from the punishment of our sins. Christianity has become a religion of lawlessness. But listen carefully to what John goes on to write,

> Everyone who sins breaks the law; in fact, sin is lawlessness. But
> you know that he appeared so that he might take away our sins.
> And in him is no sin. No one who lives in him keeps on sinning.
> No one who continues to sin has either seen him or known him. (I
> John 3:4–6)

Are we listening carefully to these words that were passed on to us by the Apostle John, who heard Jesus speak? John is not speaking about a salvation from the punishment for our sins, without a salvation from the sins themselves. This great salvation message is not an easy message, and will require that we become empowered to overcome sin. John understood that the standard of righteousness for this great salvation is high, no less than walking as Jesus walked! And if we are not yet convinced of the content of John's teaching of the plan of salvation, consider what he then writes,

> Dear children, do not let anyone lead you astray. He who does what
> is right is righteous, just as he is righteous. He who does what is
> sinful is of the devil, because the devil has been sinning from the
> beginning. The reason the Son of God appeared was to destroy the
> devil's work. No one who is born of God will continue to sin, because
> God's seed remains in him; he cannot go on sinning, because he
> has been born of God. (I John 3:7–9)

John did not preach an easy salvation message. John did not teach that salvation comes by simply *believing in Jesus* and then we will not be punished for our sins. John taught that to be saved we must accept Jesus teachings with regard to the overcoming of sin. John preached a salvation from our sins, not a salvation from only the punishment of our sins.

So what would John say to the *born-again Christian* today, who continues to walk in sin, and who is content in relying on the *grace* of God to cover his sins, rather than the *grace* of God to empower him to overcome his sins and walk in obedience to God's commands? If we are really listening carefully to these words passed on to us from John, we will begin to see that we have become a double-minded people, thinking we are righteous and wicked at the same time. If John were preaching today, he would confront our double-minded faith!

The Message of James

The Apostle James was a second disciple who heard Jesus speak. James also wrote a letter that is included in the New Testament. What did James believe about the great salvation message that he had heard Jesus announce? James does not specifically use the term *salvation* in his letter, and this in itself is a commentary on his beliefs. The message of James is really a message of defining the *faith* of God's people. James deals with the content of what we are to believe and the way we are to live out that belief. He asks two questions that will help us to understand the plan of salvation James preached. He asks, *"What good is it, my brothers, if a man claims to have faith but has no deeds? Can such faith save him?"* (James 2:14) Then James answers his own questions about this *saving faith* by saying,

> Show me your faith without deeds, and I will show you my faith by what I do. You believe that there is one God. Good! Even the demons believe that—and shudder. You foolish man, do you want evidence that faith without deeds is useless? Was not our ancestor Abraham considered righteous for what he did when he offered his son Isaac on an altar? You see that his faith and his actions were working together, and his faith was made complete by what he did. And scripture was fulfilled that says, "Abraham believed God, and it was credited to him as righteousness," and he was called God's friend. You see that a person is justified by what he does, not by faith alone . . . As the body apart from the spirit is dead, so faith without deeds is dead. (James 2:18–26)

James did not teach that salvation comes through a simple mental acknowledgement of Jesus but instead through a changed life of obedience, which is repentance from sin. James also writes about the importance of perseverance through trials in order to receive the crown of life that God has promised. James emphasizes that we must not just listen to God's word; we must do God's word. Our faith must be verified through our acts of obedience, not just a belief in our minds. He stresses that the righteousness that God requires of us is made complete only through our acts of obedience. James writes,

> Submit yourselves, then, to God. Resist the devil, and he will flee from you. Come near to God and he will come near to you. Wash your hands, you sinners, and purify your hearts, you double-minded. (James 4:7–8)

There is nothing in the Book of James that would lead one to believe that salvation is obtained by simply saying a prayer of confession of your sins and then thanking Jesus for dying on the cross to save us from the punishment for our sins. James is clearly calling us to have more than an intellectual faith; we must have an active faith, which includes obedience to God's commands. The fact that James stresses persevering through tests only makes sense in the context of overcoming sin. Again, the salvation plan preached by James was not an easy salvation plan.

The Message of Peter

A third disciple of Jesus who wrote two letters that appear in the New Testament is the Apostle Peter. What did Peter say about the great salvation plan that was announced by Jesus? Peter stressed the sanctifying work of the Holy Spirit for the purpose of obedience to Jesus. He, like James, also speaks of the refining fire of trials that prove our faith to be real. Peter refers several times to the salvation message spoken of through the Prophets, and he speaks of the grace of God as a power to be holy as God is holy. He urges believers to live in reverent fear of God. He clearly preaches the need to abstain from sinful desires that war against our souls, and that we cannot live as the pagans live. He refers to Jesus as the example for us, emphasizing that Jesus committed no sin.

Here are a few examples of Peter's writings in this regard. *"He (Jesus) himself bore our sins in his body on the tree, so that we might die to sins and live for righteousness . . ."* (1 Peter 2:24). Peter emphasis that a believer must turn away from sin and that a believer ". . . *not live the rest of this earthly life for evil human desires, but rather for the will of God"* (I Peter 4:2). Peter tells us to obey the gospel of God! That does not sound like a simple confession of sins, with the expectation that we will no longer be punished for our sins if we are Christians. He writes, *"If it is hard for the righteous to be saved, what will become of the ungodly and the sinner?"* (I Peter 4:18)

In his second letter, Peter speaks of being sure of one's salvation through a life of self-control and godliness. He states that God has given us everything we need to possess these character traits. He says we have been cleansed from our past sins. He again confirms that the Old Testament Prophets spoke the inerrant word of God! He speaks of the need for righteousness and warns us to remember what happened to angels who sinned. Peter warns us to stay on the narrow path and that we are slaves to whatever masters us. Contrary to today's belief by many that salvation cannot be lost, Peter talks about being careful not to lose our salvation by turning away from God. He says that God does not want any to perish, but all to come to repentance. Peter writes that we must be found spotless, blameless, and at peace with God. He warns us to be careful not to be carried away by the error of lawless men and or to fall from our secure position. Finally, he tells us to grow in the grace and knowledge of our Lord and Savior, Jesus Christ. Peter's preaching makes sense only if salvation is from our sins, and not simply from the punishment of sins. These letters make sense only if God's grace is the power to overcome our sins, not God's decision to overlook our sins.

A Word from Jude

Finally, it is helpful to briefly consider the short book of Jude, brother of James, whom it can be presumed may have also heard Jesus teach the great salvation message. Jude specifically addresses the message that has been handed down once for all times to the saints, as he begins,

> Dear friends, although I was very eager to write to you about the salvation we share, I felt I had to write and urge you to contend for the faith that was once for all entrusted to the saints For certain men whose condemnation was written about long ago have secretly slipped in among you. They are godless men, who change the grace of our God into a license for immorality and deny Jesus Christ our only Sovereign and Lord. (Jude 3–4)

Jude goes on to remind us what had happened to God's own people and even to His angels who chose to walk in disobedience to God's commands. Jude finishes with a doxology that confirms his belief that it is possible to walk in complete righteousness before God, as he writes,

> To him who is able to keep you from falling and to present you before his glorious presence without fault and with great joy—to the only God our Savior be glory, majesty, power and authority, through Jesus Christ our Lord, before all ages, now and forevermore! Amen. (Jude 24–25)

Conclusion

Before the birth of Jesus, God revealed through the words of an angel, why there is such power in the name of Jesus. The name of Jesus announces the purpose for which Jesus was sent into the world; it was to save the people from their sins. It was not to save the people in their sins. It was not to simply save the people from the punishment for their sins. There is great power in the name of Jesus because Jesus came to redeem God's people from their sins. Jesus came to destroy sin by empowering us to walk in righteous obedience to God's commands, just like he did.

Jesus' preaching is summarized by his message *"Repent, for the Kingdom of Heaven is at hand."* To repent from sin is to stop sinning. It is to overcome sin. And this is what Jesus taught. Jesus did not come to give the people the label *Christian*. Jesus came to actually redeem the people back to God's original intent, to walk with free will, yet in total obedience to God's Word. Jesus' teachings were not easy. Jesus did not teach salvation through a one-time sinner's prayer. Jesus taught the people that they must do everything possible to stop sinning, even if it means gouging out an eye or cutting off an arm.

Jesus did not come to lower the standard of righteousness required of God's people to enter the Kingdom of Heaven. Jesus came to empower us to rise to God's never-changing standard. Jesus did not teach that we will be judged simply by the thoughts and conclusions in our minds, but instead that we would be judged by the fruits of our thoughts, which are our actions. Jesus taught that salvation is only through a narrow gate and a narrow path, and that few will find it. But Jesus also taught us that God has made a way for every person to be saved if they chose to totally submit to God's ways. Jesus taught us that anything less than everything is nothing to God. He tells us that if we hang on to this life we will lose it. And Jesus' message remained the same after his death and resurrection.

Jesus passed on God's great salvation plan to his disciples who heard him speak. The Apostles are not the authors of God's salvation plan, and we cannot interpret their writings in a way which is inconsistent with the Law and the Prophets or with the recorded teachings of Jesus. Jesus' disciples often viewed Jesus' teachings on salvation as hard teachings. But the Apostles John, James, and Peter, who were closest to Jesus, all passed on the great salvation from our sins message that Jesus had taught them. They all taught that a true believer must stop sinning and that salvation was more than simply being labeled as a believer. These Apostles who heard Jesus speak did not teach an imputed righteousness; they taught a real righteousness in which the people of God walk in actual obedience to God's commands.

The Fear of the Lord

A Place of Beginning

We have been asking some very important and challenging questions about the foundations of today's Christian faith. This has not been easy, but if you have come this far on the journey to rediscover the ancient path that leads to life, you will now be rewarded with the keys to unlocking the door to a great treasure! Recall the words of the Prophet, Isaiah:

> The Lord is exalted for He dwells on high. He will fill Zion with righteousness and justice. He will be the sure foundation for your times, a rich store of salvation, and wisdom and knowledge. The fear of the Lord is the key to this treasure. (Isaiah 33:5–6)

If the previous chapters have caused discomfort for those who have previously been comfortable with their lives as *Christian sinners,* this is a good thing. If an awakening has taken place in your understanding of the standard of righteousness God has established in His great salvation plan, give thanks to the Lord! Hopefully the question that you are now asking is, How can I stay on this narrow path, by walking in total obedience to God's commands? If this is the question in your mind, then rest assured that God's Word will give you the answer. The God-ordained source of the power unto righteousness comes from walking in the fear of the Lord!

The fear of the Lord is the activating element of God's amazing grace. The fear of the Lord is the power we need to overcome our sins by walking in righteous obedience to God's directions for life. This fear of the Lord has been lost over time, and the result has been a religion of powerless Christianity. Rediscovering the fear of the Lord will bring the spark that ignites the next Great Awakening! The fear of the Lord is the source of the power unto righteousness that we have been longing for. Restoring the fear of the Lord into the hearts of the people is God's providential way of empowering His people to overcome their sins without violating their free will.

God is calling His people to a place which will prepare them for entry into the Kingdom of Heaven. This is a place that was known in generations past but a place that few Christians today even believe exists. Because there are so few people who have been to this place, there are very few people who can testify about it today. While history tells us that there is great glory and power in this place, many Christians will still refuse to go there. This is true even though God's Word clearly warns all of us that we must find this place if we are to be reconciled to God. There will come a day when every one of us, Christian and non-Christian alike, will find ourselves in this place, but tragically, for most people it will be too late!

Our Bibles tell us that God required the greatest men and women of His story to find this place. Noah had to find it in order to have the strength to build the great ark which would carry him and his family to safety at the time of the great flood. Abraham had to find this place before God could bless him as the father of the Nation of Israel, through whom God would bless all nations. Moses found this place as God called him to deliver the Law to God's people. The great Kings David and Solomon found this place and wrote extensively about it in the Psalms and Proverbs. The early Church described in the Book of Acts lived in this place at the time of its greatest power and influence in the world. Jesus' mother, Mary, sang about the importance of this place for generations to come. Even Jesus, the Messiah, found this place and delighted in it. What is this place? It is a place called *The Fear of the Lord.*

The fear of the Lord is the key that will unlock the door to the next Great Awakening. Carefully listen once again to the word of the Lord, spoken through His Prophet, Isaiah:

> The Lord is exalted, for he dwells on high; he will fill Zion with justice
> and righteousness. He will be the sure foundation for your times, a
> rich store of salvation and wisdom and knowledge. The fear of the
> Lord is the key to this treasure. (Isaiah 33:5–6)

The fear of the Lord is the key to unlocking the door to the greatest treasure we can seek, entry into the Kingdom of Heaven. As Isaiah tells us in this passage, the fear of the Lord is the key to establishing a sure foundation for our times. The fear of the Lord is the key to finding the great salvation plan of God. It is the key to gaining the wisdom and the knowledge we need to accomplish our God-ordained purpose in life. The time has come to pick up this key and put it into the door. The times are urgent, as the foundations of our faith are crumbling, but it is not too late if we will only listen carefully to God's directions!

American Christians have been praying fervently for revival for many years. It is hard to question the sincerity of the emotions behind these prayers. Our prayers do not lack in emotion or in sincerity. What our prayers are lacking is an *under-standing of the fear of the Lord,* and the *knowledge of God.* But God has told us how to restore this *understanding* and this *knowledge.* Listen carefully to the words of wisdom written in Proverbs 2:1–5:

> My son, if you accept my words, storing up my commands within
> you, turning your ear to wisdom and applying your heart to under-
> standing, and if you call out for insight and cry aloud for under-
> standing, and if you look for it as for sliver and search for it as for

hidden treasure, then you will understand the fear of the Lord and
find the knowledge of God.

God has told us how to restore knowledge and wisdom to our lives, and the place
of beginning for each of these treasures is rediscovering the fear of the Lord. In the
words of the great King Solomon, whom God had gifted with unsurpassed wisdom,
"*The fear of the Lord is the beginning of knowledge*" (Proverbs 1:7). He has also told
us that "*The fear of the Lord is the beginning of* wisdom" (Psalm 111:10).

But do we have ears to listen carefully to these words of wisdom of King Solomon?
Remember the warning the Lord gave His people through our foundational passage
from the Prophet Jeremiah: "*I am about to bring destruction upon this people, the
fruit of their plans. Because they have not listened to my words and have rejected
my law*" (Isaiah 6:19). And remember the words spoken to us through the writer of
Hebrews: "*So we must listen very carefully then, to the truth that we have heard, or
we may drift away from it . . .*" (Hebrews 2:1).

We must pause here, and make sure that we are really listening to God's words.
Everyone would agree that having *knowledge* is necessary for us to live a mean-
ingful and productive life. Ignorance is dangerous. God's word says that the fear
of the Lord is the beginning of knowledge, but what exactly is *knowledge*? Noah
Webster's 1828 American Dictionary of the English Language defines *knowledge*
as "a *clear and certain perception of that which exists, or of truth and fact . . .*" We
need to *know* what the true facts are to make the right decisions in life. This is what
it means to know the *truth*. And as we have seen earlier, the only source of this truth
is God. Therefore, the fear of the Lord comes from having the *knowledge of God*.
Remember what Jesus said: "*Now this is eternal life: that they may know you, the
only true God, and Jesus Christ, whom you have sent*" (John 17:3).

The same is true of *wisdom*, which Noah Webster defines as ". . . *the right use
or exercise of knowledge . . .*" Wisdom is knowledge rightly applied. It is interesting
that Webster continues with a comment that in *Scripture Theology*, "*wisdom is true
religion; godliness; piety; the knowledge and fear of God, and sincere and uniform
obedience to his commands . . .*" So where do we get this wisdom? King David
again said, "*The fear of the Lord is the beginning of wisdom*" (Psalm 111:10). He
went on to tell us, "*Blessed is the man who fears the Lord, and finds great delight
in His commands*" (Psalm 112:1). This verse confirms the great value of walking in
the fear of the Lord! Blessings come to those who fear the Lord, and the fear of the
Lord comes to those who delight in His commands. If we are willing to listen, we will
soon understand why this is true.

This may come as a surprise to many today, but the fear of the Lord is also a
place of healing for our bodies! "*Fear the Lord and shun evil, this will bring health
to your body and nourishment to your bones*" (Proverbs 3:7–8). It is not a coincidence that as we have lost the fear of the Lord in our lives, there has been a cor-
responding increase in physical illnesses and disease in our bodies. We are living
in a culture that fears cancer and disease more than we fear God. Most of us have
heard Proverbs 3:7–8 before, but have we really listened to it? Do we understand
the connection between fearing the Lord and physical health? Why does the fear

of the Lord bring health to our bodies, and nourishment to our bones? We will soon find the answer to this question.

What about security? We are we living in a time of ever-increasing fear of terrorism, both domestic and foreign. We fear for the well-being of our children and grandchildren, and for the first time in many generations, most people do not believe that the next generation will experience the prosperity we have experienced in the past. Seldom has there been a time in this nation when we have been more fearful about our economic and environmental future. Yet, God's Word tells us, *"He who fears the Lord has a secure fortress, and for his children it will be a refuge. The fear of the Lord is a fountain of life, turning a man from the snares of death"* (Proverbs 14:26–27). Do we understand why the fear of the Lord will provide us with this security in our lives?

In past generations of Americans, one of the highest compliments that a person could receive was to be considered a *"God fearing"* person. But this term is seldom used today, and for many it would not necessarily even be received as a compliment. But God's word tells us that those who are *God fearing* will be protected from their enemies, will receive all the provisions of life that they need, and will ultimately receive salvation. The Bible tells us, *"Surely His salvation is near those who fear him, that his glory may dwell in our land"* (Psalms 85:9) and *"The angel of the Lord encamps around those who fear him, and he delivers them . . . Fear the Lord, you his saints, for those who fear him lack nothing"* (Proverbs 34:7, 9).

If all of these blessings will come to those who fear the Lord, then what about those who do not fear the Lord? Answering this question will begin to expose our double mindedness. Is salvation also near those who do not fear God? Is the angel of the Lord also encamped around those who do not fear God? Will those who do not fear God also lack nothing? How we answer these questions will determine how far we have drifted away from the truth and toward our present double-minded faith. King David once wrote, *"An oracle is in my heart concerning the sinfulness of the wicked; there is no fear of God before his eyes"* (Psalm 36:1). To conclude that all of these blessings of God will come to the wicked as well as the righteous, even if they do not fear God, is to be double minded. If we are really listening carefully to God's Word we will not come to this conclusion. Instead, if we are listening carefully, the real question will become, "Do I really fear the Lord?"

The Fear of the Lord in the Old Testament

The greatest men and women throughout the history of God's people had to find this place called *the fear of the Lord* before they could be used by God to accomplish His purpose through their lives. It will be helpful to look more closely at the lives of a few of these great men and women of the Bible. Let us begin with the account of Noah, and the great flood, in Genesis 6:5–9, which begins,

> The Lord saw how great man's wickedness on the earth had become,
> and that every inclination of the thoughts of his heart was only evil

all the time. The Lord was grieved that he had made man on the earth, and his heart was filled with pain. So the Lord said, "I will wipe mankind, whom I have created, from the face of the earth—men and animals, and creatures that move along the ground, and birds of the air—for I am grieved that I have made them." But Noah found favor in the eyes of the Lord. This is the account of Noah. Noah was a righteous man, blameless among the people of his time, and he walked with God.

As we will see in greater detail later, Noah was one of God's most important men in all of history. At a time when God made the observation that mankind had become so wicked that He had no choice but to send the great flood of judgment upon the earth, God found Noah to be a righteous man. God warned Noah of the coming flood, and instructed him in detail as to how to build an ark for his survival. But how could Noah find the strength and faith to spend the many years, and likely his entire fortune, in building a huge ark in preparation for flood, at a time when most Bible scholars believe the people had never even seen a heavy rain! Noah would certainly face years of great ridicule, even among his own relatives and friends. How would God empower Noah to persevere? The answer can be found in Hebrews 11:7, which says,

> By faith Noah, being warned of God of things not seen as yet, **moved with fear**, prepared an ark to the saving of his house; by which he condemned the world, and became an heir of the righteousness which is by faith. (emphasis added)

And consider the great patriarch, Abraham. God had made a promise to Abraham, that even in his old age he and his wife, Sarah, would give birth to a son. And through this son, Isaac, God would make Abraham the father of a nation of people who would be set apart for God to be a blessing to all nations. Yet long after this initial promise was made to Abraham, and after the miraculous birth of his son, Isaac, God still had to put Abraham to a great test. It would likely be the most difficult test of Abraham's life. God instructed Abraham to take his son, Isaac, and to sacrifice him on the altar. We can only speculate what thoughts went through Abraham's mind, as he walked with his son up onto the mountain and as he lifted the knife over his son as the Lord had instructed. For most Christians today this command by God makes no sense. What possible reason could God have in giving this command to Abraham? But the reason is clearly given to us in Genesis 22:12, as Abraham lifted the knife over his son, the Angel of the Lord said,

> "Do not lay a hand on the boy. Do not do anything to him. **Now I know that you fear God,** because you have not withheld from me your son, your only son." (emphasis added)

Did we listen carefully to God's Word? The purpose of this great test of Abraham was to determine whether Abraham truly feared the Lord! Why was it so important for God to know that Abraham truly feared Him more than anything else in the world? And why is it still so important today that we fear this unchanging God? We will soon see.

There once was a great man of God named Solomon, who at a very young age had become the king of the great nation of Israel. One night, in a dream, the Lord spoke to Solomon, and said, *"Ask for whatever you want me to give you."* In his response, Solomon asked for *". . . a discerning heart to govern your people and to distinguish between right and wrong."* The Lord was pleased with Solomon's request, and He granted it saying, *"I will do what you have asked. I will give you a wise and discerning heart, so that there will never have been anyone like you, nor will there ever be"* (I Kings 3:4–12).

Not only did God give Solomon this great wisdom, He also blessed Solomon with power, possessions, and pleasure that were almost beyond all comprehension. In this wisdom, King Solomon wrote the book of *Ecclesiastes,* and at the conclusion of this book, after considering everything he had experienced in his life, including his great power, possessions, and pleasure beyond our imaginations, Solomon makes a declaration that we need to hear again today. In searching for the true meaning and purpose in life, Solomon comes to the following conclusion:

> *"Now all has been heard; here is the conclusion of the matter: Fear God and keep his commandments, for this is the whole duty of man."* (Ecclesiastes 12:13)

Why would Solomon come to this conclusion? Why both *fear God* and *keep his commandments?* Why not just keep God's commandments? Wouldn't that be enough? Could it be that Solomon, in his God-given wisdom, understood something that we have lost? Could it be that Solomon understood that without the fear of the Lord in our hearts, it would not be possible for us to obey God's commandments?

The Fear of the Lord in the New Testament

The need for the fear of the Lord in the hearts and minds of the people did not end with the closing of the Old Testament Scriptures. It continued from generation to generation. Listen to the words of Mary, the mother of Jesus, who sang, *"And His mercy is upon them that fear Him from generation to generation"* (Luke 1:50). And for those who believe that this fear of the Lord ended at the cross, God has chosen to record the story of a man named Ananias and his wife, Sapphira, who were blessed with experiencing the church in its pinnacle of Pentecost power. This was a time when people were receiving the first-hand teaching of the Apostles as they were filled with God's Holy Spirit. And in the midst of this vibrant church, Ananias somehow thought he could be dishonest with God. The shocking consequence for his sin was an immediate and final judgment in the form of instant death. How could this happen in the New Testament Church? What about the New Testament concepts of grace, forgiveness, and mercy? This happened after Jesus had gone to the cross to die for the sins of all believers! Why wasn't Ananias seen by God as simply a sinner saved by grace as we define it in today's Christianity? Do we really understand why this happened to a Christian?

One thing we do know about this New Testament incident is that it had an impact upon the people. We are told, *"And great fear seized all who heard what had happened."* (Acts 5:5). And just in case we missed it, it happens again with his wife, Sapphira, who commits the same sin, she lies to God. And Peter tells her,

> How could you agree to test the Spirit of the Lord? Look! The feet of the men who buried your husband are at the door, and they will carry you out also. At that moment she fell down at his feet and died. Then the young men came in and, finding her dead, carried her out and buried her beside her husband. **Great fear seized the whole church and all who heard about these events**. (Acts 5:9–11) (emphasis added)

Are we listening carefully to this New Testament account of Ananias and Sapphira? Would this experience make a person think twice about joining this church? Was this the end of the growth of the Church? No, the opposite happened, as we are told in Acts 9:31: *"It (the Church) was strengthened; and encouraged by the Holy Spirit, it grew in numbers, **living in the fear of the Lord.**"* (emphasis added)

The Apostle Paul also saw the need for the fear of the Lord in the New Testament Church. He urged the believers to *"Submit yourselves to one another in the fear of the Lord"* (Ephesians 5:21). And he taught of the importance of the fear of the Lord in salvation itself when he said, *"Wherefore, my beloved, as you have always obeyed, not as in my presence only, but now much more in my absence, work out your own salvation with fear and trembling"* (Philippians 2:12).

The Apostle Peter understood the teachings of Jesus, and he also urged the New Testament believers to live in this place called *the fear of the Lord,* when he wrote,

> As obedient children, do not conform to the evil desires you had when you lived in ignorance. But just as he who called you is holy, so be holy in all you do; for it is written: "Be Holy, because I am holy." Since you call on a Father who judges each man's work impartially, live your lives as strangers here in reverent fear. (I Peter 1:14–17)

But if none of the words or the accounts of these great men and women of the Bible have persuaded you to see the need for God's people to again fear God, then consider the word of the Lord spoken through the Prophet Isaiah about the Son of Man and Son of God, Jesus, himself. Isaiah writes,

> And there shall come forth a rod out of the stem of Jesse, and a Branch shall grow out of his roots; and the spirit of the Lord shall rest upon him, the Spirit of wisdom and understanding, the Spirit of counsel and of power, **and the Spirit of knowledge and of the fear**

of the Lord—and he will delight in the fear of the Lord. (Isaiah 11:1–3) (emphasis added)

How many Christians today understand this passage? Did Jesus really fear God? Why would Jesus fear God? What exactly did Jesus fear? Why would God fill Jesus with the Spirit of the fear of the Lord? Could it be that this was the power Jesus needed to overcome all sin? If so, is it possible that God would do the same for us today?

Recall again, the last prophetic Word spoken by God in the Old Testament Scriptures, in the book of Malachi. God declares the problem by saying *"These people do not fear me, says the Lord."* Malachi 3:5 God then says something very important for His people to hear again today. It is the unchanging word, of an unchanging God, with and unchanging plan, as God speaks through Malachi:

> Then those who feared the Lord, spoke with each other. And the Lord listened to what they said. In His presence a scroll of remembrance was written to record the names of those who feared Him and loved to think about Him. They will be my people, says the Lord, on the day that I act they will be my own special treasure . . ." (3:16–17)

Who did the Lord listen to? Whose names will be written on the scroll of remembrance? Who will be God's own special treasure? What about a people who no longer fear God? What about God's people today? Does it make sense to conclude that the names of those who do not fear the Lord will also be written on this Scroll of Remembrance? The time for double-minded faith has come to an end!

The Fear of Sinning Against God

So what exactly does it mean to fear God? What is it that we fear? These are critical questions for our Christian culture to ask. Over time we have drifted away from the truth about what it means to fear God. We have lost an understanding of the fear of the Lord. This drift has gone something like this: to fear God is really to revere God, and to revere God is really to respect and honor God, and to respect and honor God is really to love God. We then come to the conclusion that if we love God, then we must also fear God. But is this necessarily true? Is loving God the same as fearing God?

If we teach a man to love God, without first teaching him to fear God, then we have actually done that man a great disservice. We have wrongly defined God, because everyone who knows the true God, as He has defined Himself, will first and foremost fear God. So why should we fear God? Do we fear that God will do something that will cause us pain or discomfort? The answer is *yes,* but our understanding must go deeper than this. Would God ever allow or even cause pain upon a man or woman whom He loves? The answer is again *yes,* and with good reason.

But to understand the basis for the fear of the Lord we must understand when and why God would allow or even inflict pain upon His own people. The reason is set forth in the words of Proverbs:

> *"My son, do not despise the Lord's discipline and do not resent his rebuke, because the Lord disciplines those he loves as a father the son he delights in."* (Proverbs 3:11–12)

And consider these words spoken by God through King David, a man after God's own heart:

> If his sons forsake my law and do not follow my statutes, if they violate my decrees and fail to keep my commands, I will punish their sin with the rod, their iniquity with flogging; but I will not take my love from him, nor will I ever betray my faithfulness. (Proverbs 89:30)

God will allow us to experience pain or discomfort when we sin. And this pain or discomfort serves a two-fold purpose for those who desire to be God's people. First, the pain signals to us that something is wrong. It tells us that we are sinning. And second, the pain is intended to persuade us to repent from that sin. This is similar to the purpose of pain in our bodies, which warns us when there is something wrong. The fear of God, then, is really the fear of sinning against God. This needs to be repeated. *The fear of God is the fear of sinning against God.*

We do fear that God will cause or allow some pain or discomfort in our lives, but if we know the purpose of that pain, we will use it to our advantage. Just as pain is a great motivator to address physical problems in our bodies, pain helps us to understand that there is something wrong in our lives. Either there is something not rightly aligned with God's commands, or God is allowing us to grow through a test of our faith. In each case, however, the pain is not meant by God to continue beyond either our repentance or the passing of a test of our faith.

Some may argue that it is cruel and unfair to link all pain with sin. They will argue that some pain is just inevitable in a fallen world. But this conclusion requires us to conclude that God is either unable or unwilling to take the pain away. This conclusion cannot be accepted if we view this issue through the lens of who God is. Pain cannot be more powerful than God. This connection between evil or sin and pain is confirmed in the well-recognized Prayer of Jabez, found in I Chronicles 4:9–10, where we are told,

> Jabez was more honorable than his brothers. His mother had named him Jabez, saying "I gave birth to him in pain." Jabez cried out to the God of Israel, "Oh, that you would bless me and enlarge my territory! Let your hand be with me, and keep me from harm, so that I will be free from pain. And God granted his request.

The word *harm* is translated in the King James Bible, and other translations, as *evil*. To be kept from evil would therefore be to be kept from pain. Again, some pain may be an element of a test that God is allowing us to walk through, to prove the reality of our faith. But if this is the case, the pain is not intended to last forever. If the pain is a part of a test, then God must make it possible for us to pass this test and to overcome that pain. God takes no pleasure in the pain of his people, including the eternal pain called *judgment*. Recall the word of the Lord spoken through the Prophet Ezekiel, as the Lord was speaking to His people who were refusing to repent from their sins:

> Son of man, say to the house of Israel, 'This is what you are saying: "Our offenses and sins weigh us down, and we are wasting away because of them. How then can we live?" Say to them, 'As surely as I live, declares the Sovereign Lord, I take no pleasure in the death of the wicked, but rather that they turn from their ways and live. Turn! Turn from your evil ways! Why will you die, O house of Israel? (Ezekiel 33:10–11)

Every person who does not fear sinning against God, will eventually sin against God. A person who fears sinning against God more than he fears anything else in his life is a person who has the power to overcome all sin and to walk in righteous obedience to all of Gods commands. God's word tells us that we are *"fearfully and wonderfully made"* (Psalm 139:14). Fear is the greatest motivator in our lives, and this is by God's design. We will always walk in fear. The decision we must make is to decide what it is that we will choose to fear. If we choose to fear God, then all other fears will fade away. If we fear sinning against God more than we fear not receiving the pleasure that any particular sin will bring us, then we will have found the power to overcome that sin.

Jonathan Edwards and Charles Finney: Sparks in the two Great Awakenings

To better understand what it means to fear the Lord and why it is so critically important to the next Great Awakening, it will be helpful to look to a time when God's people had a better understanding of this concept of the fear of the Lord. More than 250 years ago, there was a preacher named Jonathan Edwards, who understood the fear of the Lord very well. Throughout American history, Jonathan Edwards has been viewed as maybe the greatest theologian that has ever walked on American soil. He lived from 1703 to 1758, and God used him as a spark to ignite the First Great Awakening in America. Edwards was a great thinker, and while not known as a great orator, Jonathan Edwards has also been credited with delivering what many consider to be one of the greatest sermons ever delivered in American history, a sermon preached during the First Great Awakening. This message is entitled, "Sinners in the Hands of an Angry God." This sermon was first delivered in Enfield, Connecticut on July 8, 1741. From this sermon it is clear that Jonathan Edwards understood the concepts of both sin and the fear of the Lord in a way that very few people today understand them.

Jonathan Edwards understood the true nature and character of God as omnipotent, omniscient, absolutely righteous, absolutely just, and unchanging. His preaching helped the people understand that they could not carry their unrepented sins into the presence of the true and holy God. In this sermon Edwards gives a warning to all *sinners* that they are in the hands of an angry God. He often refers to *wicked* Israelites, who were walking on a path to destruction, believing that their label as God's chosen people would save them from this destruction. The same can be said of wicked Christians today, who are walking on this same path of destruction, while placing their faith in their label as *Christians*. Jonathan Edwards' message awakened the people to the truth that wicked Christians of his time would come to the same place of destruction.

Before considering portions of this sermon we need to correctly define a term Jonathan Edwards uses throughout this message. That term is the word *wicked*. This word is seldom used today. Many today may even question whether there is even such a thing as a *wicked Christian*. We again need some help from Noah Webster, who in his 1828 American Dictionary, defined the term *wicked* as ". . . *a person who lives in sin, transgressors of divine Law . . ."* This would be in contrast to a *righteous* man whom Webster defined as ". . . *one who is holy in heart, and observant to the divine commands in practice . . ."* To put it simply, a wicked man is a sinner. Therefore, Edwards was saying that every man who sins is in the hands of an angry God. This would be true regardless of his label as an Israelite or as a Christian.

Calling a person who commits sin a *wicked* person may offend many of us today. But we are not the first to be offended in this way. As we have seen in previous chapters, two thousand years ago Jesus was teaching the Jews, and we are told in John 8:31–36 that Jesus said to the Jews who had believed him: *"If you hold to my teaching, you are really my disciples. Then you will know the truth, and the truth will set you free."* This offended them, and they responded, *"We are Abraham's descendants and have never been slaves of anyone. How can you say that we shall be set free?"* Jesus replied, *"**I tell you the truth, everyone who sins is a slave to sin.** Now a slave has no permanent place in the family, but a son belongs to it forever. So if the Son sets you free, you will be free indeed."* (emphasis added)

Jesus was speaking to the Jews who believed in him. Jesus was warning these believers that if they sin, then they are slaves to sin. The Jews were offended by these words because they had the label of being God's chosen people, the descendants of Abraham. Many of today's Christians will also be offended by these words for the same reason. We have become comfortable with the label *Christian sinners saved by grace* so that we think we are an exception to the rule of absolute justice and righteousness, just as the Jews did at the time of Jesus. When listening to Jonathan Edwards speak about wicked men, remember that he is speaking to everyone who is sinning, whether they consider themselves to be a believer or not!

This sermon, "Sinners in the Hands of and Angry God," deserves to be read in its entirety, and hopefully many will choose to read the entire sermon. In fact for those who truly desire the power which will come through restoring the fear of the

Lord into our lives, this sermon should be read several times. But for the purpose of this book, only highlights of some of the most relevant quotes from this sermon will be cited. This will be done in the form of an interview. In effect, Jonathan Edwards will take the witness stand, and his testimony will be through direct quotes from this great sermon, "Sinners in the Hands of an Angry God."

The interview begins with the question:

Mr. Edwards, in your famous sermon, "Sinners in the Hands of an Angry God," you have chosen Deuteronomy 32:35 as your foundational verse: "*Their foot shall slip in due time.*" In this verse God is speaking to His own chosen people, the Israelites, who continued to walk in sin. I would like you to begin by telling us what will happen to wicked men who carry their unrepented sin into the presence of God.

> *There is nothing that keeps wicked men at any one moment out of hell, but the mere pleasure of God. God is restrained by no obligation to preserve wicked men for one moment. God does not lack the power to cast wicked men into hell at any moment… God cannot only cast wicked men into hell, He can do it easily. There is no fortress or any defense against the power of God. The earth trembles at God's rebuke. Who are we to think we will stand before Him in our wickedness.*

> *Wicked men deserve to be cast into hell; so that divine justice never stands in the way, it makes no objection against God's using his power at any moment to destroy them. On the contrary, justice calls aloud for an infinite punishment of their sins. Divine justice says of the tree that brings forth such grapes of Sodom, "Cut it down, why should it use up the soil?"*

Mr. Edwards, it has been over 250 years since you preached this sermon, and today's Christianity is focused primarily on God's great love for all men, even sinners. Do you really believe that Christians who continue to walk in sin will one day find themselves in hell?

> *They are already under a sentence of condemnation to hell . . . the sentence of the law of God, that eternal and immutable rule of righteousness that God has fixed between him and mankind . . . stands against them; so that they are bound over already to hell… So that every unconverted man properly belongs to hell; that is his place; from thence he is . . . it is the place that justice, and God's word, and the sentence of his unchangeable law assign to him.*

But what about Christians who attend church every Sunday, worshipping and thanking God for the forgiveness of their sins? Could God really be angry with them?

> *Wicked men are now the objects of that very same anger and wrath*
> *of God that is expressed in the torments of hell. . . . . Yes, God is*
> *a great deal more angry with great numbers that are now on earth;*
> *with many that are now in this congregation, who it may be are at*
> *ease, than he is with many of those who are now in the flames of hell.*

So a Christian who continues to walk in sin is just one step from destruction?

> *The wrath of God burns against them, their damnation does not*
> *slumber; the pit is prepared, the fire is made ready, the furnace is*
> *now hot, ready to receive them; the flames do now rage and glow.*
> *The glittering sword is whet, and held over them, and the pit hath*
> *opened its mouth under them"*

We just considered the words of Jesus, from John chapter 8, where he said that everyone who sins is a slave to sin. He then went on to call them *sons of the devil.* Could it be that Christian sinners actually belong to Satan, without knowing it?

> *The devil stands ready to fall upon them . . . They belong to him;*
> *he has their souls in his possession, and under his dominion. The*
> *Scripture represents them as his goods (Luke 11:12). The devils*
> *watch them; they are . . . like greedy hungry lions that see their*
> *prey, and expect to have it, but are for the present kept back. If God*
> *should withdraw his hand, by which they are restrained, they would*
> *in one moment fly upon their poor souls.*

So if God truly loves us, then He must do everything it takes to turn us away from sin and toward obedience to His commands, or it will be our sins which will destroy us?

> *Sin is the ruin and misery of the soul; it is destructive in its nature;*
> *and if God should leave it without restraint, there would need nothing*
> *else to make the soul perfectly miserable. If sin was not restrained,*
> *it would immediately turn the soul into a fiery oven, or a furnace of*
> *fire and brimstone.*

Mr. Edwards, it is likely that most Christians today are actually quite comfortable with their concept of God's love and mercy for sinners and that if they are sincere in their love for Jesus, they will not end up in hell. Is it possible that they are deceiving themselves?

> *Almost every natural man that hears of hell, flatters himself that*
> *he shall escape it; . . . and that his schemes will not fail. They*
> *hear indeed that there are but few saved, and that the greater part*
> *of men that have died heretofore are gone to hell; but each one*

imagines that he lays out matters better for his own escape than others have done.

So I hear you say that false religious beliefs about sin and salvation will cause the demise of many. Is this true?

If we could speak with them (those that have died and gone to hell) and inquire of them, one by one, whether they expected, when alive, and when they used to hear about hell, ever to be the subjects of that misery; we doubtless, should hear one and another reply, "No, I never intended to come here; I had laid out matters otherwise in my mind; I thought I should contrive well for myself: I thought my scheme good… But death came upon me unexpectedly… God's wrath was too quick for me.

I fear, Mr. Edwards, that today's Christians have fallen asleep to the reality of sin and hell. We have become so casual in our understanding of what true conversion is. Please continue.

The use of this awful subject may be for awakening unconverted persons in this congregation… This which has been said is true of all who are unconverted. This is true whether you are aware of it or not. The only thing that keeps you from hell at this very moment is the "mere pleasure of God." If God should withdraw his hand, nothing will keep you from falling into this pit. The unconverted man is a burden upon creation. . . . the creation groans with you; the creation is made subject to the bondage of your corruption, not willingly; the sun does not willingly shine upon you to give you light to serve sin and Satan; the earth does not willingly yield her increase to satisfy your lusts; nor is it willingly a stage for your wickedness to be acted upon; the air does not willingly serve you for breath to maintain the flame of life in your vitals, while you spend your life in the service of God's enemies…

Your words help us see the urgency of the times, Mr. Edwards. We need to hear more.

The bow of God's wrath is bent, and the arrow made ready on the string, and justice bends the arrow at your heart, and strains the bow, and it is nothing but the mere pleasure of God, and that of an angry God, without any promise or obligation at all, that keeps the arrow one moment from being made drunk with your blood. Thus all you that never passed under a great change of heart, by the mighty power of the Spirit of God upon your souls; all you that were never born again, and made new creatures, and raised from being dead in sin, to a state of new, and before altogether unexperienced light and life, are in the hands of an angry God... However unconvinced you may now be of the truth of what you hear, by and by you will be fully convinced of it.

My purpose in presenting your testimony today is to restore the fear of the Lord back into the hearts of God's people. Please give us more thoughts on the wrath of God, and its importance in our understanding of God's great salvation plan.

Consider whose wrath it is: it is the wrath of the infinite God... Jesus understood this wrath when he said, "And I say unto you, my friends, be not afraid of them that kill the body, and after that, have no more that they can do. But I will forewarn you whom you shall fear; fear him, which after he hath killed, hath power to cast into hell; yea, I say unto you, fear him" (Luke 12:4–5).

Our only hope in overcoming our sins, as God desires, is to allow the fear of sinning against God to become our greatest fear in life. Is God's wrath worthy of this much fear?

Consider this, you that are here present, that yet remain in an unregenerate state. That God will execute the fierceness of his anger, implies, that he will inflict wrath without any pity. When God sees your torment to be so vastly disproportioned to your strength, and sees how your poor soul is crushed, and sinks down, as it were, into an infinite gloom: he will have no compassion upon you, he will not . . . in the least lighten his hand; there shall be no moderation or mercy, . . . he will have no regard to your welfare, nor be at all careful lest you should suffer too much in any other sense, than only that you shall not suffer beyond what strict justice requires... As God spoke through the Prophet Ezekiel, "Therefore will I also deal in fury; mine eye shall not spare, neither will I have pity; and though they cry in mine ears with a loud voice, yet I will not hear them"(Ezek. 8:18).

Many Christians today will find these words difficult to accept, Mr. Edwards. Would God really not hear the cries of His own people?

How awful are those words which are the words of the great God.. As spoken through the Prophet Isaiah, "I will tread them in mine anger, and will trample them in my fury, and their blood shall be sprinkled upon my garments, and I will stain all my raiment" (Isaiah 63:3). "God will not only hate you, but he will hold you, in the utmost contempt; no place shall be thought fit for you, but under his feet to be trodden down as the mire of the streets."

Mr. Edwards, it is almost as if God's wrath against sin has become invisible to God's people today. Help us to see it again, so that we have the power to turn away from our sins and live!

> *God hath had it on his heart to show to angels and men, both how excellent his love is, and also how terrible his wrath is... Consider Romans 9:22 which says, "What if God, willing to show his wrath, and to make his power known, endured with much longsuffering the vessels of wrath fitted to destruction?" God will one day "call upon the whole universe to behold that awful majesty and mighty power that is to be seen in it." "And the people shall be as the burnings of lime, as thorns cut up shall they be burnt in the fire. Hear ye that are far off, what I have done; and acknowledge my might. The sinners in Zion are afraid; fearfulness hath surprised the hypocrites . . ." (Isaiah 33:12–14).*

Many Christians today will reject these words, Mr. Edwards, because they are trusting in Jesus to stand with them, in their sins, on the great and dreadful day of the Lord. Many today believe that Jesus will argue their case before God the Father, so that they will be spared this eternal suffering. What are your thoughts?

> *You (those who are wicked) shall be tormented in the presence of the holy angels, **and in the presence of the Lamb**: and when you shall be in this state of suffering, the glorious inhabitants of heaven shall go forth and look on the awful spectacle, that they may see what the wrath and fierceness of the Almighty is; and when they have seen it, they will fall down and adore that great power and majesty... "And it shall come to pass, that from one new moon to another, and from one Sabbath to another, shall all flesh come to worship before me, saith the Lord. And they shall go forth and look upon the carcasses of the men that have transgressed against me; for their worm shall not die, neither shall their fire be quenched, and they shall be an abhorring unto all flesh" (Isaiah 66:23–24) (emphasis added)*

Because we focus primarily on God's love and forgiveness in today's Christianity, rather than on sin and repentance, many today believe that the worst-case scenario for those who will not spend eternity with God will be an eternal state of unconsciousness, or sleep. What is your understanding of this eternal separation from God which we call hell?

> *It would be dreadful to suffer this fierceness and wrath of Almighty God one moment; but you must suffer it to all eternity... Your punishment will indeed be infinite... There is reason to think, that there are many in this congregation now hearing this discourse, that will*

actually be the subjects of this very misery to all eternity. We know not who they are, or in what seats they sit, or what thoughts they now have. It may be they are now at ease, and hear all these things without much disturbance, and are now flattering themselves that they are not the persons, promising themselves that they shall escape. If we knew that there was one person, and but one, in the whole congregation, that was to be subject to this misery, what an awful thing would it be to think of! But, alas! Instead of one, how many is it likely will remember this discourse in hell?

I would like you to conclude this portion of your testimony, Mr. Edwards, with the words that you used to close your great sermon, "Sinners in the Hands of an Angry God."

And now you have an extraordinary opportunity, a day wherein Christ has thrown the door of mercy wide open, and stands calling and crying with a loud voice to poor sinners; a day wherein many are flocking to him, and pressing into the kingdom of God… Therefore, let everyone that is out of Christ, now awake and fly from the wrath to come. The wrath of Almighty God is now undoubtedly hanging over a great part of this congregation: Let everyone fly out of Sodom: Haste and escape for your lives, look not behind you, escape to the mountain, lest you be consumed."

This ends the first segment of testimony from Jonathan Edwards. May this testimony be a spark that ignites the next Great Awakening in America as it did in the First Great Awakening! God's people must again fear God. We must fear His wrath upon all sin, and we must remember that sin only exists within a sinner. Rocks don't sin. Animals don't sin. Trees don't sin. Only moral agents commit sin, and the only moral agents that God created are men and angels. Sin is a decision to disobey God's directions for life, His commands. Sin is not something that happens to us. Sin is, was, and always will be the source of all of our problems. God must punish all sins because He is absolutely righteous and absolutely just. And if we are the sinner, His wrath falls upon us. The unchanging Law tells us that the wages of sin is death. The foundation that is laid for the fear of the Lord in God's people is very clear, so why have we lost this fear of God?

We have lost the fear of the Lord because we have changed the great salvation message of God. We have drifted away from the truth, and we have become indifferent to the salvation message that was delivered by the angels, that was announced by the Lord Jesus, and that was passed on to us by the Apostles. This drift has been happening for many generations since the Great Awakening preachers of our nation's history. We have just heard portions of Jonathan Edwards' message, "Sinners in the Hands of an Angry God," which identified the problem of sin. This sermon, as great as it was in awakening the people to sin and the wrath of God against all sinners, does not set forth the solution to the problem, which is God's great salvation plan! For that we must look to a second sermon delivered by Jonathan Edwards, entitled "The Manner in which the Salvation of the Soul is to be Sought."

The foundational scripture verse for this sermon may surprise many. It is not a passage from any of the New Testament writers, but instead comes from Genesis 6:22, which says, *"Noah did everything just as God commanded him."* In this message, Edwards urges all of us to do the same if we are to be saved from the coming flood of judgment against our sins.

The study of this sermon will lead us to an important understanding about God and about His great salvation plan. While God is omnipotent and omniscient, He does have self-imposed limits as to what He can do. In other words, there are things that God will never do. It is very important to know what these things are. For example, God cannot act in opposition to His own character, which is reflected in His Word. Because God is absolutely righteous and absolutely just, His judgment of man at the time of the great flood also had to be absolutely just and righteous. It is critically important in the understanding this message of Jonathan Edwards we are about to hear to acknowledge that justice would not allow God to punish man for his sins unless God had first made it possible for man to actually be righteous.

This point needs to be stated again. If actual righteousness is not possible for man, then God would be unjust in punishing man for his wickedness. This is true because it is God who created man, and it is God who has determined what is possible for man. It is easy to presume that God, in His anger, could just wipe out all of mankind and start over. But this is not true! At the time of the great flood, God had to find a righteous man on the earth, or He could not bring judgment upon the earth. This is because without at least one righteous man, wicked men could have claimed that actual righteousness was not possible. If there were no righteous men, then wicked men would have had a valid defense, based upon the circumstantial evidence, that God had not made righteousness possible, and therefore God would be unjust to punish their wickedness.

This understanding opens the door to a greater understanding of the statement made by the writer of Hebrews who wrote;

"By faith Noah, when warned about things not yet seen, in holy fear built an ark to save his family. By his faith he condemned the world and became heir of the righteousness that comes by faith" (Hebrews 11:7).

Again, the challenge for us today is to really listen to the Word of God. What was it that gave Noah the strength to persevere in the building of the ark? It was the fear of the Lord! And why did Noah's faith condemn the world, not save it? Because it took away any defense that the wicked may have had against God's righteous judgment through the great flood. Consider the answers to these two questions as we listen to the testimony of Jonathan Edwards from his great sermon, "The Manner in which the Salvation of the Soul is to be Sought."

The foundation passage from scripture for this message is from Genesis 6:5–9:

> *The Lord saw how great man's wickedness on the earth had become, and that every inclination of the thoughts of his heart was only evil all the time. The Lord was grieved that he had made man on the*

earth, and his heart was filled with pain. So the Lord said, "I will wipe mankind, whom I have created, from the face of the earth, men and animals, and the creatures that move along the ground, and the birds of the air—for I am grieved that I have made them. But Noah found favor in the eyes of the Lord. This is the account of Noah. Noah was a righteous man, blameless among the people of his time, and he walked with God.

Then in Genesis 6:22, we are told, *"Thus did Noah; according to all that God commanded him, so did he."*

This second Jonathan Edwards sermon may be even more important for today's Christians to hear than "Sinners in the Hands of an Angry God" was to the people in 1741. If we listen carefully to the content of this next sermon, our eyes will be opened to the great drift that has taken place in the great salvation message over the past 250 years. Again, it will be wise to study this entire sermon, but its message will be condensed here through a series of questions, with Edward's responses in the form of quotes from this second sermon, "The Manner in which the Salvation of the Soul is to be Sought."

The interview begins:

Mr. Edwards, can you explain why you chose this scripture passage from Genesis as the foundation for a message on salvation?

> *We may observe Noah's obedience. He obeyed God: thus did Noah. And his obedience was thorough and universal: according to all that God commanded him, so did he. He not only began, but he went through his work, which God had commanded him to undertake for his salvation from the flood. To this obedience the apostle refers in Hebrews 11:7, "By faith Noah, being warned of God of things not seen as yet, moved with fear, prepared an ark to the saving of his house." Therefore, we too should be willing to engage in and go through great undertakings, in order to our own salvation.*

In this message, you have established three major premises: (1) There is a work, or business, which man must undertake if he is to be saved; (2) this work, or business, is a great undertaking; and (3) men should be willing to enter into this undertaking, even though it is great, because it is for their salvation, and because it is not impossible. Please begin by explaining the first premise.

> *If we would be saved, we must seek salvation. For although men do not obtain heaven of themselves: they do not go thither (there) accidentally, or without any intention or endeavors of their own... The work we have to do is not an obedience only to some, but to all the commands of God; a compliance with every institution of worship; a*

diligent use of all the appointed means of grace; a doing of all duty towards God and towards man. This must be the one thing they do. They must be ready to part with pleasures and honor, estate and life, and to sell all, that they may successfully accomplish this business. This is the import of taking up the cross, of taking Christ's yoke upon us, and of denying ourselves to follow Christ... Men must not only be diligent in the use of the means of grace, and be anxiously engaged to escape eternal ruin, til they obtain hope and comfort; but afterwards they must persevere in the duties of religion, til the flood comes, the flood of death.

Mr. Edwards, it would appear that you have already gone on to the second premise as well. This *something* which a man must do to be saved is already appearing to be a very great undertaking. Many Christians today will be concerned that you are saying we must earn our salvation through works. Is that what you are saying?

Men are not saved on account of any work of theirs, and yet they are not saved without works. . . . Though it be not needful that we do anything to merit salvation, which Christ hath fully merited for all who believe in him; yet God, for wise and holy ends, hath appointed, that we should come to final salvation in no other way, but that of good works done by us. ... So God hath appointed that man should not be saved without this undertaking and doing this work of which I have been speaking; and therefore we are commanded to work out our own salvation with fear and trembling (Phil. 2:12).

This makes sense, Mr. Edwards. Please move to your second premise. Just how great of an undertaking is our salvation?

Man was made for business and not idleness and the main business for which he was made, was that of religion. Man's business brings glory to God! God gave man mental and physical ability to do things, not to be idle. Why would God's plan of salvation reward idleness? God's plan of salvation thus promotes the end of stirring up in man to use his facilities and talents for God's purpose. This is the wisdom of God!

Again, this seems to make much sense. Why would God's plan of salvation be to simply persuade people to say a one-time prayer and then go to church each Sunday? This would not serve God's redemptive purpose for creation. Please continue.

It becomes the wisdom of God so to order it, that things of great value and importance should not be obtained without great labor and diligence. . . . If great things were in common easily obtained, it would have a tendency to cause men to slight and undervalue them. Men commonly despise those things which are cheap, and which are obtained without difficulty.

This too makes sense. It would not make sense that our salvation would be gained without much effort. Salvation in today's Christianity is greatly undervalued due to the teaching that it is obtained by simply saying a one-time prayer. So you are clearly saying that salvation is more than a prayer.

It is a business of great labor and care. There are many commands to be obeyed, many duties to be done, duties to God, duties to our neighbor, and duties to ourselves. There is much opposition in the way of these duties from without... We must battle against the things of this world which tempt and hinder us... There is a great opposition from within . . .We must battle our own emotions, will and deceitful heart...

It is a constant business... This is a business which must be followed every day... We must deny ourselves and pick up our cross daily. There is no relaxation or vacation from this business. If we relax from time to time we lose everything...

It is an undertaking of great expense... We must, therein sell all; we must follow this business at the expense of our substance, of our credit among men, the good will of our neighbors, at the expense of all our earthly friends, and even at the expense of life itself...

*Sometimes we must wait a long time before we obtain comfort in this business. God may actually 'hide His face' from us for a time. It may seem at times that we actually are moving backward rather than forward **in the business of overcoming sin**. And we may have to pass through times of despair before we obtain some saving comfort.* (emphasis added)

This is a critical observation. Overcoming sin is never easy to do, but God did not say it would be easy. Please go on.

Because this business is so great, it requires much instruction, consideration, and counsel... There is no business wherein men stand in need of counsel more than in this... There are many more wrong ways to do this work, than there are right ways.

This could be the reason that so many Christian's today don't see the need for continuing education in our churches. If we feel that we have our salvation in our pocket, then the rest is just extra credit for those who desire it. What you are saying is that salvation is not a point in time; it is a lifetime journey.

> *This business never ends till life ends… We cannot rest on the past accomplishments… Past attainments and past success will not excuse us from what remains for the future, nor will they make future constant labor and care unnecessary to our salvation.*

This is precisely what the Prophet Ezekiel warned the people in Ezekiel 33 when he said, "*A righteous man, if he turns from his righteousness and does evil, will not be allowed to live because of his former righteousness.*" This was God's warning to His people! This will upset the *salvation in your pocket* believers today, Mr. Edwards. But I am convinced that your conclusions are correct. Salvation is truly a great endeavor. What about those who plan to wait until tomorrow to make this great commitment?

> *The greater part of men therefore choose to put it off, and keep it at as great a distance as they can. They cannot bear to think of entering immediately on such a hard service, and rather than do it, they will run the risk of eternal damnation by putting it off to an uncertain future opportunity.*

> *Men who neglect this great work, when they are drawing near to death, may cry out and confess their past sins, and they may promise future reformation, but it will prove in vain for them… God hath numbered their days and finished them; and as they have sinned away the days of grace, they must even bear the consequences, and forever lie down in sorrow… The destruction, when it shall come, will be infinitely terrible.*

Mr. Edwards, this view of salvation as a great endeavor will be rejected by many, if not most Christians today. It would seem to be impossible to obtain. Isn't this an impossibly high standard?

> *Though the work which is necessary in order to man's salvation is a great work, **yet it is not impossible.** However difficult it be, yet multitudes (like Noah) have gone through it, and have obtained salvation by the means. It is not a work beyond the faculties of our nature, nor beyond the opportunities which God giveth us. If men will but take warning, and hearken to counsel, if they will but be sincere and in good earnest, be seasonable in their work, take their opportunities, use their advantages be steadfast, and not wavering; they shall not fail. (emphasis added)*

Jesus does teach that nothing is impossible for God. In this message you are brutally honest with those who profess to want salvation. Give us this challenging invitation to salvation.

> *I would have you sit down and count the cost; and if you cannot find*
> *it in your hearts to engage in a great, hard, laborious and expensive*
> *undertaking and to persevere in it to the end of life, pretend not to*
> *be religious. Indulge yourselves in your ease; follow your pleasures;*
> *eat, drink, and be merry; even conclude to go to hell in that way, and*
> *never make any more pretenses of seeking your salvation.*

I would like you to finish your testimony, Mr. Edwards, the way you finished this
great sermon.

> *You have been once more warned today, while the door of the ark*
> *yet stands open. You have, as it were, once again heard the knocks*
> *of the hammer and axe in the building of the ark, to put you in mind*
> *that a flood is approaching. Take heed therefore that you do not still*
> *stop your ears, treat these warnings with a regardless heart, and still*
> *neglect the great work which you have to do lest the flood of wrath*
> *suddenly come upon you, sweep you away, and there be no remedy.*

This ends the testimony of Jonathan Edwards. May his words again spark an awakening in God's people today!

If we have listened carefully to how Jonathan Edwards just described salvation,
we will see the great drift away from God's great salvation plan that has occurred in
the American Christian Church over the past 250 years. While this drift may have
been motivated by a desire to make salvation sound easy so that more people will
be *saved,* we should be reminded of the writing of the Apostle Peter, who warned
about those who come to know the Lord and then later turn back to their sins when
he wrote, *"It would have been better for them not to have known the way of righteousness, than to have known it and then to turn their backs on the sacred command that was passed on to them"* (2 Peter 2:21).

This is the danger of luring people into the Church with an easy salvation message. It is easier to tell people that God has taken away the consequences for our
sins by sending Jesus to die in their place than it is to tell people that to receive this
forgiveness they must repent from their sins. We have allowed a counterfeit salvation to evolve. Counterfeits always contain a great deal of truth. A counterfeit dollar
bill looks good to the untrained eye, and a counterfeit salvation looks good to the
untrained Christian. These are very difficult words to hear, but they are words that,
if received in humility, can spark the next Great Awakening.

In the great salvation plan of God, our salvation is from our sins. In the counterfeit salvation message, our salvation is from the punishment of our sins, even
though we continue to sin. This counterfeit salvation message is widely accepted
because this is what many Christians want the salvation message to be. But if sin
is something we do, a choice we make, then what sense does it make to say we
are saved from our sins even though we continue to sin? If we are saved from sin,
which is disobedience to God's commands, then we must by definition be saved to

obedience to God's commands. This is not complicated. Salvation is not simply from punishment; it is to obedience.

Again, to really understand what salvation from sin is, we must understand what *sin* really is. Sin is not an illness. Sin does not happen to us. Yes, we have a *sin nature,* but that means we have an inclination to disobey God's commands. We are by nature self-centered. This is a necessary element of having free will. Remember that sin is a choice, a decision to disobey God rather than to obey God. We must not broaden the definition of *sin* to include temptation. If it is a sin to be tempted, then it truly is impossible to overcome all sin because we cannot avoid all temptations. But temptation cannot be sin, because Jesus was tempted in all ways, yet he did not sin. Temptation is not sin. Sin is a choice that we make when faced with temptation. Sin occurs when we choose to disobey God's commands.

The counterfeit salvation plan is also the result of expanding the definition of sin to include *sins of omission.* This belief leads people to reject God's great salvation from sin plan because it again leads to the conclusion that overcoming all of our sins is impossible. But if failing to do every good thing that could be done is a sin, then Jesus had to have sinned, because he did not go to every village that he could have gone to, and he did not help every person in every village he visited. Jesus did not heal every person in every town. Yet Jesus did not sin by not doing everything that he possibly could have done. Jesus did do everything that His Father told him to do. And if we do everything that God tells us to do, we are not committing a sin of omission. There were limits as to what Jesus was able to do as the Son of Man, and there are limits to what we are able to do. If God specifically tells us to do something and we do not do it, then we have disobeyed God, and we have sinned. But we must not overbroadly define sin to include the sins of omission, or we will reject the great salvation plan of God.

If we conclude that it is impossible to overcome all of our sins, then we are really blaming God for our sins. God is the One who has determined what is possible for mankind. God created us with abilities and also with limits. To say that God created us without the ability to walk in complete obedience to His Law is actually blaming God for our sins. But if God has made total obedience to His commands possible and we choose not to obey, then sin is our fault. Some may say that we will only have the power to walk in complete obedience to God when we get to heaven. But this would be delayed righteousness, and God would never choose to delay righteousness. We do not honor God by teaching that His plan was to delay righteousness until after we die rather than to empower us to overcome our sins while we are still alive. Delayed righteousness would not serve God's redemptive purpose for His creation.

Yet today, a majority of Christians do not believe that God has made a way for them to overcome all of their sins and to actually walk in complete obedience to His commands at all times. Those who believe that God has made a way for us to overcome all sins are likely to be called *legalistic.* For generations now we have stressed God's love, mercy, and forgiveness but have neglected the concepts of repentance from sins and righteousness through obedience to God's Law. We know that *repentance* and *righteousness* are valid concepts of our Christian faith because we hear Jesus say, "*Repent, for the Kingdom of Heaven is at hand*" and "*Seek first the kingdom of God, and His righteousness*" (Matthew 4:17 and Matthew 6:33). Yet we have drifted away from the meaning of these words. We have come to believe that repentance is a one-time prayer rather than a lifetime walk and that righteousness is a label God gives us rather than an actual state of being. We have come to believe that God's great plan was to save us from the punishment of our sins rather to empower us to turn from our sins and go and sin no more.

This drifting is not new to our generation. This was also the problem of the American Church at the time of the Second Great Awakening in the 1800s. And just as God used Jonathan Edwards as a spark in the First Great Awakening, God used Charles Finney as a spark in the Second Great Awakening. Charles Finney was a highly intelligent and well-trained lawyer who walked in the manifest power of the Holy Spirit. His preaching was controversial within the Church at that time, and it will be controversial to many today. But one thing cannot be denied: history has recorded the transformation of lives that took place when Charles Finney preached. And one of the issues that he preached on was the issue of *salvation from sin* as opposed to *salvation from the punishment of sin.* Today's Church needs to again hear the testimony of Charles Finney.

Before we hear the testimony of Charles Finney, we should again recall the foundational verses from Hebrews 2:1–4, for they have great relevance to Finney's messages:

> So we must listen very carefully then, to the truth we have heard, or we may drift away from it. **The message God delivered through angels has always proved true,** and the people were punished for every act of disobedience and every violation of the Law. What makes us think that we can escape, if we are indifferent to this great salvation, that was announced by the Lord Jesus himself. It was passed on to us by those who heard him speak. And God verified the message through signs, wonders, various miracles, and by giving gifts of the Holy Spirit whenever He chose to do so. (emphasis added)

The testimony of Charles Finney will help us to understand what this message delivered by angels is, and why it is critical to the next Great Awakening. In Matthew 1:21, the angel of the Lord spoke to Joseph, regarding his wife Mary. The angel said to Joseph, "*She will give birth to a son, and you are to give him the name Jesus, because he will save his people from their sins.*" Could this be the message that the writer of Hebrews s referring to? We must listen very carefully to hear what God has spoken through the angels. There is great power in the name of Jesus, and this verse will help us to understand why this is true.

This verse gives us a good opportunity to see how easily we can drift from the truth when we do not listen carefully to God's Word. Most of us would be alarmed if someone intentionally changed God's Word, but sometimes the change is not in the actual words we read but in the way we listen to those words. For example, a counterfeit of this passage would be that the angel said to Joseph, *she will give birth to a son, and you are to give him the name Jesus, because he will save the people from the punishment of their sins.* Can we tell the difference? This second statement is a true statement, but it is a counterfeit of the real message spoken by angels.

Listen now to the testimony of the Second Great Awakening revivalist, Charles Finney. The quotes in this testimony are taken from Finney's sermons "Holiness Essential to Salvation," "Christ Magnifying the Law," "Way to be Holy," and "Jesus, A Savior from Sinning." A foundational verse Finney used for his messages on salvation was none other than Matthew 1:21: "*She will give birth to a son, and you are to give him the name Jesus, because he will save his people from their sins.*" In his message "Holiness Essential to Salvation," Finney makes three points: (1) salvation from sin is the great necessity of man; (2) Jesus has undertaken this work; and (3) many fail of this salvation.

The testimony begins:

Mr. Finney, what do you mean by your first point, that *salvation from sin* is the great necessity of man? Shouldn't this be obvious to most Christians?

> *Salvation consists in being* **saved from sin***; and the reason why many persons are not saved is that they are unwilling to accept salvation on such a condition, they are unwilling to give up their sins; but if they will not be persuaded to be saved from their sins, and become sanctified, if they will not relinquish and renounce their sin, they never can be saved." "Many persons will even pray to God that he will save them, but they really do not desire that for which they ask, they do not mean what they say; to get men to consent to relinquish their sins, is the great difficulty." "God cannot consent to this for man. Jesus cannot do it for man. Man must submit his will by consenting to the relinquishment of his sin. Man must choose this, and* **this choice must be continuous and complete***.* (emphasis added)

Your testimony is accurate Mr. Finney. Christians today do not generally want to be saved from sinning; what they really want is to be saved from the consequence of their sins. Please continue.

> *Man must voluntarily consent to be saved, or Jesus himself cannot possibly save him. Man is a moral agent, and he is addressed by God as such, and therefore, in order to his salvation, he must voluntarily consent to relinquish sin, and have his mind brought into obedience with the law of God... Many are not saved because they seek forgiveness while they do not forsake their sins... Again, many persons fail of this salvation because they are waiting for God to fulfill conditions which it is naturally impossible for Him to fulfill, and*

*which they themselves must fulfill, and which God is endeavoring
to persuade and influence them to fulfill.*

I agree, Mr. Finney. Over 150 years after your preaching, many today believe that salvation is something that God does for us, or even to us, and that all we need to do is say *thank you.* What are your thoughts on this?

*God never requires of us to perform an impossibility, nor does he
accomplish that for us which we can do ourselves. Don't be shocked
at this, for it is truth.*

But many Christians today believe that salvation is really based entirely on the work of the Holy Spirit.

*They pretend that they are waiting for the Holy Spirit to save them
and convert them; now, mark, every moment they wait they are
grieving and resisting the Holy Spirit.*

The Christian culture today is increasingly built on a foundational belief that we are justified only by our faith, and not by what we do. Therefore many Christians today simply consider themselves to be sinners saved by grace, and few Christians even attempt to actually go and sin no more. They believe that this would be justification by works. What are your thoughts?

*While some of the Apostles were still living, many persons came to
regard the gospel as a system of indulgence,—that men were to be
justified in sin rather than be saved from sin: thus they too had an
entirely false view of the gospel of Christ… Now, no man who lives
in sin can be justified, because no man can be pardoned who lives
in any form of iniquity. The Apostle tells you plainly that those who
commit sin are the children of the devil, and while they are living in
sin they cannot enjoy the privileges of the gospel… Men cannot be
Christians unless they are holy.*

This is a very strong statement, Mr. Finney. How can we be a *sinner* at the same time that we are holy? Is there a New Testament standard of holiness that is different from actual and total obedience to God's commands?

*The moral law is as much binding upon Christians as it was upon
those to whom it was first given. Faith without love will never save
man; but let me say, that true faith is always true love. Every man
who breaks the law systematically and designedly, living in violation of its precepts, is a child of the devil, and not of God. **Let
this be thundered in the ears of the Church and the world.***
(emphasis added)

151

Many today believe that we are no longer under the Law, as were God's people in Old Testament times. Is this the *good news* of the gospel message, that we are free from the Law?

> *Now, it is very common for men to overlook this great truth, and fall into the worldly-mindedness and sinful practices of those around them. Again: multitudes are not saved because they regard the gospel as an abrogation of the moral law—a virtual repeal of it. Now, the gospel does not repeal the moral law. What saith the Apostle? "Do we make void the law through faith? God forbid! Yea, we establish the law." Now, it is true that the gospel was designed to set aside the penalty of the law,* **upon all who should be persuaded to come back to its precepts, and yield that love and confidence which the law requires.** *Now, it is frequently the case, if ministers begin to say anything about obedience to the law, the people call out against it as legal preaching! If they are roused up and urged to do that which the law of God requires of them, they tell you they want the gospel. Now, such people know nothing at all of the gospel! They make Christ the minister of sin! They seem to think that Christ came to justify them in their sin, instead of saving them from it.* (emphasis added)

So true repentance must take place before salvation takes place?

> *Justification in sin is a thing impossible! Now, how can a man be pardoned and justified, before he repents and believes! It is impossible! He must be in a state of obedience to the law of God before he can be justified! The fact is, there is a very great mistake among many people on this subject. They think that they must persuade themselves that they are justified, but they are not and never can be, till they forsake sin, and do their duty.*

Your conclusions are consistent with the plain meaning of salvation as being from our sins rather than only from the consequences of our sins. This does appear to be a great mistake that we are making again today. Please continue.

> *Multitudes make this mistake . . . they seek hope, rather than holiness: instead of working out their own salvation, they seek to cherish a hope that they shall be saved. Again, they seek to persuade themselves that they are safe, while they are in a state of condemnation... If they have certain feelings, which lead them to hope that all will be well with them at last, they are perfectly satisfied, and have no desire to be saved from sin.*

This message will not be easy for many of today's Christians to accept, Mr. Finney. Today we focus almost entirely on spreading the *good news* that God has forgiven all of our sins, and that He no longer even sees our sins because they have been covered by the blood of Jesus. The *good news* we celebrate today is that even though we are sinners, we will not be punished for our sins because we are *Christian sinners* who live under God's grace.

> *Why is it (this) good news?... How is it that the good news of the gospel as it strikes them is the good news that will justify rather than sanctify?... Does it not show, when persons lay more stress upon justification than upon sanctification, that they are more afraid of punishment than of sin? If they can but get rid of the penalty, the governmental consequence of sin, they are satisfied. Now, who does not know that the true Christian is more afraid of sin than of punishment? Yes, a great deal more! They abhor sin; and when they ever fall into sin, they are ready to curse themselves; and all the more because Christ is so willing to forgive them. The man in this condition of mind will never look upon the gospel as mere justification. Again:* **whenever the doctrine of justification comes to be more prominent in the church than sanctification, there is something wrong, there is a radical error crept into the church; there is a danger of that church losing all true idea of what the gospel is**. (emphasis added)

This does seem to be true of today's Christianity, Mr. Finney. Our focus has become primarily on forgiveness of sin rather than on repentance from sin. You close this sermon with a warning. Please give us that warning and invitation.

> *. . . let me say to everyone in this house, don't you expect to be forgiven, don't you expect to be pardoned, unless you will consent to be separated from your sins, and have the name of the Lord Jesus Christ written upon your hearts; unless your prayer is, "O Lord, write thy law upon my heart and make me holy"... Receive his name in your forehead and his law in your heart, give yourself up to him, body and soul, and rely upon it, as the Lord liveth, as Jesus liveth, you shall understand what is the salvation of God. Will you do it?*

Mr. Finney, in another message you address the importance of God's moral law in God's salvation plan. Why must we keep God's law in the forefront of the salvation message?

> *The moral law is not founded in the arbitrary will of God, for if it were He would have no rule of conduct, nothing with which to compare His own actions. But every moral agent must have some rule by which to act. Again, He must have no character at all, for character*

implies moral obligation, and moral obligation implies moral law.
Again, unless the law is obligatory on Him, benevolence in Him is
not virtue, for virtue must be compliance with obligation.

Many Christians today believe that we are no longer under the Law because of what
Jesus did for us on the cross. But you seem to be saying that without the Law there
can be no salvation. Please explain this further.

If He could and should abolish the moral law, then we could have
no moral character. We could neither be sinful nor holy . . . Christ
cannot be the end of the law in the sense that He abolishes it...
Jesus, himself, declared, "Do not think that I have come to abolish
the Law or the Prophets; I have not come to abolish them but to
fulfill them. I tell you the truth, until heaven and earth disappear,
not the smallest letter, not the least stroke of a pen, will by any
means disappear from the Law until everything is accomplished."
(Matthew 5:17–18)

Mr. Finney, in your preaching you made a very important observation about a false
understanding of salvation based upon the concept of *imputed righteousness* rather
than on *imparted righteousness*. Many today believe that there will be no consequences for the sins of Christians because Jesus' death on the cross has paid the
penalty for all of our sins, even those from which we do not repent. This is a critical
point for Christians to hear. Please give us your thoughts on the concept of *imputed
righteousness*.

If the penalty is set aside, the law is repealed, for law consists of pre-
cept and penalty... The law never aimed at imputation. This was no
part of its object... The doctrine of imputed righteousness is founded
on the absurd assumption that Christ owed no obedience to the law.
But how can this be? Was he under no obligation to be benevolent?
If not, then his benevolence was not virtue. He certainly was just as
much bound to love God with all his heart, and soul, and strength,
and mind, and his neighbor as Himself, as you are.

We do seem to forget that Jesus was the Son of Man, who was tempted in all ways,
and therefore he was clearly obligated to obey God's law. If he was not the Son of
Man, then he cannot be the standard of righteousness for men and women today.
Why is it that we look for this theoretical imputed righteousness rather than actual
imparted righteousness?

It would seem that the great mass of professed Christians are
looking to Christ to forgive their sins and secure their pardon; but this
is all. They look for no sanctifying influence or agency from Jesus
Christ. In place of this they resort to a notion of Christ's imputed

righteousness. It is remarkable that so many Christians have set-tled down in this notion of an imputed rather than imparted righ-teousness; on the notion that Christ, instead of imparting, imputes righteousness to his people; instead of begetting in them personal holiness, makes over to them the credit of his own holiness, while they are yet unsanctified; instead of making them holy in fact, only accounts them holy in law, while they are really sinful. This is a most strange and singular doctrine indeed. I am well aware it is not sin-gular in the sense of being uncommon or out of fashion; but it surely is most strange in view of either Bible teachings, or the essential nature of things.

My hope, Mr. Finney, is that today's Christians will again hear your call to rely upon the fear of the Lord to give us the power to overcome our sins rather than rely upon a theoretical imputed righteousness to excuse our sins. Please give us a final thought on this.

Imputation is not, and never was, the end or object of the law. The end which it seeks is righteousness or true obedience... Righteousness is obedience to the Law.... Confidence or faith is essential to all hearty obedience to any law.

The purpose of including the testimonies of these two great American revivalists, Jonathan Edwards and Charles Finney, is not to persuade today's Christians to become disciples of these two men. We must be disciples of only Jesus, the Christ, who is our Savior. But just as we can learn from those who learned from Jesus, the Apostles, we can also learn from the teachings of great Christian teachers of the past and of the present. When we listen to the preaching of these two great revival-ists, however, we should be prompted to ask whether their preaching is supported by the Word of God. We need to test their words against the truth of God's Word, not simply against the opinions of other men. Studying the preaching of these two men will also help us to see the great drift away from God's great salvation plan, which has continued to occur over the last 250 years of American Christian history.

Conclusion

The fear of the Lord is the fear of sinning against God. The fear of the Lord is the key to experiencing the next Great Awakening. It is the power unto righteousness, the power to overcome sin and to enter the Kingdom of Heaven. Restoring the fear of the Lord into the hearts of God's people is God's ordained way of empowering us to walk in righteous obedience to God's directions without violating our free will. The fear of the Lord is the beginning of knowledge and wisdom, and it will be the foundation for our times.

God's people have lost an understanding of the fear of the Lord because we have redefined who God is and what His great salvation plan is. We have attempted to change God's Law by taking away the God-ordained consequences of our sins. Without the fear of the Lord in our hearts, overcoming our sins is impossible. All of the great men and women of God's story walked in the fear of the Lord. Even Jesus himself walked in the fear of the Lord, and he delighted in it. We too must again understand the fear of the Lord, and this will happen when we find the knowledge of the true God and of his never changing great salvation plan.

To Lose the Law is a Fatal Flaw

"Blessed is the man who fears the Lord, who finds delight in his commands."
(Psalm 112:1)

The Power unto Righteousness

*"I will give them singleness of heart and action, **so that they will always fear me for their own good and the good of their children after them**. I will make an everlasting covenant with them: I will never stop doing good to them, **and I will inspire them to fear me, so that they will never turn away from me**."* (Jeremiah 32: 39–40) (emphasis added)

*"I have **hidden your word in my heart** that I might not sin against you."* (Psalm 119:11) (emphasis added)

"And I will put my Spirit in you and move you to follow my decrees and be careful to keep my laws." (Ezekiel 36:27)

For many years people across this nation have been praying for a *revival*. This is the theme of many contemporary songs and books, and there is a passage of Scripture that often forms the foundation of the prayers that have been prayed in this regard. We have considered this passage from II Chronicles 7:14 in prior chapters, but this verse deserves a closer examination. These are the words of the Lord, spoken to King Solomon:

> If my people, who are called by my name, humble themselves and
> pray and seek my face and turn from their wicked ways, then will I
> hear from heaven and forgive their sins and heal their land.

This passage forms a solid foundation for our prayers for revival, but simply getting more people to recite this prayer over and over will not be enough to spark the next Great Awakening. What we need to do is really understand and obey what God is telling us in these words. We must again *listen carefully* to what God is saying. This passage is directed at God's own people, not toward the nonbelievers, and the first observation that we need to make is that it is a *conditional promise* God is making with His people. It takes the form of an *"if"* and *"then"* statement. God says *if* His people do these things, *then* He will respond accordingly. God has not yet responded by healing our land, so it is reasonable to conclude that God's people have not yet done what He has told us we must do. We will now examine each of the requirements set forth in this conditional promise of God, to see where we may have failed to give God what He requires of us.

The first requirement of God's people is to humble ourselves and pray. We have previously looked at the requirement of humbling ourselves before God. The greatest challenge for today's Christians in this regard will be to humble ourselves by letting go of our traditional beliefs about the nature of God and about what His great salvation plan is if those traditional beliefs are not consistent with the truth of God's Word. This has been the issue that we have been addressing throughout this book, and we will not go into it further here. But we do need to humble ourselves in our understanding of what it means to really *pray* to God. It is easy to presume that we have met the requirement of prayer, but we must be careful not to come to this conclusion too quickly. Prayer is a very personal aspect of our relationship with God, but we need to humble ourselves by rethinking what prayer really is, and maybe even more importantly, what prayer is not!

When most of us pray, we spend the vast majority of our time first telling God what the problem is and then telling Him how we want Him to solve the problem. But when we look at prayer through the lens of who God is, a God who is omniscient, who knows all things, this makes no sense. Obviously an omniscient God knows what our problems are without us telling Him, and He knows how to solve the problem without our advice. But if we don't need to tell God what the problem is, and if we don't need to tell Him how to solve the problem, then what is it that we are to tell Him? Is it possible that prayer is not really about telling God anything? There is nothing wrong with bringing our problems and petitions to God or with telling Him how much we love Him and thank Him for all He has done for us. This is praise to God, and God's Word tells us that God inhabits the praises of His people. But is it possible that we are missing one of the most important aspects of what prayer really is?

In generations past, when parents taught their children to pray, they would often begin by bowing their heads and kneeling down before beginning to speak the prayer. Many did this simply out of tradition because this is the way their parents taught them to pray. We need to rediscover the reason for this posture of prayer. We bow our heads and get down on our knees as a posture of humility before God, and this is a good and wise thing to do. It shows that we honor God. Yet in today's Christian culture the trend is away from taking this kneeling or bowing posture before the Lord. This may be another step of rebellion against *legalism* that has been growing with each generation, but prayer is very much about protocol and taking a humble posture when approaching the true and holy God of the universe. We would be wise to return this posture of prayer as we seek to enter the presence of God with our prayers and petitions.

But this posture of *prayer* is more than physical. We must also rightly align the rest of our lives, in both words and deeds, with God. We should remember that prayer includes the process of rightly aligning our entire lives with God in body, soul, and spirit. When we think of prayer in this way, we can understand and apply passages from our Bible such as I Thessalonians 5:17, which tells us to pray continually. If we think of prayer only as a time of petitioning God for what we need, this passage makes little sense. But if prayer includes the process of rightly aligning our lives with God, we can and must literally pray continually. And if we understand prayer to include rightly aligning our lives with God's directions, then when we pray for another person, what we are really doing is helping that person to rightly align themselves with God as well! Praying is so much more than telling God our problems and pleading for Him to help us. It is rightly aligning our entire lives with God's directions, with His Law.

God then tells His people that we are to seek His face. As we have seen, seeking the face of God is a great undertaking, which cannot be done in a casual manner. Moses once asked God to let him see His glory, and God responded:

> I will cause all my goodness to pass in front of you, and I will proclaim my name, the Lord, in your presence. I will have mercy on whom I will have mercy, and I will have compassion on whom I will have compassion. But," He said, "you cannot see my face, for no one may see me and live." Then the Lord said, "There is a place near me where you may stand on a rock. When my glory passes by, I will put you in a cleft in the rock and cover you with my hand until I have passed by. Then I will remove my hand and you will see my back; but my face must not be seen. (Exodus 33:19–21)

God was pleased that Moses desired to see Him, and God did let Moses get a glimpse of His glory as He passed by. And God does tell us to seek His face in II Chronicles 7:14, so how are we to do this? And why is it important to God that we have a desire to seek the face of God?

Seeking the face of God is more than praise and worship, as good as these may be. Seeking God's face is actually seeking righteousness, which again is perfect obedience to God's Law, His directions for life. Consider the following verse from the Psalms in this regard: *"For the Lord is righteous, He loves justice; upright men will see His face"* (Psalm 11:7) Also consider Psalm 17:15, *"And I, in righteousness, will see your face, when I awake I will be satisfied with seeing your likeness."* As we have seen earlier, to seek the face of God is to seek to know who the true God really is. It is to seek to understand His character, and to know His desires for us and for His creation. It is the very pursuit of God. Seeking the face of God is seeking the knowledge of God.

God then commands His people to turn from their wicked ways. This is God's call to true *repentance* as we have previously addressed. God cannot return to us until we first return to Him. And to return to Him means we must return to following His decrees. There is no repentance without obedience to God's Law. God has made a way for us to repent through the cross, but God cannot repent for us. Jesus cannot repent for us. The Holy Spirit cannot repent for us. Repentance is something each of us must choose to do, and God has given us everything we need to do it.

The next statement in II Chronicles 7:14 is critical to our understanding of what God is asking of us before He will answer our prayers. God says that *if* His people do all of these things, *then* He will hear from heaven . . . Did we listen carefully to what God just said? If we do these things, then He will hear our prayers. So what if we do not do all of these things? Will God still hear our prayers? Would it make sense to conclude that God will hear our prayers regardless of whether we do these things? The answer is *"No!"* God will not even hear our prayers if we do not do the prerequisite things He has told us to do. If God does not hear our prayers, He cannot not answer our prayers.

God is not simply waiting for us to pray more often or even for more people to pray. These are good things, but they are not what God is waiting for. God is waiting for us to learn to really *pray,* which is to rightly align our words and deeds with His desires, with His Word. We have missed this critical relationship between righteousness and prayer. All prayers are not equal, and all prayers are not heard by God! The Apostle James wrote, *"The prayer of a righteous man is powerful and effective"* (James 5:16). If the prayers of a righteous man avail much, then how much do the prayers of a wicked man avail? Does God even hear the prayers of a wicked man?

It is time for us as God's people to humble ourselves and to admit that if we do not rightly align with God as He is commanding us in this verse, then He will not hear our prayers, no matter how sincere they are! The reason God is not responding to our prayers is not a problem with God; it is a problem with us. We do not have to beg God to do what He already desires to do. If we rightly align ourselves with God's directions, then God will hear our prayers, because that is what God has said He will do. If we do not rightly align ourselves with God's directions, then God will not hear our prayers, because that is what God has said. The Apostle John writes in I John 5:14–15, *"This is the confidence we have in approaching God: that if we ask anything in accordance with his will, we know that he hears us. And if we know that he hears us, whatever we ask, then we know that we have what we ask of him."*

It is time to stop trying to get more people to *pray* more prayers and to instead get God's people to actually align themselves, and their prayers, with God's will! Then God will hear our prayers. And the Apostle Paul tells us that we can know the will of God if we stop conforming to the ways of the world. He writes, *"Be not conformed any longer to the patterns of this world, but be transformed by the renewing of your minds. Then you will be able to test and approve what God's will is, His good, pleasing and perfect will"* (Romans 12:2). Conforming to the world is actually *wickedness* in God's eyes, and conforming to His Word, His commands, is *righteousness.* This is why the fervent prayers of a righteous man avail much, while the fervent prayers of a wicked man avails nothing.

The proposition that God does not hear the prayers of all people and that all prayers are not created equal is likely to be offensive to many Christians today, whose traditional belief is that God hears every person's prayer in the same way, whether they are a *sinner* or a *saint.* But this is not what God's Word tells us. The prayers of a righteous man avail much, but the prayers of a wicked man avail nothing. Consider the following passages from Psalms and Proverbs in this regard:

> *"Come and listen, all you who fear God; let me tell you what he has done for me. I cried out to him with my mouth; his praise was on my tongue.* **If I had cherished sin in my heart, the Lord would not have listened***; but God has surely listened and heard my voice in prayer. Praise be to God, who has not rejected my prayer or withheld his love from me!"* (Psalm 66:16–20) (emphasis added)

> **"If anyone turns a deaf ear to the law, even his prayers are detestable."** (Proverbs 28:14) (emphasis added)

> *"The Lord is near to all who call on him,* **to all who call on him in truth***. He fulfills the desires of* **those who fear him***; he hears their cry and saves them."* Psalm 145:18–19) (emphasis added)

For God to hear the prayers of His people and to then heal our land will require God's people to be righteous, to be rightly aligned with God's Law. The question then becomes, How will God's people find this place of righteousness that God requires of us before we receive the power of God in answer to our prayers? We need the power unto righteousness even before we approach God with our petition for revival in our land, but where will we get this power? The answer is by placing God's Law upon our hearts, that we may fear God and obey His commands. Just as God put the Spirit of the fear of the Lord in His Son, Jesus, He will put this same spirit in us to empower us to walk in obedience to His commands. God spoke this truth through the Prophet Ezekiel when He said, *"And I will put my Spirit in you and move you to follow my decrees and be careful to keep my laws"* (Ezekiel 36:27).

There is power in finding delight in God's Law. The blessings of God will come to those who delight in God's Law! Consider the following Psalms in this regard:

> Blessed is the man who does not walk in the counsel of the wicked, or stand in the way of sinners, or sit in the seat of mockers, but his delight is in the Law of the Lord. And on this Law he meditates, day and night, he is like a tree planted by streams of waters, which bears fruit in season, whose leaf does not wither, whatever he does prospers. (Psalm 1:1–3)

> *"Blessed is the man who fears the Lord and finds great delight in His commands."* (Psalm 112:1)

The fear of the Lord is the key to unlocking the door to the next Great Awakening. As we have just seen, it is the point of beginning of knowledge and of wisdom. God's Word tells us that it is the power unto righteousness. How do we restore the fear of the Lord into the hearts of God's people? The answer is not complicated; it happens when we come to know the true God. To know the true God will always result in the restoration of the fear of God, because anyone who knows God will fear God. The standard of righteousness required to be reconciled to the true God will strike fear into our hearts. This standard of righteousness, which reflects God's character, is revealed to us through God's Law. To know God, we must know His Law. Remember that the Law is not an arbitrary set of rules to be followed. The Law is a reflection of the character of God. When we place God's Law into our hearts, we are actually placing His character and nature into our lives! The only way to put the fear of the Lord back into our hearts is to know the true God. And the good news is that when we come know the true God, we will have restored the fear of the Lord back into our hearts!

God emphasized the importance of knowing Him, when He spoke these words through the Prophet, Jeremiah:

> This is what the Lord says, 'Let not the wise man boast in his wisdom. Let not the strong man boast in his strength. Let not the rich man boast in his riches. But let him who boasts, boast in this, that he knows and understands Me. I am the Lord who exercises kindness, righteousness and justice upon the earth. In these I am well pleased.' Thus says the Lord. (Jeremiah 9:23–24)

Jesus emphasized the foundational importance of knowing God in receiving eternal life with God when he said, *"Now this is eternal life: that they may know you, the only true God, and Jesus Christ, whom you have sent"* (John 17:3). To know and understand God, we must know and understand His Law. And not only must we know God's Law, but if we want to walk in God's blessings, then as set forth in the verses above, we must actually delight in God's Law! But is it possible to actually delight in the Law?

If you doubt that loving God's Law is possible, stop here and read Psalm 119 in its entirety. This is the longest chapter in our Bibles, and in every verse the Psalmist proclaims the blessings, joy, and strength that we receive from God's Law! Don't read Psalm 119 just to get through it; read it to really hear what it is saying to us about God's Law. Here are just a few additional verses from the other Psalms with regard to the importance of placing the Law into our hearts so that we can walk in righteousness through the power of the fear of the Lord:

> *The Lord has dealt with me according to my righteousness; according to the cleanness of my hands he has rewarded me. For I have kept the ways of the Lord; I have not done evil by turning from my God. All his laws are before me; I have not turned away from His decrees. I have been blameless before him and have kept myself from sin. (Psalm 18:20–23)*

"The mouth of the righteous man utters wisdom, and his tongue speaks what is just. The law of his God is in his heart; his feet do not slip." (Psalm 37:30–31)

"I desire to do your will, O my God, your law is within my heart." (Psalm 40:8)

"Teach me your way, O Lord, and I will walk in your truth; give me an undivided heart, that I may fear your name." (Psalm 86:11)

"But from everlasting to everlasting the Lord's love is with those who fear him, and his righteousness with their children's children, with those who keep his covenant and remember to obey his precepts." (Psalm 103:17)

Listen again to our foundational verse spoken through the Prophet Jeremiah:

This is what the Lord says, 'Stand at the crossroads, and look. Ask for the ancient paths, ask where the good way is, and walk in it, and you will find rest for your souls. But you said, 'We will not walk in it.' I appointed watchmen over you and said 'Listen to the sound of the trumpet' but you said, 'We will not listen.' Therefore, here O nations, observe O witnesses what will happen to them. Hear O earth, for I am about to bring destruction upon this people, the fruit of their schemes. **Because they have not listened to my words, and have rejected my law.** (Jeremiah 6:16–19) (emphasis added)

We are called to not only humble ourselves and pray, but also to fear God, which is to fear sinning against God more than all other fears in life. This fear of the Lord must be present in the hearts of God's people for us to be blessed by God, as set forth in these Psalms:

"All the ways of the Lord are loving and faithful for those who keep the demands of His covenant." (Psalm 25:10)

"The Lord confides in those who fear him, He makes His covenant known to them." (Psalm 25:14)

"How great is your goodness, which you have stored up for those who fear you . . ." (Psalm 31:19)

"The eyes of the Lord are on all those who fear Him, on those whose hope is in his unfailing love . . ." (Psalm 33:18)

163

> "*The angel of the Lord encamps around those who fear him, and he delivers them.*" "*Fear the Lord, you his saints, for those who fear him lack nothing.*" (Psalm 34: 7 and 9)

> "*Come, my children, listen to me; I will teach you the fear of the Lord.*" (Psalm 34:11)

For those who continue to believe that all of us are destined to remain sinners saved only from the punishment of our sin, not saved from sinning, consider the following words from the Psalms and Proverbs:

> "*To the wicked God says, 'What right have you to recite my laws or take my covenant on your lips?*" You hate my instruction, and cast my words behind you.*" (Psalms 50:16)

> "*God, who is enthroned forever, will hear them and afflict them— men who never change their ways and have no fear of God.*" (Proverbs 55:19)

> *How long will you simple ones love your simple ways? How long will mockers delight in mockery and fools hate knowledge? If you had responded to my rebuke, I would have poured out my heart to you and made my thoughts known to you. But since you rejected me when I called and no one gave heed when I stretched out my hand, since you ignored all my advice and would not accept my rebuke, I in turn will laugh at your disaster; I will mock when calamity over- takes you—when calamity overtakes you like a storm, when disaster sweeps over you like a whirlwind, when distress and trouble over- whelm you.* **Then they will call to me but I will not answer; they will look for me but will not find me. Since they hated knowl- edge and did not choose to fear the Lord, since they would not accept my advice and spurned my rebuke, they will eat the fruit of their ways and be filled with the fruit of their schemes.** (Proverbs 1:22–31) (emphasis added)

To activate the power of II Chronicles 7:14 will require us to humble ourselves by letting go of our traditional beliefs if they are in opposition to God's Word. It will require us to truly *pray* from a posture of righteous alignment with God's Law. It will require us to *seek the face of God* by knowing the true God and His standard of righteousness, which is foundational to his great salvation plan. And finally, we will need to *turn from our wicked ways,* which is true repentance. We must turn from our sins and toward obedience to His commands. Finally, we must remember that *anything less than everything is nothing to God!*

This will not be easy. This will require everything we have. This will take great power, which will come only from the grace of God, which begins with the fear of the

Lord in our hearts. The fear of the Lord is the key to unlocking the door to the next Great Awakening. It is time to place this key in the door. It is time to really discover how to walk in this power unto righteousness all of the days of our lives.

The Truth Will Set You Free From Your Sins

My son, **if you accept my words and store up my commands within you**, turning your ear to wisdom and applying your heart to understanding, and if you call out for insight and cry aloud for understanding, and if you look for it as for silver and search for it as for hidden treasure, **then you will understand the fear of the Lord and find the knowledge of God.** For the Lord gives wisdom and from his mouth come knowledge and understanding. He holds victory in store for the upright, he is a shield to those whose walk is blameless, for he guards the course of the just and protects the way of his faithful ones. Then you will understand what is right and just and fair—every good path. **For wisdom will enter your heart, and knowledge will be pleasant to your soul.** Discretion will protect you, and understanding will guard you. Wisdom will save you from the ways of wicked men, from men whose words are perverse, who leave the straight paths to walk in dark ways, who delight in doing wrong and rejoice in the perverseness of evil whose paths are crooked and who are devious in their ways. (Proverbs 2:1–15) (emphasis added)

What will happen if we restore the love of God's Word back into our lives by writing His Law upon our hearts? The answer to this question will become clear if we learn to see God's Law as His directions for life rather than an arbitrary set of rules through which God manipulates His people. To love the Law is really to restore the fear of the Lord back into our hearts. This is true because to know God's Law is really to know and understand God, because God's Law reflects God's character. To write God's Law on the tablets of our heart is therefore to put God's character into our hearts. In Proverbs we are told, *"My son, do not forget my teachings, but keep my commands in your heart, for they will prolong your life many years and bring you prosperity"* (Proverbs 3:3).

The result of restoring the Law into our hearts is a long and prosperous life! When we restore the Law into our hearts, we restore the fear of sinning against God into our lives, because knowing the Law is not just knowing God's commands; it is also knowing the consequences for disobeying God's commands. When we fear sinning against God more than we fear anything else in life, we become empowered to overcome our sins. And when we overcome the sin in our lives, we begin to walk in the power of righteousness that God originally intended us to walk in! As the Psalmist tells us, *"Blessed is he who fears the Lord, and finds delight in His commands."* (Psalm 112:1)

So let us take this one step at a time and make sure that we understand how to reach this place called *the fear of the Lord,* which God's Word calls the key to the treasure of salvation, wisdom, and knowledge. As God has spoken through His Prophet, Isaiah, this will be the sure foundation for our times! This will be the spark in the next Great Awakening in our land.

While we have addressed the issue of *sin* several times, we need to take this step one more time if we are to restore the fear of the Lord and its power back into our lives. Sin is disobedience to God's commands. Sin is always disobedience to God's Law, to His directions for life. Sin is not something that happens to us. We sin because we choose to sin. Sin is a choice.

We must not confuse *temptation* with sin. It is critically important to make a distinction between sin and temptation. Temptation is not sin. Temptation is the opportunity to sin, an invitation to disobey God. Jesus was tempted in all ways yet he did not sin. Sin is something that we can choose to do when faced with temptation. We do have an inclination to sin because we are by nature self-centered. This is a necessary element of our free will, and the free will of mankind is the second most powerful force in the universe. This is true because it was God's original intent for mankind and for His creation. The fact that we have free will, however, does not in itself make us sinners. It is what we choose to do with our free will that will determine who we are in the eyes of God.

We cannot avoid all temptation. We should do all we can to avoid temptation, but we cannot fully eliminate all temptation from our lives. As long as we have free will, which will be for all of eternity, we will also have temptations. Even after we enter the Kingdom of Heaven we will still have free will. God chose to give man free will as part of His original intent, which was in all ways good, and God is returning us to His original intent. We will always have free will because this is what God desires. But in the Kingdom of Heaven we will have something that has been lost: we will have the power to walk in total righteous obedience to all of God's commands!

But how will this be possible? God is not going to overpower our wills with His Holy Spirit so that we cannot sin against Him. This would take away our free will. So how has God ordained it to be possible to have free will and yet to walk in total and complete obedience to His commands? The answer is that He will write His Law upon our hearts. This is the *new covenant* that God spoke of through the Prophet Jeremiah, who said:

> This is the covenant I will make with the house of Israel after that time," declares the Lord. "**I will put my law in their minds and write it on their hearts**. I will be their God, and they will be my people. No longer will a man teach his neighbor or a man his brother saying, 'Know the Lord,' because **they will all know me**, from the least of them to the greatest," declares the Lord. (Isaiah 31:33–34) (emphasis added)

It is critical to our awakening that we understand and accept that we will have free will for all of eternity in the Kingdom of Heaven. In other words, those who enter the

Kingdom of Heaven will continue have the choice to either obey or disobey God. We are not going to lose this gift of free will. But we will always obey God because we will be walking in the light of truth, the power of God's Word, His Law. We will have God's Law written on our hearts. We will know both God's commands and the consequences of disobeying those commands. We will fear sinning against God more than anything else. We will *understand the fear of the Lord,* and we will have found *the knowledge of God.*

A simple illustration may be helpful here. The people in the Kingdom of Heaven are like a man who is sitting in a room with a red hot stove in the corner. This man has the ability to choose whether or not to go over and press his hand against the hot stove at any time. But he will never choose to do it. He is not a fool, and he does not desire the pain of touching that stove. He knows the truth. He may, for some reason, be tempted to touch the stove, but he has the power to choose wisely. When we enter the Kingdom of Heaven, we will have the power to overcome all temptations and to walk in complete obedience to God's Law! We will walk in the fear of the Lord and in the knowledge of God. And the exciting truth is that God's plan is that we are to enter the Kingdom of Heaven before we die.

When God's Law is written in our hearts and on our minds, something powerful happens to us; we are moved to obey those commands. To understand why this happens we must again remember that the Law is both the commands of God and the consequences for disobedience to these commands. If we think of the Law as just the commands, without the consequences, we will miss the power. As stated earlier, the commands, without the consequences, turn God's Law into suggestions for better living. There is no real power in mere suggestions. There is power in the Law, the commands of God. So when the whole Law is written on our heart and minds, it means that we live in the constant awareness of God's standard of righteousness. This is a life lived in the fear of the Lord because we live with a constant fear of sinning against God.

Some may say that this doesn't sound like a great way to live, in constant fear of sinning against God. But they have not listened carefully to God's word, and they do not understand the joy and blessings of God that come to those who are living in the fear of the Lord, to those who live in complete obedience to His directions for life. We will rejoice in walking in this power over sin. Remember that Jesus lived in this fear of the Lord, and He delighted in it! The Prophet Isaiah foretold the people about Jesus:

> The Spirit of the Lord will rest on him—the Spirit of wisdom and of understanding, the Spirit of counsel and of power, the Spirit of the knowledge and of the fear of the Lord—and he will delight in the fear of the Lord. (Isaiah 11:2–3)

If Jesus delighted in the fear of the Lord, then we should delight in the fear of the Lord as well. And when we understand why the fear of the Lord really is the key to unlocking the treasures of righteousness and therefore also to receiving the blessings of God, we too will forever delight in living in the fear of the Lord!

Fear God or Fear Everything Else

So how does this fear of the Lord really work to empower us to overcome our sins? Most Christians today are not all that interested in fearing the Lord because they have been taught that *fear* is only a negative concept. Our lives today are filled with fear. We fear losing our jobs. We fear not having enough money to retire. We fear not getting a good grade. We fear not winning a ballgame. We fear getting sick. We fear losing the ones we love. We fear failing in our relationships. We fear not getting the pleasures we want out of life. For many, the greatest fear in life is the fear of physical death. We fear so many things, and we don't really have a desire to add fearing God to the list. But what we do not understand is that the reason we fear is because *we are fearfully and wonderfully made.* This is written in Psalm 139:14. God placed this fear in all of us, and for a good reason. We cannot escape fear, but we can make it work for us rather than against us. And we can overcome all other negative fears if we place our fear in the right place: the fear of sinning against God. If we truly fear God, then all other fears will fade away.

Fear is the greatest motivator in our lives. While many of our fears cause us distress, some of our fears are for our own good. For instance, as in the illustration above, we should fear touching a hot stove. We should also fear jumping off a 1,000 foot cliff. We should fear losing all of our money at a casino, or consuming too much alcohol. We should fear breaking our civil laws. These are positive fears, which benefit our lives and our society. But the greatest *positive fear* we can have in our lives is to fear sinning against God. If we do not fear sinning against God we will sin against God. To fear sinning against God is a very good and necessary fear. We need to live in this fear of the Lord by restoring God's Law into our hearts so that we can overcome our sins. The Psalmist understood the power of this fear when he prayed, "*I have hidden your word in my heart so that I may not sin against You.*" (Psalm 119:11)

Learning to fear God is not a new concept. In what many Biblical scholars consider the oldest book of the Bible, the book of Job, we are introduced to a man whom God held in high regard, Job. In the very beginning of this story, we are told, "*In the land of Uz there lived a man whose name was Job. This man was blameless and upright; he feared God and shunned evil.*" This description of Job was repeated by God to Satan after God had allowed Satan to test Job's faith and his fear of the Lord. "*Then the Lord said to Satan, "Have you considered my servant Job? There is no one on earth like him; he is blameless and upright, a man who fears God and shuns evil. And he still maintains his integrity, though you incited me against him to ruin him without any reason*" (Job 2:3). God reveals the source of Job's power to walk in righteousness in this passage of Scripture. Job is a blameless and upright man because He fears God and shuns evil. If Job did not fear God, he could not shun evil.

Recall again how God delivered His Law to the people and then spoke these words through His servant Moses. God delivered the Law to the people through the sound of His own voice so that the people would fear Him and therefore be empowered to obey His commands:

168

> When the people saw the thunder and lightning and heard the trumpet and saw the mountain in smoke, **they trembled with fear.** They stayed at a distance and said to Moses, "Speak to us yourself and we will listen. But do not have God speak to us or we will die." Moses said to the people, "Do not be afraid. **God has come to test you, so that the fear of God will be with you to keep you from sinning.** (Exodus 20:20) (emphasis added)

Did we listen carefully to what God said to His people? Why was God testing His people? It was to determine whether the people feared Him. And why was it so important that the people feared God? Because the fear of God would keep them from sinning! God's Word could not speak this truth any more clearly. But we have come to a point in time when most Christians do not have ears to hear what God is saying. God has not changed. God's plan for His people has not changed. The only thing that has changed is God's people. Today's Christians need to fear God no less than God's people at the time of Moses. We need to fear God so that we can walk in obedience to His directions for life!

Recall again the words of King Solomon, who had been given the gift of incomparable wisdom from God. After considering all of the power, pleasures, and the possessions he had experienced in his life, blessings beyond anything we can imagine today, Solomon came to this final conclusion:

> *"Now all has been heard; here is the conclusion of the matter: Fear God and keep His commandments, for this is the whole duty of man."* (Ecclesiastes 12:13)

Solomon understood this connection between the fear of God and the power to walk in obedience to God's commands. Solomon would have technically been correct if he had simply concluded that the whole duty of man is to obey God's commands. Obedience is righteousness, and there is nothing more than could be expected of man than to walk in righteous obedience to God. But Solomon, in his God given wisdom, concluded, *fear God and obey His commands,* because he knew that if we do not fear God, we cannot keep His commands. Without the power that comes from fearing God, from the fear of sinning against God, Solomon knew that we would eventually fall into sin.

There is a practical application of this relationship between fearing God and overcoming sin that we can receive, and more importantly, that we can apply in our day-to-day lives. It again begins with the understanding that every sin we commit is the result of a decision we make. We sin because we choose to sin. Sin does not happen to us. We do not sin by mistake; we sin because we decide to disobey God rather than obey God. And at the very core of every decision we make is the concept of *fear.* We may not think of our decisions this way, but fear governs every decision we make, and this is a God-established principle of life. At the very core of our souls is this God-ordained truth: we are fearfully and wonderfully made, and we make every decision in our lives based upon what we fear most.

To illustrate this relationship between *fear* and every decision we make, consider a practical example. Let us presume that we are faced with a temptation to do something we know is wrong. For example, we discover a $100 bill on a park bench. We are then faced with a temptation to simply pick it up and walk away. The reason that we would choose to take the $100 bill is that we *fear* not getting the pleasure of possessing it. We fear walking away without it. If there are no other competing fears, we will take the item even though it is not ours. But there are other fears that should come into play. We may fear being seen taking the item, and then accused of stealing it. We may fear the embarrassment that this will cause us. We may even fear being charged with the crime of theft. If any of these fears are greater than the fear of not getting the pleasure of taking the $100 bill, then we will choose not to take it. But if the fear of not getting the pleasure of taking possession of the $100 is greater than the fear of the consequences for taking the item, then we will put it in our pocket and walk away. Our actions will be governed by our greatest fear!

Another example of this truth would be a man who faces the temptation of looking at a pornographic image on the Internet. The fear that compels the man to click on the button and look at the image is the fear of not getting the pleasure of viewing the image. To overcome this temptation, there must be a greater fear in the man as a consequence of looking at the image. If there is no greater fear in this man of the consequences of looking at the image, he will choose to click the button. If the man does not have a fear that anyone will ever know that he looked at the image, then the fear of the consequences of looking at the image may not be strong enough to stop him. But if the man knows the true God, and if he knows that to look at the image would be a sin against this God, and if He knows that God's eyes are always upon him, then this man should have enough fear to overcome the temptation. This, however, presumes that the man also understands that the wages of sin is death. If he believes this truth, he will not look at the pornographic image because his fear of not getting the temporary pleasure of viewing the image is greatly overpowered by his fear of sinning against God!

But if the man in the above illustration is a typical Christian in today's culture, the fear of God has been removed from his heart. His fear of sinning against God has been lost due to his belief that God loves him just the way he is. Today's typical Christian believes that he is just a sinner saved by grace, or even that God no longer sees his sins because they are covered by the blood of Jesus. He knows that to look at the pornographic image is clearly a sin, but he believes that he is a *Christian sinner* who will not be punished for his sins. There is no longer a belief in this Christian sinner that the wages of sin is death. Instead, he believes that the wages of sin, because he is a Christian sinner, is no longer death, it is eternal life. After he looks at the pornographic image, this man simply plans to confess his sin and then to thank God for loving him so much that he has been forgiven for this sin. This man will continue on with his life trying to overcome his sins in his own strength, and without the fear of the Lord in His heart. And this man will fail!

This man knows that God does not want him to sin, and he also knows that he will probably feel guilty after he has looked at the image, but these fears are not as strong as his fear of not getting the pleasure of looking at the pornographic picture.

170

This man will sin, and according to Jesus' words in John 8:31–35, he will fall into the category of '*everyone who sins*' and he will not enter the Kingdom of Heaven. This man's ignorance of the truth will not save him from eternal destruction. The only power that would have saved this man from his sin would have been the true fear of the Lord in His heart and mind. Tragically, this fear of the Lord has been lost due to his belief in a *new salvation* plan of God, a salvation plan void of true repentance and without the power of the fear of the Lord.

The fear of the Lord acts as a filter in our soul. Every decision we make is processed through this filter. If we have God's Law written on our hearts and we understand the consequences of our sin is separation from God, which is death, then we have the power within us to overcome all sin. When we fear sinning against God more than we fear not receiving the temporary pleasure we may find in our sins, then we will have the true grace of God dwelling within us. We will have the power to walk on the *ancient path* that leads us into the Kingdom of Heaven.

The fear of the Lord is the key to entering the Kingdom of Heaven because only the righteous will enter this Kingdom. The Kingdom of Heaven is a place where the King's commands are obeyed, not disobeyed. This is what a kingdom is, the domain of the king. It is a place where the King's law is always obeyed. As we have seen, the Law and the Prophets and then Jesus and the Apostles all taught that only the righteous, not the wicked, will enter this Kingdom. And the fear of the Lord is the only power unto righteousness. The true grace of God is the power to overcome our sins. The counterfeit grace of God, which eliminates the fear of sinning against God by removing the consequences for sin, will not empower us to walk in righteous obedience to God's directions. This counterfeit grace of God lacks the power to overcome sin. The true grace of God is the power unto righteousness, the power to overcome our sins. The true grace of God begins with the fear of the Lord!

Putting the Key in the Door

We have identified the key to our salvation from sin, which is the fear of the Lord. But we must also put this key into the door. How do we put the fear of the Lord back into our hearts and minds? The answer has been stated many times in the above paragraphs, but it cannot be overemphasized. To restore the fear of the Lord into our hearts and minds, we must first know who the true God is. We must seek the face of God, and then we will know who He really is. If we do this correctly we will discover, as the writer of Hebrews discovered:

> "*Therefore, since we are receiving a kingdom which cannot be shaken, let us be thankful, and so worship God acceptably with reverence and awe, for our God is a consuming fire*" (Hebrews 12:28–29).

This passage references back to the Book of the Law where God revealed a critical truth about Himself when He spoke through Moses: "*For the Lord your God is a consuming fire, a jealous God"* (Deuteronomy 4:24). Is God really a jealous God? The answer is a resounding, "Yes!" He is jealous for the hearts of His people. He will not tolerate any adulterous thoughts or deeds in the ones He loves. He has made a way for us to be holy as He is holy! We are to love and serve Him alone, at all times and forevermore!

To put this key back into the door we must acknowledge that this consuming fire God has not changed. We must come to understand and accept that the great salvation plan of God is a plan to save us from our sins, not to simply save us from the punishment of our sins. If we change the great salvation plan of God to salvation from only the punishment of sins, we will lose the fear of God, and if we lose the fear of God, we lose the power unto righteousness. If we lose the power unto righteousness, we lose the ability to accept God's invitation to salvation, His invitation to cross over the line from death to life. When we lose the power to overcome sin and to be restored to righteous obedience to God's Law, then we lose the power to enter into the Kingdom of Heaven!

Many Christians today may reject the fear of the Lord as the key to their salvation. They may put their confidence instead in the unconditional love, grace, and mercy of God. They may rest their assurance on the statement that perfect love casts out all fear in support of their belief that the real power in their lives is their love for Jesus and God's unconditional love and forgiveness of their sins. Many today have placed their traditional belief in God's unconditional love for sinners as the foundation of their faith, not the fear of the Lord. But what is this perfect love that casts out all fear? Do Christians today really understand the love of God? Most Christians today define *love* as an emotion of pleasure. When we say that we *love* something, we usually mean that it brings us pleasure.

When Christians today say that they love Jesus, what they mean is that they find pleasure in Jesus. But how did Jesus respond to those who professed to love him? Jesus said, "*If you love me, then keep my commandments*" (John 14:15). And who did Jesus say that he and his Father would love? Was it those who simply found the emotion of pleasure in him? No! Listen to what Jesus said about what our love relationship with God is to be. He said, "*Whoever has my commands and obeys them, he is the one who loves me. And whoever loves me will be loved by my Father, and I too will love him, and show myself to him*" (John 14:21). We should find great pleasure in Jesus, but our simple emotion of pleasure is not enough!

How does God define this perfect love? Perfect love does overcome fear, but that is because perfect love, as God has defined it, is called righteousness! Perfect love reflects the nature of God, who is perfect love. But the perfect love of God is not the emotion of pleasure in all things. The perfect love of God finds pleasure in that which is good, and it hates that which is evil. God loves obedience, and God hates disobedience. God loves righteousness, and God hates wickedness. If we are to be reconciled to this true God, then we must also be reconciled to this truth and to the perfect love of God, which is called *righteousness*. To love God is to hear, fear, and obey His commands.

God's wisdom calls out to us in Proverbs 8:13: "*All who fear the Lord will hate evil. That is why I hate all pride, arrogance, corruption and every kind of perverted speech."* If we are wise, we too will love what God loves and hate what God hates. We too will love righteousness, and we will hate evil. And when we truly walk in this righteous obedience to God's Law, as the people who fear God, we will awaken to the dawn of a new day. This is the day spoken of by the Prophet, Malachi: *"But for you who fear my name, the sun of righteousness will rise with healing in its wings"* (Malachi 4:2).

Conclusion

Restoring the whole Law of God, His commands and the consequences for disobedience of those commands, will restore the fear of the Lord into our hearts. This is the God-ordained power unto righteousness that today's Christianity is missing. This righteousness is required of us if our prayers are to be heard by a holy God. God's promise to hear our prayers, to forgive our sins, and to heal our land is conditioned upon this righteousness. Prayer itself includes the process of rightly aligning our entire lives with God's Word, with His commands.

To know God's Law is to know God's character and nature. When we write God's Law upon our hearts, we actually place the character and nature of God within us. This is righteousness, and it begins the process of seeking the face of God and of finding the knowledge of God. When we find the knowledge of God, we find eternal life.

Writing God's Law upon our hearts will give us the knowledge of God, which leads to the fear of the Lord. This is the power to overcome our sins and to enter the Kingdom of Heaven. Sin does not happen to us; sin is a choice that we make. The power to overcome sin comes to us when we fear sinning against God more than we fear anything else. We were fearfully and wonderfully made by God, and we cannot avoid all fear, but we can choose to place our fear in the right place. When we learn to fear sinning against God, then all other fears will be overcome. This is the only way to truly be set free from our sins. When the fear of the Lord is restored to our hearts, it becomes a filter through which all of our decisions are made. When this happens, we are truly set free from our sins, and we are free to walk in righteous obedience to our God.

The love of God is really righteousness. God loves that which is good, and He hates that which is evil. God loves obedience, and God hates sin. As God's people we must love what God loves and hate what God hates. Because God loves us, He must do whatever it takes to turn us away from our sins because they will lead to eternal separation from God, which is death. God's love is grounded in God's Law.

173

God Verified the Message

So we must listen carefully then, to the truth which we have heard, or we may drift away from it. The message God delivered through angels has always proved true, and the people were punished for every violation of the law, and for every act of disobedience. What makes us think that we can escape if we are indifferent to this great salvation, which was announced by the Lord Jesus, himself. It was passed on to us by those who heard him speak and **God verified the message through signs, wonders, various miracles, and by giving gifts of the Holy Spirit whenever He chose to do so**. (Hebrews 2:1–4 NLT) (emphasis added)

As stated earlier, the first and foremost purpose of this book is to give God something to testify to. God is the audience of One to whom this book is written. If there is to be any transformational power in the words of this book, it will be because God is pleased with its content. For His story tells us that God desires to testify on behalf of His sons and daughters. The desire of God's people should be to say *yes* and *amen* to God's Word, to His directions for life. And His story tells us that God desires to then say *yes* and *amen* back to His people in the form of manifesting His power and glory. The great and dreadful day of the Lord will be a day of this great testimony of God, just as was spoken through the Prophet Malachi. The lives of God's people should be directed toward being prepared for this day to come.

To prepare for God's testimony it will be helpful to recall again the Word of the Lord, spoken through the Prophet, Malachi, which closed the Old Testament Scripture, as Jesus and the Apostles referred to it:

Look, I am sending you My Prophet, Elijah, before that great and dreadful of the Lord arrives. His preaching will turn the hearts of the fathers back to their children and the hearts of the children back to their fathers. Otherwise, I will come and strike the land with a curse. (Malachi 4:5–6)

174

This was the last Prophetic Word of the Lord, spoken to His people, as recorded in the Old Testament. After God spoke these words to His people, there would be 400 years of silence. This fact alone should lead us to listen very carefully to these words. Why would God be silent for the next 400 years? Why will God send His Prophet Elijah once again before the great and dreadful day of the Lord arrives? What exactly did Elijah preach the first time he came, and what will his preaching be in the future?

Elijah was one of God's greatest prophets. Yet the Biblical accounts of Elijah's days are not great in number. Elijah comes on the scene rather suddenly, when he is first mentioned in I Kings 17. We are told that he was a Tishbite. Elijah was sent by God at a time when His people had one of their most wicked leaders, King Ahab. God's people had drifted far from God, and God's prophets had been persecuted and killed at the direction of Jezebel, King Ahab's wife. The people had become worshippers of Baal, and the land was filled with at least 850 false prophets. God had used Elijah to get the people's attention by shutting up the heavens so that no rain would fall for three years. During these years of drought, God hid Elijah away from the King and the people, and God miraculously provided for Elijah's needs.

After the drought had accomplished its great and devastating impact upon the land, God sent Elijah back to King Ahab. But before Elijah was ordered to return, he was told by God to go to Sidon, where God had plans for Elijah. Elijah's experience in Sidon prepared him for what God was about to have him do, and this experience will also help prepare us for what we must do if we too are going to experience the next Great Awakening. In Sidon, a widow had been preparing a last meal for herself and her son because they were down to nothing. We are then given a glimpse of the manifest power in which Elijah walked, as God performs great miracles of provision and healing in the widow's life. God uses Elijah's faith and his words to raise the Widow's dead son to life, and the Widow responds to this miraculous sign with words we need to hear. She says:

> "*Now I know that you are a man of God and that the word of the Lord from your mouth is the truth.*" (I Kings 17:24)

God's manifest power upon Elijah's life was His testimony to this widow that Elijah was a true *man of God*. It is interesting to note that the Apostle James, in his closing words, referred to this great Prophet Elijah in a very interesting and challenging way. He said:

> The prayers of a righteous man are powerful and effective. **Elijah was a man just like us**. He prayed earnestly that it would not rain on the land for three and a half years. Again he prayed, and the heavens gave rain, and the earth produced its crops. My brothers, if one of you should wander from the truth and someone should bring him back, remember this: **Whoever turns a sinner from the error of his way will save him from death and cover over a multitude of sins**. (James 5:16–20) (emphasis added)

175

The Apostle James was calling out to the people of his time that *Elijah was a man just like us!* James was calling the people back to the place of original intent that God has for all men and women who choose to believe in His great salvation plan! We need men like Elijah again today! But what we really need is *to be* men like Elijah today. This is not a gender-specific statement. We need women to walk in the faith, the purpose, and the power of Elijah as well! The culture today, including the majority of the Christian culture, is in need of an encounter with the true God. And God has always chosen to work through people who are wholly committed and aligned to His truth and purpose. We need to be the *manifest sons and daughters* of God that the Apostle Paul wrote that the entire creation is waiting for God to reveal. But we can't just wait for God to send these *manifest sons;* instead we need to seek first the kingdom of God and His righteousness so that we can be these manifest sons. What we need is nothing short of another experience like the people of God had on Mount Carmel, as God manifested Himself to the people through His servant, His manifest son Elijah!

Consider this historical account of Elijah as he returned to confront the wicked King Ahab and the people of God who had drifted away into Baal worshipping. This account can be found in I Kings 18:16–39. Neither the King nor the people were happy to see Elijah. The King called Elijah the *troubler of Israel.* It should be noted here that if we walk in the way of Elijah today and choose to carry God's truth back to His people, it is likely that we will find a similar reception. But Elijah said, *"I have not made trouble for Israel . . . But you and your father's family have. You have aban-doned the Lord's commands and have followed the Baals. Now summon the people from all over Israel to meet me on Mount Carmel"* (I Kings 18:18–19).

Elijah then makes a very important statement to the people of Israel. *"Elijah went before the people and said "How long will you waver between two opinions? If the Lord is God, follow him; but if Baal is God, follow him."* This is important because it gives us insight into what had happened to Israel. They had become double-minded, in that they thought they were continuing to follow the true God, but they had added to their worship of God, the worship of false gods, which are Baals. The definition of the word *Baal* includes *"any deity other than the true God"* (Vines Complete Expository Dictionary).

The people had drifted away from the true God, but they didn't realize it. They had become double-minded and did not know it. The same can be said of today's Christians. We too have become double-minded. The substance of our faith has drifted away from the truth through our evolving traditional beliefs about who God is and about what God's great plan of salvation is. We are now guilty of redefining God as we want Him to be, or at least as we think we want Him to be, and we have done the same with His great salvation plan. And because this drift has been gradual, we have not seen it happening. Just as at the time of Elijah, the time has now come for us to choose which God, and which salvation plan we are going to follow and believe! This is the ultimate test that God is bringing upon His people again today.

Elijah had been sent by God to His people to bring them to a crossroads deci-sion. The time had come for the people to choose which God they were going to worship and serve. And mere words would not be enough to awaken the people to repentance. It is important for us to listen carefully to the words of Elijah's invitation to the people to come up to Mount Carmel for this time of decision:

> You have abandoned the Lord's commands and have followed the Baals. Now summon the people from all over Israel to meet me on Mount Carmel. And bring the four hundred and fifty prophets of Baal and the four hundred prophets of Asherah, who eat at Jezebel's table.
>
> So Ahab sent word throughout all Israel and assembled the prophets on Mount Carmel. Elijah went before the people and said, "**How long will you waver between two opinions?** If the Lord is God, follow Him; but if Baal is God, follow him."
>
> **But the people said nothing**.
>
> Then Elijah said to them, "I am the only one of the Lord's prophets left, but Baal has four hundred and fifty prophets. Get two bulls for us. Let them choose one for themselves, and let them cut it into pieces and put it on the wood but not set fire to it. I will prepare the other bull and put it on the wood but do not set fire to it. Then you call on the name of your god, and I will call on the name of the Lord. The god who answers by fire—he is God."
>
> Then all the people said, "What you say is good." (I Kings 18:18–24) (emphasis added)

The false prophets of Baal did their best to call upon the power of their false gods, but to no avail. Elijah actually mocks them as they call out to their gods. But Elijah knew the truth. Elijah had faith in the true God. Elijah feared God more than he feared anything else, including what the people would do to him if God did not come through. Elijah prayed:

> O Lord, God of Abraham, Isaac and Israel, let it be known today that you are God in Israel and that I am your servant and have done all these things at your command. Answer me, O Lord, answer me, so these people will know that you, O Lord, are God, and that you are turning their hearts back again. (I Kings 18:36–37)

God honored Elijah's faithful obedience. The fire came down from heaven in a way that we can barely imagine! And when God provided His testimony by fire, there was no room for any more doubt about which God was the true God:

> Then the fire of the Lord fell and burned up the sacrifice, the wood, the stones and the soil, and also licked up the water in the trench.

> When all the people saw this, they fell prostrate and cried, "The Lord—He is God! The Lord—He is God! (I Kings 18:38–39)

We are truly in the need of the days of Elijah again. The time has come for the people of God to again fear the Lord so that the sun of righteousness will rise again, with healing in its wings, just as the Lord spoke through the great Prophet Malachi:

> The Lord almighty says, 'The day of judgment is coming, burning like a furnace. The arrogant and the wicked will be burned up like straw on that day. They will be consumed like a tree roots and all. But for those who fear my name, the sun of righteousness will rise, with healing in its wings, and you will be set free, leaping for joy, like a calf let out to pasture. On the day when I act you will tread upon the wicked as though they were dust under your feet.
>
> Remember to obey the instructions of my servant Moses. All of the Laws and regulations that I gave him on Mount Sinai, for all of Israel.
>
> Look, I am sending you my Prophet, Elijah, before that great and dreadful day of the Lord arrives. His preaching will turn the hearts of the fathers back to their children, and the hearts of the children back to their fathers, otherwise I will come and strike the land with a curse. (Malachi 4, NLT)

Today's generation of Christians is faced with a great test, and it is God who is testing us. We are in the same position as God's people were in during the days of the Prophet, Ezekiel, who was sent by God as a watchman on the wall to warn the people that the sword of judgment is in the hands of the Lord. It is God's judgment against our unrepentant sins which we must fear. The time has come to redirect our fears to the only place that will save us from that which we fear.

Our problem is not with global warming. It is not with economic disaster or the greed of Wall Street. It is not with the epidemics, infirmities, or cancers we face. Our problem is not with Washington politicians or with the *other* political party. It is not the terrorists around the world that we should fear. We should fear only one thing. We should fear the sword of judgment in the hands of an angry God. God's wrath is directed squarely at the unrepentant sins of His own people. Our problem is, was, and always will be the fact that we, God's people, have drifted away from God's Law and toward disobedience, which is sin. All of the great and seemingly unsolvable problems we are facing are really only manifestations of the real problem. The real problem is that we have drifted away from the true God and away from His great plan of salvation, and until we repent and turn back to God on these issues, there will be no escaping the sword of judgment that is coming in the form of all of these other problems we face.

God truly is a faithful and loving God who will give us exactly what we choose, blessings or curses. We have the same choice that God's people have always had.

It is set forth clearly in Scripture, but only to those who choose to seek the face of God. We are no different than God's people were at the time of Josiah and the rediscovery of the Book of the Law. Deuteronomy 28 applies to us just as it applied to God's people at that time. The words spoken through the prophet to King Asa in II Chronicles 15:2–4, now apply to us as well. We too have been for a long time without the true God, without a teaching priest and without the Law. And just like God's people then, it is only the great *distress* that God allows, or even brings against His people, that will cause us to seek the Lord, that He may be found by us. Our only hope is to awaken and turn back to the true God, by again obeying His Word.

Conclusion

Great awakenings require the testimony of God, and God will never give false testimony. If we want to see God manifest His presence in our lives, in the Church, and in the nation, then we must give God something to testify to. That something is called *truth* and *righteousness*. The purpose of this book is to give God something to say "yes" and "amen" to, just as He has done in generations past. The purpose of this book is to speak the truth about God and His great salvation plan. We must turn away from our double-minded ways. We too must choose which God we are going to serve and worship. When we choose wisely, God will testify, and change will happen.

The Next Great Awakening

A Pendulum or a Plumb Line

In previous chapters we have examined the substance of the next Great Awakening, an awakening from the drift that has occurred in our understanding of who God is and what His great salvation plan really is. We have considered Great Awakenings recorded in Scripture, and we have listened to the preaching of two of America's past Great Awakening preachers, Jonathon Edwards and Charles Finney. We have listened to the Law and the Prophets of the Old Testament, to the teachings of Jesus, and to the teachings of the Apostles with regard to God's never-changing standard of righteousness. We have discovered the key to unlocking the treasures of God's blessings, the fear of the Lord, which is the power unto righteousness. We have established a foundation of scriptural truth, upon which the next Great Awakening can take place, but only if we choose to build upon it. As we contemplate this great task set forth before us, it will be wise to recall that, "*Unless the Lord builds the house, its builders labor in vain*" (Psalm 127:1). For it is really God who will accomplish this building project, called the next Great Awakening, through His people.

But is it really possible for America to experience another Great Awakening? At the center of our Bibles, the very middle verse, we find the words of a Psalm 118:8. This is the mathematical center of the Bible, and while some may point out that the chapters and verses in our Bibles are not inspired by God, this verse at the very heart of our Bibles is worthy of our attention: "*It is better to take refuge in the Lord, than to trust in man*" (Psalm 118:8). Another Great Awakening is possible, if we trust in the Word of God rather than in the opinions of man.

As stated earlier, when God speaks, truth comes forth from His mouth. This *truth* is the *Law,* which is the *Word of God.* The Word of God is the plumb line of absolute truth, which forms the only firm foundation upon which we can experience the next Great Awakening. The next Great Awakening will take place as a result of the transition from a culture based upon the traditions of man to a culture based upon the Word of God. When the secular culture is built upon the opinions of men, the law becomes nothing more than a set of rules for manipulation by those in power, and the law functions like a pendulum swinging back and forth from liberal to conservative. The result is eventually either gridlock or tyranny in our civil government. And when the Christian culture is built upon the opinions of men, the law again operates like a pendulum, swinging back and forth from legalism to lawlessness. The result in the Church is eventually a Body of Christ that is divided and powerless to impact the secular culture. But when we humble ourselves by submitting our lives to the Word of God, the Law functions as a plumb line in both the Church and the State, which empowers us to enter the Kingdom of Heaven, a place where God's Law is obeyed and where God's blessings flow.

When we build our culture upon the laws of man, rather than upon the Law of God, the two great institutions of the Church and the State begin to drift toward destruction, which is what God has warned us of in our foundational verse from the Prophet Jeremiah:

This is what the Lord says:

> "**Stand at the crossroads and look;**
> **ask for the ancient paths**,
> ask where the good way is, and walk in it,
> and you will find rest for your souls.
> But you said, 'We will not walk in it.'
> I appointed watchmen over you and said,
> 'Listen, to the sound of the trumpet!'
> But you said, 'We will not listen.'
> Therefore hear, O nations;
> observe O witnesses,
> what will happen to them.
> Hear O earth:
> **I am bringing disaster on this people,**
> **the fruit of their schemes,**
> **because they have not listened to my words**
> **and have rejected my law."** (Jeremiah 6:16–19) (emphasis added)

The disaster of which this verse speaks is one of our own design! God will give us what we choose, the fruit of our own schemes. Disaster comes through our own plans, our own laws. When our civil laws become rules of manipulation by those in power, we live under tyranny. And when our religious doctrines are based upon the opinions of men, not on the Word of God, then the Church becomes fragmented and powerless. This is not new, but it is fatal to any culture, including a Jewish culture and a Christian culture. To live in the liberty God desires us to live, both our civil and religious cultures must be based upon the plumb line of God's truth.

The next Great Awakening will require America to *rediscover, reform, revive, and restore*. First, we must rediscover our heritage, it is our God ordained inheritance which has been established through the lives of the generations that have gone before us. Second, we must reform our government, but this reform is much more than political reform, it is a return to self-government from the hearts of the people. Third, we must revive the Church, for it holds the key to America's moral authority and because Great Awakenings must always begin in the Church. And fourth, we must restore the family, which is God's ordained institution for passing on His blessings from generation to generation. Without these four elements, there can be no Great Awakening in America.

Rediscovering our Heritage

"A nation which does not remember what it was yesterday, does not know what it is today, nor what it is trying to do. We are trying to do a futile thing if we do not know where we have come from, or what we have been about" President Woodrow Wilson (*Role of Pastor's and Christians*, David Barton 3).

There are two books that will be instrumental in laying a solid historical foundation of understanding of our American Heritage. These two books are *The Light and the Glory,* by Peter Marshall and David Manuel, and *Original Intent,* written by David Barton. These two books are likely to be controversial to those who want to deny God's providential hand upon America. But the strength of these two books is not in the opinions of these well-respected authors. It is instead in the well-documented words of the men and women who actually lived our American history. These two books are important because they rely upon original source documentation of the words of our American ancestors themselves. They allow us to come to our own conclusions with regard to the hearts and minds of the generations that have gone before us. It is time for this generation of Americans to rediscover our American heritage by looking directly to the words of our ancestors rather than relying only on contemporary historians or fictional novelists to recreate our nation's history within the framework of their own preconceived beliefs and agendas.

To understand our American heritage we must begin our inquiry at a time long before the Revolutionary War in 1776. We must go back another 284 years, to 1492, when Christopher Columbus first set sail on his famous voyage across the Atlantic Ocean. This is the point of beginning of *The Light and the Glory,* and the question raised in that book was, "Did God have a plan for America?" *The Light and the Glory* is an amazing story in search of the hand of God in the different periods of our nation's beginning. *(Light and Glory 22)* After reading *The Light and the Glory,* which is filled with direct quotations from the people who lived this history themselves, it will become clear that God has always had a plan for America! And while America cannot be considered the *New Israel* from a Biblical sense, because God's Word does not support such a conclusion, there can be no doubt that God's providential hand has been upon America from the time of Columbus through the Revolutionary War.

Today's generation of American Christians needs to listen to the words of the men and women who have given us our American Heritage. To hear how God was speaking to those who have gone before us will help us to hear what this unchanging God is speaking to us today. The first person we should listen to is Christopher Columbus, who believed that God had called him to carry the light of Christ into this new land. We should then introduce ourselves to the many nameless Pilgrims who survived almost inconceivable physical and emotional challenges, and when given the opportunity to return to their homeland, refused that opportunity because they felt that they had been called by God to be stepping stones for future generations. We need to rediscover the army of Puritans who, led by John Winthrop, established the foundational principles of righteousness and obedience that God demands from His people. These principles have formed the cornerstone of American liberty and law. And finally, we need to hear the words of our Founding Fathers, those who were willing to pledge their lives, their liberty, and their fortunes to the purpose of establishing the American Experiment.

Rediscovering our American heritage is beyond the scope of this book and will require effort on the part of those who are willing to be used by God in the next Great Awakening. But it is worthwhile to consider the testimony of just a few of these important people of America's history, beginning with a quote from Christopher Columbus with regard to the call upon His life:

> It was the Lord who put into my mind (I could fell his hand upon me) the fact that it would be possible to sail from here to the Indies. All who heard of my project rejected it with laughter, ridiculing me. There is no question that the inspiration was from the Holy Spirit, because He comforted me with rays of marvelous inspiration from the Holy Scriptures . . .

> I am a most unworthy sinner, but I have cried out to the Lord for grace and mercy, and they have covered me completely. I have found the sweetest consolation since I made it my whole purpose to enjoy His marvelous presence. For the execution of the journey to the Indies, I did not make use of intelligence, mathematics or maps. It is simply the fulfillment of what Isaiah had prophesied . . .

> No one should fear to undertake any task in the name of our Saviour, if it is just and if the intention is purely for His holy service. The working out of all things has been assigned to each person by our Lord, but it all happens according to His sovereign will, even though He gives advice. He lacks nothing that it is in the power of men to give Him. Oh, what a gracious Lord, who desires that people should perform for Him those things for which He holds Himself responsible! Day and night, moment by moment, everyone should express their most devoted gratitude to Him. (Light and Glory 17)

Over the next one hundred years after Columbus, there would be many who would cross the Atlantic Ocean to America. They would come to America for various reasons; some to escape persecution in Europe, others to seek gold, and some for the purpose of carrying the Gospel to a new land. But it would not be until 1620, with the arrival of the Pilgrims, that the Light of the Gospel would for the first time establish a permanent foothold upon the American soil. The Pilgrims were the first group of Christians who lived in accordance with a faithful obedience to God's Word in a sustained manner which was worthy of the providential blessings of God. *The Light and the Glory* makes this observation about the Pilgrims:

> These Pilgrims were a mere handful of Light-bearers, on the edge of a vast and dark continent. But the Light of Jesus Christ was penetrating further into the heart of America. William Bradford (a leader of the Pilgrims) would write with remarkable discernment, "As one small candle may light a thousand, so the light kindled here has shown unto many, yea in some sort to our whole nation . . . We have noted these things so that you might see their worth and not negligently lose what your fathers have obtained with so much hardship. (Light and Glory 144)

Within a decade of this small group of Pilgrims landing the *Mayflower* on America's shores, the true army of light, the Puritans, began to invade the darkness that was America at that time. It is the Puritans, more than any other group of people in American history, who laid the foundation for God's providential blessings upon America. The Puritans, unlike the Pilgrims, did not come to America out of persecution or by necessity. They came to America out of choice. This group of committed Christians believed what Jesus had taught, that God's people are to pray that the Kingdom of Heaven would come to earth. The call of the Puritans was to bring the Kingdom of Heaven to America. "*They actually believed . . . what few people have, before or since: that the Kingdom of God really could be built on earth, in their lifetimes . . . They knew that they were sinners. But like the Pilgrims, they were dedicated to actually living together in obedience to God's laws, under the Lordship of Jesus Christ*" (Light and Glory 145).

The Light and the Glory goes on to conclude, "*The Puritans were the people who, more than any other, made possible America's foundation as a Christian nation. Far from merely fleeing the persecutions of the King and Bishop, they determined to change their society in the only way that could make any lasting difference: by giving it a Christianity that worked*" (Light and Glory 146). After studying the writings of the Puritans, Peter Marshall and David Manuel came to the conclusion that the key word in the lives and success of the Puritans, which empowered them to be used by God in such a mighty way, was the word *covenant*. They conclude, "*. . . it is a word almost never heard in American life today, for it speaks of a commitment to Christ and to one another which is deeper and more demanding than most of us are willing to make. And as a consequence, most of us modern American Christians are of little use to God in the building of His Kingdom. For the building of that Kingdom, as the Puritans demonstrated, requires total commitment*" (Light and Glory 146).

The Light and the Glory dedicates one entire chapter to understanding *the Puritan way.* The Puritans understood God's standard of righteousness in a way that few contemporary Christians do today. They understood that if the blessings of God were not being experienced, the first step that must be taken is to do a self-examination of their lives to see if they are living in obedience to God's commands.

The Puritan faith was in a God who desires to bless the obedience of His people but also in a God who will curse that same people who choose to continue in their sins. "*There is no question that the Puritans took sin seriously—far more seriously than most American Christians today. But they had good reason: they knew that the very success or failure of God's New Israel hung on their willingness to deal strongly with sin—in themselves first, but also in those who had been called with them to build the Kingdom. Indeed, there could be no compromise where the presence of sin was concerned*" (*Light and Glory* 172).

Puritan discipline was strict by today's standards. "*The reason it was strict (and enforced by civil law), was that they all felt that the entire fabric of their covenant life together depended on living in proper order and in joint obedience to the laws of God. Thus when one sinned, it affected them all*" (*Light and Glory* 172). Puritan discipline was directed toward repentance, which they understood was a prerequisite to God's forgiveness (*Light and Glory*, 173). The Puritans believed that if they truly loved one another, then they would do whatever it takes to lead one another toward repentance from their sins. The Puritan way is revealed in the famous words of the Puritan leader, John Winthrop, who when landing upon the shores of America wrote:

> Thus stands the cause between God and us: we are entered into covenant with Him for this work. We have taken out a Commission; the Lord hath given us leave to draw our own articles . . . If the Lord shall please to hear us, and bring us in peace to the place we desire, then hath He ratified this Covenant and sealed our Commission, and will expect a strict performance of the Articles contained in it. But if we shall neglect the observance of these Articles . . . the Lord will surely break out in wrath against us.

> Now the only way to avoid this shipwreck and to provide for our posterity, is to follow the counsel of Micah, to do justly, to love mercy, to walk humbly with our God. For this end, we must be knit together in this work as one man . . . We must hold familiar commerce together in all meekness, gentleness, patience and liberality. We must delight in each other, make one another's condition our own, rejoice together, mourn together, labor and suffer together, always having before our eyes our Commission and Community in this work, as members of the same body. So shall we keep the unity of the Spirit in the bond of peace . . .

> We shall find that the God of Israel is among us, when ten of us shall be able to resist a thousand of our enemies, when He shall make us a praise and glory, that men of succeeding plantation shall say, "The Lord make it like that of New England." For we must consider that we shall be as a City upon a Hill, the eyes of all people are upon us; so that if we shall deal falsely with our God in this work we have undertaken and so cause Him to withdraw His present help

from us, we shall be made a story and a byword through the world.
(Light and Glory, 161–162)

The Puritan's had found the knowledge of God. They understood the fear of the Lord,
which is the fear of sinning against God. This understanding allowed the Puritans
to be empowered by God to accomplish His purpose for them in establishing our
American Heritage.

It was upon this foundation of righteous obedience to God's Word, God's directions for life, that America experienced its first Great Awakening. For just as God's
people, Israel, repeatedly drifted away from God's Law and away from His blessings, the early Americans, including the Puritans, also drifted away from God as they
became complacent in their obedience to His directions for life. This drift was noted
in *The Light and the Glory:*

> One of the greatest mysteries that we faced in our search was the
> question of what finally became of the Puritans. They had seemed
> to be prospering in every way—the hard times were behind them,
> there was plenty of good land and plenty to eat, spacious houses,
> and they were living in peace with the Indians. Spiritually, for the
> most party, they were deeply committed, obedient, and fulfilling
> the terms of the covenant. And God was blessing them beyond all
> measure . . . Then, like a fire slowly dying down, the spiritual light
> began to dim, until, by the beginning of the 1700's, what had been
> a blazing light of the Gospel of Christ had become only a faint glow
> from smoldering embers. What had gone wrong? (209)

The drift occurred because the Puritans began to compromise their covenant with
God. And His story of the American Puritans became much like His story of Israel.
God is faithful, even when His people are not. But God's faithfulness is to His Word,
to His unchanging Law, and to His plan, not to the wants and desires of the people.
The words that God had spoken to King Asa in II Chronicles 15:2–3, would come to
now apply to the American Puritans:

> The Lord is with you, if you are with Him. If you seek Him, He will
> be found by you, but if you forsake Him, He will forsake you. For a
> long time Israel was without the true God, without a priest to teach,
> and without the law.

The Puritan's stopped seeking God with all of their hearts, with all of the souls, and
with all of their strength. And just as God had rewarded the Puritan's obedience with
great blessings, He would punish their disobedience with great curses. And while
the preachers in the pulpits warned the people not to turn God's blessings into idols,
not to forget the source of their blessings, and not to break their covenant with God
to walk in His ways, eventually the people stopped listening. *The Light and the Glory*
makes the following observation:

The ministers could see it coming, and Sunday after Sunday they had warned their congregations with such passage from the Word of God as:

> Take heed lest you forget the Lord your God, by not keeping his commandments and his ordinances and his statutes . . . lest, when you have eaten and are full, and have built goodly houses and live in them and when your herds and flocks multiply, and your silver and gold is multiplied, and all that you have is multiplied, then your heart be lifted up, and you forget the Lord your God . . . Beware lest you say in your heart, "My power and the might of my hand have gotten me this wealth." You shall remember the Lord your God, for it is he who gives you power to get wealth; that he may confirm his covenant which he swore to your fathers, as at this day. And if you forget the Lord your God and go after other gods and serve them and worship them, I solemnly warn you this day that you shall surely perish. (Deuteronomy 8:11–14; 17–19)

And this was exactly what was beginning to happen in God's New Israel, just one generation after the arrival of the first comers. For faith was not something that could be passed on from generation to generation, or imparted by baptism or the partaking of Holy Communion. In order for faith to come to flower, it must be planted in the soil of gratitude. (213)

The Puritan parents were either unable or unwilling to teach the following generations how to walk in this covenant relationship with their God, and with the passing of the original American Puritan generation, the following generations continued to compromise their covenant with God. They even established what was called the "Half-Way Covenant" for those who wanted to continue to be a part of the institution of the Church but did not want to walk in complete obedience to God's directions for life.

This Puritan drift and its devastating consequences are clearly set forth in a poem of Michael Wigglesworth entitled "God's Controversy with New England," which was a favorite in Puritan classrooms:

> Our healthful days are at an end and sicknesses come on
> From year to year, because our hearts away from God are gone.
> New England, where for many years you scarcely heard a cough,
> And where physicians had no work, now find them work enough.
> Our fruitful seasons have been turned of late to barrenness,
> Sometimes through great and parching drought, sometimes through rain's excess.
> Yea now the pastures and corn fields for want of rain do languish;

> The cattle mourn and hearts of men are filled with fear and anguish.
> The clouds are often gathered as if we should have rain;
> But for our great unworthiness are scattered again.
> We pray and fast, and make fair shows, as if we meant to turn;
> But whilst we turn not, God goes on our field and fruits to burn.
> (Light and Glory 221)

When the light is removed, the darkness invades, and this is precisely what happened throughout American history. The latter part of seventeenth century America is an example of this truth. As the light of truth diminished, the manifestations of darkness began to thrive in the form of occultism and witchcraft, which began to flourish in America. But just as we have seen in the Old Testament history of God's people, Israel, where God sent His prophets such as Elijah, Jeremiah, Ezekiel, and Malachi to turn the hearts of the people back to Him, God used great preachers of revival to awaken His people in America.

It began with Jonathan Edwards in 1734, who we have heard from in previous chapters preached a salvation message that was much different than contemporary Christianity preaches. There were several great preachers in this time period, but none were more effective than George Whitefield, who felt called to come to America from England to carry this message of revival to the American Church. George Whitefield did not preach a casual Christianity message. He preached that one must repent from their sins, accept Jesus' atoning death, and then totally commit oneself into God's hands. God gave Whitefield an almost supernaturally powerful voice, with which He called the people into true conversion, rather than membership into any denominational belief. From the courthouse steps in Philadelphia, where the streets were jammed with people intently listening to his every word, he declared:

> *"Father Abraham," cried Whitefield, "whom have you in heaven? Any Episcopalians?"*
> *"No!" Whitefield called out, answering his own query.*
> *"Any Presbyterians?"*
> *"No!"*
> *"Any Independents or Seceders, New Sides or Old Sides, any Methodists?"*
> *"No! No! No!"*
> *"Whom have you there, then, Father Abraham?"*
>
> *"We don't know those names here! All who are here are Christians—believers in Christ, men who have **overcome** by the blood of the Lamb and the word of His testimony."*
>
> *"Oh, is that the case? Then God help me, God help us all, to forget having names and to become **Christians in deed and in truth!**"*
> (*Light and Glory* 248) (emphasis added)

It was the preaching of men such as George Whitefield that brought the Body of Christ together in America. It was this preaching that began to bring about the unity of the people of America into the *one nation under God,* which we were destined to become. And it was this preaching that prepared the hearts and minds of the men who would become the Founding Fathers of the American Revolution.

One young man, named Benjamin Franklin, who was then in his thirties, heard Whitefield preach in Philadelphia and later wrote in his popular *Poor Richard's Almanac,* "*It was wonderful to see the change soon made in the manners of our inhabitants, from being thoughtless or indifferent about religion, it seemed as if all the world were growing religious, so that one could not walk through the town in an evening without hearing psalms sung in different families of every street"* (*Light and Glory* 248). During one period of time, George Whitefield would preach a hundred times in six weeks, riding through the back roads of New England, and this would include preaching up to four times each day, usually for an hour or two per sermon!

The First Great Awakening prepared the American soil for the Revolutionary War and also for the formation of the American experiment of a government for the people, of the people and by the people. Tragically, what had been common knowledge about the faith of our Founding Fathers in generations of the past has been all but lost to today's generation of Americans. It is beyond the scope of this book to correct this problem, but it is this book's intent to inspire those of this generation who desire to be used by God in the next Great Awakening to rediscover the faith of the men and women to whom we owe so much. In addition to *The Light and the Glory,* which introduces us to a few of these Founding Fathers, there are two additional resources that will help establish with certainty that the vast majority of America's Founders were God-fearing men who believed in the inspired truth from the Word of God. While some of their terminology may seem foreign to us today, it is clear that their hearts were turned toward the true God and His unchanging Word.

The first book that will lay this foundation of historical truth is *Christianity and the Constitution,* written by John Eidsmoe. In this scholarly history book, John Eidsmoe addresses the substance of the faith of our most prominent Founding Fathers such as George Washington, James Madison, John Adams, Thomas Jefferson, and Patrick Henry, as well as the faith of lesser known Founding Fathers such as John Witherspoon, Gouverneur Morris, Samuel Adams, Roger Sherman, and several others. This book also reveals the biblically based concepts that formed our Constitution and our current Republic. The second book that will help this generation rediscover our American heritage is *Original Intent,* which was written by one of our generation's most well-respected and qualified national historians, David Barton, the founder of *Wallbuilders,* an organization dedicated to presenting America's forgotten history. Without the decades of laborious work done by men like John Eidsmoe and David Barton it would be very difficult for the average American today to have confidence in the truth that our nation was founded upon Biblical principles.

For the limited purpose of this book, we will begin our brief look at the Founding Fathers with a statement of Benjamin Rush, signer of the Declaration of Independence, who wrote,

> I sat next to John Adams in Congress, and upon my whispering to
> him and asking him if he thought we should succeed in our struggle

with Great Britain, he answered me, **"Yes—if we fear God and repent of our sins."** This anecdote will, I hope, teach my boys that it is not necessary to disbelieve Christianity or to renounce morality in order to arrive at the highest political usefulness or fame. (Original Intent 100) (emphasis added)

As David Barton concludes, with regard to his study of the original intent of the Founding Fathers who participated at that *Congress* at which the above words were spoken, *"The Declaration of Independence was actually a dual declaration: a Declaration of Independence from Britain and a Declaration of Dependence on God"* (*Original Intent* 100).

Several years after the Declaration of Independence had been signed, and after the Revolutionary War had been won, one of our most famous Founding Fathers, Benjamin Franklin, addressed President Washington at the Constitutional Convention:

Mr. President: The small progress we have made after four or five weeks close attendance and continual reasonings with each other— our different sentiments on almost every question, several of the last producing as many noes as ayes is, methinks, a melancholy proof of the imperfection of the human understanding . . . In this situation of this Assembly, groping as it were in the dark to find political truth, and scarce able to distinguish it when presented to us, how has it happened, sir, that we have not hitherto once thought of humbly applying to the Father of lights, to illuminate our understanding? In the beginning of the contest with Great Britain, when we were sensible of danger, we had daily prayer in this room for the Divine protection. Our prayers, sir, were heard, and they were graciously answered. All of us who were engaged in the struggle must have observed frequent instances of a superintending Providence in our favor. To that kind of Providence we owe this happy opportunity of consulting in peace on the means of establishing our future national felicity. And have we now forgotten that powerful Friend: Or do we imagine we no longer need His assistance? **I have lived, sir, a long time, and the longer I live, the more convincing proofs I see of this truth—that God governs in the affairs of men. And if a sparrow cannot fall to the ground without His notice, is it probable that an empire can rise without His aid? We have been assured, sir, in the Sacred Writings, that "except the Lord build the House, they labor in vain that build it." I firmly believe this: and I also believe that without His concurring aid we shall succeed in this political building no better than builders of Babel; we shall be divided by our little partial local interests; our projects will be confounded, and we ourselves shall become**

190

a reproach and byword down to future ages. (Original Intent 110-111) (emphasis added)

What is most striking about this statement by Benjamin Franklin is that of all of the most well-known Founding Fathers, he may be one of the least God-fearing men of the entire group. Yet, when compared to the political leaders of today's culture, this statement would likely be viewed as the statement of a religious fanatic! How far we have drifted.

The Founders and the Rule of Law

The founding fathers of this nation had an understanding of the Rule of Law that has now all but disappeared. Listen to just a few of their statements about what the Law really is, and where it comes from:

> "Human law must rest its authority ultimately upon the authority of that law which is divine . . . Far from being rivals or enemies, religion and law are twin sisters, friends, and mutual assistants. Indeed, these two sciences run into each other." James Wilson, Signer of the Constitution, and US Supreme Court Justice (Original Intent 324)

> "Laws will not have permanence or power without the sanction of religious sentiment—without a firm belief that there is a Power above us that will reward our virtues and punish our vices." House Judiciary Committee, 1854 (Original Intent 325)

> "The law . . . dictated by God Himself is, of course, superior in obligation to any other . . . It is binding over all of the globe, in all countries, and at all times. No human laws are of any validity if contrary to this." Alexander Hamilton, Signer of the Constitution (Original Intent 337)

> "The . . . law established by the Creator . . . extends over the whole globe, is everywhere and at all times binding upon mankind . . . This is the law of God by which he makes his way known to man and is paramount to all human control." Rufus King, Signer of the Constitution (Original Intent 337)

So what exactly is the *Rule of Law?* There are three foundational documents that will help us understand this term. The first document is the Declaration of Independence, which begins with these words:

> We hold these truths to be self-evident, that all men are created equal, endowed by their Creator with certain unalienable rights, among these are life, liberty and the pursuit of happiness. That

> *to secure these rights, governments are instituted among men,*
> *deriving their just powers from the consent of the governed.*

The second document is the United States Constitution, which in its Preamble states,

> We the people of the United States, in order to form a more per-
> fect Union, establish justice, insure domestic tranquility, provide for
> the common defense, promote the general welfare, and secure the
> blessings of liberty to ourselves and to our posterity, do ordain and
> establish this Constitution for the United States of America.

The third document is the Minnesota State Constitution, which in its Preamble is very similar to the preambles of several other state constitutions throughout our nation, and which declares,

> We the people of the State of Minnesota, grateful to God, for our
> civil and religious liberty, and desiring to perpetuate its blessings
> and to secure the same to ourselves and to our posterity, do hereby
> establish and ordain this constitution.

When the Founders penned these words they actually established the rule of law in this state and nation. This Rule of Law has led to the generations of blessings that we have experienced. The Rule of Law looks like this:

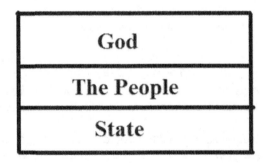

At the top is the true and sovereign God of the universe. This is not just any god; it is the Judeo-Christian God of the Bible. This was the God that our founders knew and served. At the time that these documents were written, America was not a reli-giously pluralistic culture. The principles that formed this nation were Biblical prin-ciples. In a ten-year study of over 15,000 political writings from 1760 through 1805, and after isolating 3,154 quotations and then documenting the original sources of those quotations, it was determined that the vast majority of ideas and philosophies that formed the foundation of our nation came from men such as Montesquieu, Blackstone, Locke, and Hume, all men who were great Christian thinkers. It was also determined that the Bible itself was quoted more than any other source in developing the foundation of our government (*Original Intent* 213–226).

This true God of the Bible was acknowledged by our founders to be the source of both our civil and religious liberty. They understood that God is no less sovereign over the State than He is over the Church. And they acknowledged that if they wanted to receive the blessings that come from this true God, they must acknowledge His sovereignty over all of life and creation. Consider the words of George Washington as he delivered his Inaugural Address to the Congress:

> It would be peculiarly improper to omit, in this first official act, my fervent supplications to that Almighty Being who rules over the universe, who presides in the councils of nations, and whose providential aids can supply every human defect . . . No people can be bound to acknowledge and adore the Invisible Hand which conducts the affairs of men more than those of the United States. Every step by which they have advanced to the character of an independent nation seems to have been distinguished by some token of providential agency . . . We ought to be no less persuaded that the propitious [favorable] smiles of Heaven can never be expected on a nation that disregards the eternal rules of order and right which Heaven itself has ordained. (Original Intent 114)

And for those who doubt George Washington's faith in the true God and the importance of His continuing providential hand of protection upon our nation, these were the opening words of Washington's first proclamation of a national day of thanksgiving on October 3, 1789:

> Whereas, it is the duty of all nations to acknowledge the Providence of Almighty God, to obey his will, to be grateful for his benefits, humbly to implore his protection and favor . . . that we may then unite in most humbly offering our prayers and supplications to the great Lord and Ruler of Nations, and beseech Him to pardon our national and other transgressions, to enable us all, whether in public or private stations, to perform our several and relative duties properly and punctually; to render our national government a blessing to all the people, by constantly being a government of wise, just, and constitutional laws, discreetly and faithfully executed and obeyed . . . to promote the knowledge and practice of true religion and virtue, and the increase of science, among them and us; and, generally, to grant unto all mankind such a degree of temporal prosperity as He alone knows to be best." (Christianity and the Constitution 118)

George Washington was a man who walked in the fear of the Lord!

The True Source of Liberty

The Rule of Law established through our Declaration of Independence and state and federal constitutions acknowledged that the sovereign God has delegated authority to the people. This is what *liberty* really is. Liberty is delegated authority, not sovereignty. Liberty is not absolute freedom to do whatever we want. They understood that the people's authority was limited by God's Word, His desires for us and for all of His creation. This is why the Founding Fathers consistently looked to God's Law as the foundation for our civil laws.

In the American experiment, we the people formed a limited servant government underneath us. Again, the government was under the people, not over the people. The Constitution was the tool that the people used to form a State, a civil government, underneath them as their servant. The government was given certain authority to make laws that would create an atmosphere of liberty for the people to live under. The primary purpose of civil government was to create an environment in which the people would be free live their lives in accordance with the providential purpose of the true God. This is religious liberty. When the Rule of Law is understood in this way, with God on top, then the people, and then a limited servant state, we live in the liberty that God intended for us. This is the *liberty* the founders so strongly desired. But when we change the Rule of Law, by allowing any branch of the State to move above the people, and become our ruler, then we move from an environment of liberty to an environment of *tyranny.*

Liberty is defined by Noah Webster's 1828 American English Dictionary as ". . . *freedom from undue restraints.*" The Founders understood that the *restraints* placed upon the people by the Law of God are not *undue restraints.* They understood that the Law of God is really God's directions for life, which lead to His blessings. And when God blesses His people in a nation, even those who do not believe in God experience a measure of His blessings. When God protects His people from foreign threats, the nonbelievers benefit as well. When God blesses a nation's economy, the nonbelievers also reap the economic rewards. When God sends the rain in season, it falls upon both the righteous and the wicked. Our blessings come from God, and they come to a people who live in liberty, not absolute freedom. Americans today, however, have lost an understanding of the source of our liberty. Our liberty does not come from the government. It does not come from the courts. Our liberty does not even come from the Constitution. Our liberty comes from God, and again as Thomas Jefferson so clearly warned us, we must never lose this understanding:

> *Can the liberties of a nation be thought secure when we have removed their only firm basis, a conviction in the minds of the people that these liberties are the gift of God? That they are not to be violated but with His wrath? I tremble for my country when I reflect that God is just; that His justice cannot sleep forever.* Notes on State of Virginia (Philadelphia: Mathew Justice Carey, 1794), p.237, query XVII)

Our second president of the United States, John Adams, once said, "*Our Constitution was made only for a moral and religious people. It is wholly inadequate for the government of any other*" (*Original Intent* 182). This is a very bold statement, and it is evidence of the reason that our Founders so strongly believed that *religion* and *morality* were the pillars of our civil government and were necessary for the American Experiment to succeed.

Consider just a few more of the Founding Fathers' statements in this regard, remembering that the *religion* they were speaking of is the religion of the true God of the Judeo-Christian faith:

> "*Religion must be considered as the foundation on which the whole structure rests . . . In this age there can be no substitute for Christianity; that, in its general principles, is the great conservative element on which we must rely for the purity and permanence of free institutions.*" (House Judiciary Committee 1854, *Original Intent* 326

> "*Suppose a nation in some distant region should take the Bible for their only law book and every member should regulate his conduct by the precepts there exhibited . . . What a Utopia, what a Paradise would this region be.*" (John Adams, *Original Intent* 162)

> "*True religion affords to government its surest support. Religion and morality are the essential pillars of civil society.*" (George Washington, *Original Intent* 182)

Our founding fathers gave us a *republic* not a *democracy*. Yet most Americans today would be unable to differentiate between these two types of government. In a *pure democracy,* the ultimate source of authority is the feelings of the majority of the people. In a republic, the ultimate source of authority is the law. In a *republic* the people elect men and women to represent them to secure the rule of law. Benjamin Rush, one of our greatest founding fathers, and a signer of the U.S. Constitution once wrote, "*A simple democracy . . . is one of the greatest of evils*" (*Original Intent* 335). And John Adams said in this regard, "*Remember, democracy never lasts long. It soon wastes, exhausts, and murders itself. There never was a democracy yet that did not commit suicide*" (*Original Intent* 335). There is a great difference between these two types of government. A democracy is run by politicians, who govern by looking at polls, while a republic is run by statesmen, who govern by principles of law.

David Barton summarizes this important distinction between a democracy and a republic, through the eyes of our Founding Fathers, in the following statement:

> If the source of law for a democracy is the popular feeling of the people, then what is the source of law for the American republic? According to Founder Noah Webster:

Our citizens should early understand that the genuine source of correct republican principles is the Bible, particularly the New Testament, or the Christian religion.

The transcendent values of the Biblical natural law were the foundation of the American republic. Consider the stability this provides; in our republic, murder will always be a crime, for it is always a crime according to the Word of God. However, in a democracy, if a majority of the people decide that murder is no longer a crime, murder will no longer be a crime.

America's immutable principles of right and wrong were not based on the rapidly fluctuating feelings and emotions of the people but rather on what Montesquieu identified as the "principles that do not change." Benjamin Rush similarly observed:

> Where there is no law, there is no liberty; and nothing deserves the name of law but that which is certain and universal in its operation upon all the members of the community.

In the American republic, the "principles which did not change" and which were "certain and universal in their operation upon all the members of the community" were the principles of Biblical natural law. In fact, so firmly were these principles ensconced in the American republic that early law books taught that government was free to set its own policy only if God had not ruled in an area. (Original Intent 336–337)

Reformation of Government

Self-government, from within the hearts of the people, is the key to the success of the American experiment. As Charles Carroll, signer of the Declaration of Independence once said,

> *Without morals a republic cannot subsist any length of time, they therefore who are decrying the Christian religion whose morality is so sublime and pure . . . are undermining the solid foundation of morals, the best security for the duration of free governments.* (*Original Intent* 168)

One-time Speaker of the House of Representatives, Robert Winthrop, once wrote, *"Men, in a word, must necessarily be controlled either by a power within them or by a power without them; either by the Word of God or by the strong arm of man; either by the Bible or by the bayonet"* (*Original Intent* 173).

This truth was shared by Benjamin Franklin, when he wrote, *"Only a virtuous people are capable of freedom. As nations become corrupt and vicious, they have more need of masters"* (*Original Intent* 321).

The real source of the success of the American Experiment was also seen by those who viewed it from abroad, such as Alexis de Tocqueville, *The Republic of the State of America and Its Political Institutions, Reviewed and Examined,* who after studying American history and culture concluded,

> Upon my arrival in the United States, the religious aspect of the country was the first thing that struck my attention; and the longer I stayed there, the more did I perceive the great political consequences resulting from this state of things, to which I was unaccustomed. In France I had almost always seen the spirit of religion and the spirit of freedom pursuing courses diametrically opposed to each other; but in America I found that they were intimately united, and that they reigned in common over the same country. (Original Intent 121)

The real source of American strength and prosperity has been our ability to rightly align ourselves with God's Law, which as we have seen is true *righteousness.* The great founding father, Patrick Henry, echoed this truth when he proclaimed,

> Righteousness alone can exalt them (America) as a nation. Reader! Whoever thou art, remember this; and in thy sphere practice virtue thyself, and encourage it in others. The great pillars of all government and of social life: I mean virtue, morality, and religion. This is the armor, my friend, and this alone, that renders us invincible. (Original Intent 321)

Revival in the Church

The next necessary element of the next Great Awakening is a revival within the Church. The next Great Awakening must begin with God's own people, His Church. Revival in the Church must precede the reformation of our civil government because the Church is responsible for ensuring that *we the people* are a self-governing people, who fear God more than anything else. Our constitutions are great documents, but they are just pieces of paper, and they were never intended to govern the people. Our constitutions were intended to govern the state. The Church was and is responsible to ensure that the people are self-governing so that we are worthy of the prosperity and liberty that our founding documents have given us. Unless we again become a self-governing people, we do not deserve a small limited servant government, and we are destined to live under the tyranny of an ever-increasing state. The words of wisdom of Robert Winthrop are worth repeating here: *"Men, in a word, must necessarily be controlled either by a power within them or by a power without them; either by the Word of God or by the strong arm of man; either by the Bible or by the bayonet"* (Original Intent 173).

The American Christian Church has led this nation to its greatness of the past by placing the power of self-government in the hearts of the people. But as the Church has drifted away from teaching the Law of God to the people, our culture has been led down the road to lawlessness. It may not seem as though we are becoming lawless, when the number of civil laws we have is skyrocketing out of control. But as the people become less governed by their own hearts, they require more statutory laws to govern their behavior. It is the pastors, not the politicians, who led this nation to its historic greatness, and it is the pastors, not the politicians, who must lead this culture back onto the Road to Righteousness, which is defined by God's Law. But a Church led by the emotions and the self-centered desires of the people, rather than by the Law of God, is destined to become a powerless Church within a nation in decline.

There are three foundational institutions that must be rightly aligned with each other for this nation to be restored to its greatness of the past. These three institutions are (1) the Church, which is responsible to preserve the *faith* and to insure that we remain a self-governing people, (2) the State, which is responsible for providing security to the people from foreign and domestic threats and to hold the sword of punishment for those who are not self-governing, thus maintaining an environment of liberty, and (3) the Family, which is the principle unit of order and government, which is responsible for raising and preparing the next generation. Each of these institutions has a critical role in our society and culture. Each of these three institutions has an area in which it has a sphere of sovereignty. There are certain roles for each of these institutions to play in society. There are some areas in which each of these spheres that will overlap with each other, as can be seen in the diagram below:

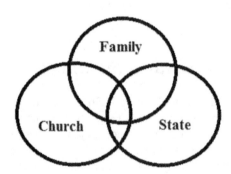

One of the greatest errors made by recent generations of Americans is to lose an understanding of the role of each of these institutions. The area where this has become the most apparent is in the area of the relationship between the Church and the State. We have allowed a false wall of separation to be built between the Church and the State that was never intended by our founding fathers. This *wall of separation* is not in the Constitution. The portion of our United States Constitution that deals with the issue of religious liberty is the First Amendment, which states: *"Congress shall make no law respecting an establishment of religion or prohibiting the free exercise thereof . . ."*

The Founder's purpose for this Amendment was to ensure that the federal government, Congress, would not establish a State church. The Founders did not want Congress to dictate a denominational preference to the people. There was absolutely no original intent on the Founders' part to prohibit the people from freely exercising their religious beliefs in the public arena. The wall was intended to protect the Church from the state, not to protect the State from the church. There was no intent in the writings of the First Amendment to eliminate God from government. Consider the words of United States Supreme Court Justice Joseph Story, often referred to as the *Father of American Jurisprudence* due to his many contributions to American law over the course of his thirty-four years of service on the Supreme Court:

> We are not to attribute this [First Amendment] prohibition of a national religious establishment to an indifference to religion in general, and especially to Christianity (which none could hold in more reverence, than the framers of the Constitution) . . . Probably, at the time of the adoption of the Constitution, and of the Amendment to it now under consideration, the general, if not the universal, sentiment in America was that Christianity ought to receive encouragement from the State . . . An attempt to level all religions would have created universal disapprobation [disapproval] if not universal indignation [anger]. (Original Intent 30)

And consider the following statement with regard to this issue made by the House Judiciary Committee 1853–1854:

> Had the people during the Revolution, had a suspicion of any attempt to war against Christianity, that Revolution would have been strangled in its cradle . . . In this age there can be no substitute for Christianity; that, in its general principles, is the great conservative element on which we must rely for the purity and permanence of free institutions. That was the religion of the founders of the republic, and they expected it to remain the religion of their descendants. (Original Intent 30)

Consider the words of former U.S. Supreme Court Chief Justice, William Rehnquist, who was appointed to the Court in 1971 and served on the Supreme Court until his death in 2005:

> *"The 'wall of separation between church and state' is a metaphor based on bad history, a metaphor which has proved useless as a guide to judging. It should be frankly and explicitly abandoned."*

The true wall of separation intended by our Constitution was the wall that prevents the federal government from establishing a state church. It is a wall that protects the people's right to worship the true God, not a wall that keeps the church from influencing the state, or prohibits God's Word from impacting our public policy. It is the church, not the state, which is to define what is *right* and *wrong*. It is the state which then has the role of ensuring that good behavior is rewarded and bad behavior is punished. History tells us the great dangers of having the state both determine what is good and evil and then to also execute judgment with its sword. A necessary element of the next Great Awakening will be the return of the church to its God-ordained role in our culture of ensuring that the hearts of the people are able to distinguish between right and wrong.

This government reform, returning self-government to the hearts of the people, will by necessity also result in a reformation of politics in this nation. When scriptural truth is again preached from the pulpit across this nation and the people again know the true God and when His great salvation plan is restored, the results will inevitably be a transformed state and federal government. As the great revivalist, Charles Finney, once said,

> The Church must take right ground in regard to politics . . . [T]he time has come that Christians must vote for honest men and take consistent ground in politics . . . Christians have been exceedingly guilty in this matter. But the time has come when they must act differently . . . God cannot sustain this free and blessed country which we love and pray for unless the Church will take right ground . . . It seems sometimes as if the foundation of the nation are becoming rotten, and Christians seem to act as if they think God does not see what they do in politics. But I tell you He does see it, and He will bless or curse this nation according to the course [Christians] take [in politics]. (The Role of Pastors & Christians in Civil Government 36).

Restoring the Family

> Here is another thing you do. You cover the Lord's altar with tears, weeping and groaning because He pays no attention to your offerings, and does not accept them with pleasure. You cry out, 'Why has the Lord abandoned us? I will tell you why. Because, the Lord witnessed the vows you and your wife made to each other on your wedding day, when you were young. But you have been disloyal to her, while she remained faithful companion, the wife of your wedding vows. Didn't the Lord make you one with your wife? And what does He want? Godly offspring from your union, so guard yourself, always remain loyal to the wife of your youth. For I hate divorce, says the Lord God of Israel. It is as cruel as putting on a victim's

bloodstained coat. So guard yourself, always remain loyal to your
wife. (Malachi 2:13–16)

God hates divorce because God's purpose and plan for marriage and family is
so good! The family is God's foundational institution. This institution existed prior to
the fall of mankind, when God ordained that marriage is to be between one man and
one woman for life. And as we have heard spoken through God's Prophet, Malachi,
the primary purpose of this institution of marriage and family is godly children. The
institution of marriage and family is God's ordained instrument of ensuring that His
people would continue to be worthy of His blessings from generation to generation.

Marriage and family are foundational to God's Law, His directions for life. The
Fifth Commandment says,

> *Honor your father and your mother, as the Lord your God has com-
> manded you, so that you may live long and that it may go well with
> you in the land the Lord our God is giving you. (Deuteronomy 5:16)*

Do we understand why honoring our father and mother results in living long, blessed
lives? The Apostle Paul's writings will help us understand the importance of honoring
our parents. He writes,

> Children, obey your parents in the Lord, for this is right. "Honor
> your father and mother"—which is the first commandment with a
> promise—"that it may go well with you and that you may enjoy
> long life on the earth." Fathers, do not exasperate your children;
> instead, bring them up in the training and instruction of the Lord.
> (Ephesians 6:1–4)

Living in a family, as God has defined and designed it, is the training ground for entry
into the Kingdom of Heaven. The family unit teaches us how to live a life of submission and obedience to God's Law, His directions for life. As the Apostle Paul teaches
in Ephesians 5:22–33, husbands are to be the head of the wife as Christ is the head
of the church. This submission of a wife to her husband is to be like the perfect submission that Jesus gave to His Father's commands, and it forms the strength of the
marriage relationship. Husbands are to love their wives as Christ loved the Church,
and gave himself up for it. Wives are to submit to their husbands as to the Lord. And
children are to obey their parents. When the family rightly aligns itself with these
instructions, God's blessings will flow into and through this family unit.

If children do not grow up in a family as set forth above, they will not be prepared to enter the Kingdom of Heaven when they become adults. If a young man
does not learn to obey his earthly father, whom he sees every day, he will have a
very difficult time obeying His heavenly Father whom he has not seen. The proper
structure and alignment of the family is critical to God's great salvation plan, as we
have been focusing on in previous chapters. Jesus confirmed God's original intent
for marriage and family when he spoke the following words:

> But at the beginning of creation God 'made them male and female.' 'For this reason a man will leave his father and mother and be united to his wife, and the two will become one flesh.' So they are no longer two, but one. Therefore what God has joined together, let man not separate . . . Let the little children come to me, and do not hinder them, for the kingdom of God belongs to such as these. I tell you the truth, anyone who will not receive the kingdom of God like a little child will never enter it. (Mark 10:6–9 and 14–15.)

If we are listening carefully to what Jesus is saying, we will understand why we must enter the kingdom of God as little children. We are not to be like little children because God desires that we remain immature and ignorant like a little child. We are to be like little children, as God intends them to be, because little children should be known for their lives of obedience to their parent's instructions, the authority figure over them. If a child is not obedient to his parents, he is not a model for salvation. Christian parenting is not simply about behavior modification to avoid embarrassment in public, Christian parenting is about teaching a child to obey his earthly father and mother, so that he will be prepared to one day obey his heavenly Father.

The family has the responsibility of not only providing a safe and loving environment for children but also for educating the next generation, and preparing them for God's purpose of stewardship and dominion over His creation. It is not a coincidence that the powers of darkness want to destroy the family as God has established it. The proper understanding and protection of the institutions of marriage and family is so foundational to God's original intent that God has used it as an illustration of His relationship with His only begotten Son, Jesus, and also as an illustration of the relationship between Christ and his body, the Church. God's Law has established the institution of marriage and family, and mankind has no authority to change that definition. Without strong families, as God has ordained, there is no hope for a nation.

Today it is the institution of marriage and family that is under the greatest cultural attacks. Is God's definition of marriage as one man and one woman really unconstitutional as so many courts today are concluding? Consider the holding of our United States Supreme Court in *Murphy v. Ramsey* (1885):

> Certainly no legislation can be supposed more wholesome and necessary in the founding of a free, self-governing commonwealth . . . than that which seeks to establish it on the basis of the idea of **the family, as consisting in and springing from the union for life of one man and one woman in the holy estate of matrimony: (the family is) the sure foundation of all that is stable and noble in our civilization; the best guarantee of that reverent morality which is the source of all beneficent progress in social and political improvement**. (emphasis added)

One Nation Under God

In our Pledge of Allegiance to the American Flag, we recite these words: *"I pledge allegiance to the flag of the United States of America, and to the republic for which it stands, one nation under God, indivisible, with liberty and justice for all."*

These are not only important words to recite, but they are words we need to understand. These words, when spoken daily, were intended to remind us of who we are as Americans, and what has made America great in the past. We have been great because we have been one nation under God, and we have been *indivisible* because we have historically acknowledged our Judeo-Christian heritage. We have been great because in the past we have embraced our diversity as a strength, but we have chosen to always move from diversity toward unity. When this nation began to seek diversity rather than seek to bring that diversity into unity, we began a great decline. That is when we left the path of being an indivisible people.

When we seek diversity we get division. Historically we have taught our children that America was a *melting pot* of cultures. But a melting pot does not remain separate and divided; it becomes one. Historically, we accepted those who had come here in search of freedom and opportunity, but we would insist that they must become what we are, Americans. In the past those who came to America did not expect America to change and become something we were never intended to be. Until recently our nation's leaders have viewed America as a *Christian nation.* This is historical truth that was clearly stated by our United States Supreme Court, when after studying over 200 years of American history came to the following conclusion: *"These, and many other matters which might be noticed, add a volume of unofficial declaration to the mass of organic utterances that this is a Christian nation"* (United States Supreme Court in 1892, in the case of *Church of the Holy Trinity v. United States*).

God has greatly blessed America. These blessings have not come without great challenges and tests, but the providential hand of God has been evident through our many struggles as a nation. For many generations America has been the hope of other nations around the world who love liberty and desire justice. But we must never forget that America has been great only because America has been good. And when America ceases to be good, America will no longer be a great nation. May the generations to come continue to sing the great anthem, *"God Bless America."* But the real question for us today is whether America will continue to be worthy of the blessings that we have received from God. If America returns to God, then God will return to America. America can only return to God by restoring His Law as the foundation of our nation, as it was in the beginning.

Conclusion

The next Great Awakening will take place when we understand that the Word of God is a plumb line, not a pendulum. The next Great Awakening will require us to rediscover our heritage because it is our God-ordained inheritance. We must revive the Church, because all awakenings begin with God's people. We must reform our government, which means we must again become a self-governing people who are governed by the fear of God within our hearts. And finally we must restore the family, which is God's foundational institution.

God has providentially had His hand upon America from the time of Columbus through the two Great Awakenings in our nation. America is not the 'New Israel' in a Biblical sense, but God has a purpose for this nation, and our Founding Fathers understood this purpose far better than we do today. We must restore the Rule of Law, which has led to the blessings, prosperity, and liberty that America has enjoyed for generations. We must reject the false doctrine of separation of church and state, which has caused this nation to reject our God-ordained purpose. We must again become a nation that embraces diversity but seeks unity. We can again become one nation under God, indivisible, with liberty and justice for all, but to do this will require the next Great Awakening.

A City on a Hill

"For we must consider that we shall be as a city upon a hill, the eyes of all people are upon us; so that if we shall deal falsely with our God in this work we have undertaken and so cause Him to withdraw His present help from us, we shall be made a story and a byword through the world" (The great Puritan leader, John Winthrop, *Original Intent* 77)

The American Christian Church is indeed at a crossroads. The time is short, but it is not too late for God's people to turn back to God. God has not changed. God's plan has not changed. He is the same God today as He was when He spoke to His people through King Solomon, and said,

> *If my people, who are called by my name, will humble themselves and pray and seek my face and turn from their wicked ways, then will I hear from heaven and will forgive their sin, and will heal their land.* (II Chronicles 7:14)

But God's people must do more than cry out to God; we must use our God-given gift of liberty to choose to turn back to God. This is what God's people did at the time of King Asa, after God spoke these words through His Prophet:

> The Lord will be with you if you are with him. If you seek him, he will be found by you, but if you forsake him, he will forsake you. For a long time Israel was without the true God, without a teaching priest, and without the law, but in their distress they sought the Lord God of Israel and he was found by them. (II Chronicles 15:2–4)

In the first chapter of this book we heard the words of God's watchman on the wall, Ezekiel, warning the people that the sword of judgment was coming against the land. As stated earlier, everything we need to know for the next Great Awakening can be found in these words of warning, but we must have ears to hear them. We will finish with these words once again, in the hope that the contents of this book have opened our ears to God's truth, so that we may take warning and live:

The Word of the Lord came to me, "Son of man, speak to your countrymen, and say to them, **"When I bring the sword against the land**, and the people of the land chose one of their men, and make him their watchman, and **the watchman sees the sword coming against the land and sounds the trumpet to warn the people**. Then if anyone hears the sound of the trumpet and does not take warning, and the sword comes and takes his life. That man's blood will be on his own head. Since he heard the sound of the trumpet and did not take warning, his blood will be on his own head. If he had taken warning he would have saved himself. **But if the watchman sees the sword coming against the land, and does not sound the trumpet to warn the people**, and the sword comes and takes the life of one of the people. That man's life will be taken for his sin, but **I will hold the watchman accountable for his blood**.

Son of man, I have made you a watchman for the house of Israel, so hear the words that I speak, and give them warning from me. If I say to the wicked man, you shall surely die, and you do not speak out to dissuade him from his ways, that man will die for his sins, but I will hold you, son of man, accountable for his blood. But if you warn the wicked man to turn from his sins, and he does not do so, that man will die for his sins, but you son of man will have saved yourself.

Therefore, Son of man, say to the house of Israel, this is what you are saying. **"Our sins and offenses weigh us down, and we are wasting away because of them. How then shall we live?"** Say to them, **"As surely as I live, declares the Sovereign Lord, I take no pleasure in the death of the wicked, but rather that they turn from their ways and live. Turn! Turn from your evil ways!** Why will you die O house of Israel?"

Son of man, say to your countrymen, **"The righteousness of a righteous man will not save him when he disobeys, and the wickedness of a wicked man will not cause him to fall, when he turns from it.** A righteous man, if he turns from his righteousness and does evil, will not be allowed to live because of his former righteousness. If I say to a righteous man, you will be saved, but then he turns from his righteousness and does evil, none of the righteous things he has done will be remembered and he will die for the evil he has done. And if I say to a wicked man, you will surely die, but then he turns from his wickedness and does what is just and right, he gives back what he has taken in pledge for a loan, returns that which he has stolen, **follows the decrees that bring life, and does no evil,** none of the wicked things he has done will be remembered against him, he has done what is just and right and he will surely live.

Yet O house of Jacob you say, "The way of the Lord is not just." But it is their way that is not just. A righteous man, if he turns from his righteousness and does evil, will die for the evil he has done, and a wicked man, if he turns from his wickedness and does what is just and right, will surely live, he will not die. Yet again, O house of Israel, you say, "The way of the Lord is not just!" **But I will judge each one in accordance with his own ways. (**Ezekiel 33:1–20) (emphasis added)

If this book has done nothing but to sound the trumpet of warning that the sword of God's judgment is about to strike this land, it will have served its purpose. This judgment is not coming simply because of the sins of the nonbelievers in our nation. This judgment is coming because God's people, those who profess to be His Church, have drifted away from the true God and away from His truth, as set forth in His great salvation plan. God's people today have lost the Law, through the teaching a new salvation plan. The sword is coming against this land because God's people have attempted to move God's plumb line, which defines good and evil, and the result has been a culture of lawlessness. There is now a famine in the land for the truth of God's Word, His Law. The teaching of this new salvation plan has removed the fear of the Lord from the hearts of the people, thereby leaving them powerless to overcome their sins. The wickedness of the nonbelievers will cause eternal judgment upon them, but their blood will be on the head of today's Christian Church, because it has failed to warn them of this truth. The only way we can avoid this sword is to repent, and the repentance that God is requiring of us is to restore the plumb line, which is God's great salvation message, a salvation from our sins.

His story tells us that there is one more Great Awakening that we should consider before we give in to the temptation of believing that there is no hope for America. This is the vision God gave to His prophet, Ezekiel, in the Valley of Dry Bones. Ezekiel testifies to this Great Awakening in chapter 37 of the book that bears his name:

The hand of the Lord was upon me, and he brought me out by the Spirit of the Lord and sat me in the middle of a valley; it was full of bones. He led me back and forth among them, and I saw a great many bones on the floor of the valley, bones that were very dry. He asked me, "Son of man, can these bones live?"

I said, "O Sovereign Lord, you alone know."

Then he said to me, "Prophesy to these bones and say to them, 'Dry bones, hear the word of the Lord! This is what the Sovereign Lord says to these bones; I will make breath enter you, and you will come to life. Then you will know that I am the Lord.'"

So I prophesied as I was commanded. And as I was prophesying, there was a noise, a rattling sound, and the bones came together,

> bone to bone. I looked, and tendons and flesh appeared on them and skin covered them, but there was no breath in them.
>
> Then he said to me, "Prophesy to the breath; prophesy, son of man, and say to it, 'This is what the Sovereign Lord says: Come from the four winds, O breath, and breathe into these slain, that they may live.'" So I prophesied as he commanded me, and breath entered them; they came to life and stood up on their feet—a vast army. (Ezekiel 37:1–10)

There could not be a greater vision of a Great Awakening than this one given to Ezekiel. God then states the purpose and meaning of this vision:

> Then he said to me: "Son of man, these bones are the whole house of Israel. They say, 'Our bones are dried up and our hope is gone; we are cut off.' Therefore prophesy and say to them; "This is what the Sovereign Lord says: O my people, I will bring you back to the land of Israel. Then you, my people, will know that I am the Lord, when I open your graves and bring you up from them. I will put my Spirit in you and you will live and I will settle you in your own land. Then you will know that I the Lord have spoken, and I have done it, declares the Lord. (Ezekiel 37:11–14)

God's people today have again drifted away from God. The Church itself at times appears to be as lifeless as these dry bones. We have drifted away from His truth, and as a result the darkness appears to be winning the battle for the soul of our nation. But we must never forget the unchanging truth that we, God's people, are the light of the world, if we exercise our free will in obedience to God's commands. We must never forget that no matter how dark the world and the culture have become, the darkness is really just the absence of the light we are to carry. Light is power. Darkness is the absence of power. The source of the light we carry is the Word of God, and there is no other power which can stand against this light. When we carry this light, the darkness must leave. The only way we will lose this battle is if we either fail to carry the light of truth, or if the light we carry has actually become darkness. The world is growing dark only because God's people have stopped carrying the light of truth into the world.

It has been said that the darkest hour is right before the dawn. We are close to the dawn of a new day, if we are willing to repent and turn back to God. But the way back to God is a narrow path. It is an ancient path, and we must seek this path with all of our hearts, all of our souls, and all of our strength. The next Great Awakening will not be easy. God will not do it for us. We, God's people, must choose to open our eyes to the sun of righteousness the Prophet Malachi said would rise with healing in its wings, but only for those who fear the Lord. While this will not be easy, it is not impossible, and the rewards are greater than anything we can imagine!

Let us close with the benediction Moses gave to the people when, after reminding the people of the need to obey all of God's commands, he said,

> **These commands that I have given you today are not too diffi-cult for you to understand or to perform.** They are not way up in heaven, so distant that you have to ask, 'Who will go up to heaven and get them for us so that we can hear and obey them?' And they are not so far across the sea that you have to ask, 'Who will cross over the sea and get them for us so that we can hear and obey them?' **No, the word is very near to you. It is in your heart and on your lips so that you can obey it.**
>
> Today I am giving you a choice, between prosperity and disaster, between life and death. **I am commanding you today to love the Lord your God, to obey his commands, laws and regulations, by walking in His ways**, then you will be blessed in the land you are entering to possess.
>
> But if your heart turns away, and you fail to listen, and if you are drawn to worship and serve other gods, then I warn you now, you will certainly be destroyed. You will not live long in the land you are crossing the Jordan to enter and possess. **Today I am giving you a choice, between life and death, between blessings and curses. I call upon heaven and earth to witness the choice that you make. O that you would choose life, so that you and your children, and your children's children might live. Choose to love the Lord, and to obey His commands, for the Lord is your life**. Then the Lord will bless you and the land that he swore to give your ancestors Abraham, Isaac, and Jacob. Deuteronomy 30:11–20 (emphasis added)

God has given His people a choice between life and death, between blessings and curses. My hope in writing this book is that God's people will want to hear these words, because these are the words God wants to hear from His people. May we choose wisely, and may it be in us as God has said!

CPSIA information can be obtained at www.ICGtesting.com
Printed in the USA
LVOW03s1805190815

450626LV00001B/1/P